FROM THIS DAY FORWARD

Other books by the author

Novels
The Windsurf Boy
The Anderson Question
The Fourth of July

Non-Fiction
The Year of the Child – Portraits of British Children
Differences of Opinion (Collected Journalism)
Bel Mooney's Somerset

Children's Books
Liza's Yellow Boat
I Don't Want To!
I Can't Find It!
It's Not Fair!
The Stove Haunting

Satire
Father Kissmass and Mother Claws (with Gerald Scarfe)

FROM THIS DAY FORWARD

AN
ANTHOLOGY
OF MARRIAGE

EDITED BY
BEL MOONEY

John Murray

First published in 1989 by
John Murray (Publishers) Ltd,
50 Albemarle Street,
London w1x 4BD

British Library Cataloguing in Publication Data
Mooney, Bel, *1946–*
From this day forward: an anthology of marriage.
1. English literature. Special subjects. Marriage –
Anthologies
I. Title
820.8'0354

ISBN 0–7195–4748–2

Text design by Ran Barnes
Typeset by Butler & Tanner
Printed and bound in Great Britain
by Butler & Tanner, Frome and London

CONTENTS

Introduction	1
Questions	7
Proposals	48
Nuptials	105
Domesticity	152
Complications	189
Accommodations	224
Celebrations	266
Reverberations	308
Acknowledgements	365
Index of Authors	371

FOR JONATHAN

Such love I cannot analyse;
It does not rest in lips or eyes,
Neither in kisses nor caress.
Partly, I know, it's gentleness

And understanding in one word
Or in brief letters. It's preserved
By trust and by respect and awe.
These are the words I'm feeling for.

Two people, yes, two lasting friends.
The giving comes, the taking ends.
There is no measure for such things.
For this all Nature slows and sings.

Elizabeth Jennings (1979)

INTRODUCTION

Love and marriage, love and marriage,
Go together like a horse and carriage,
This I tell you, brother,
You can't have one without the other.

THE POPULAR SONG I remember floating jauntily from the huge old bakelite radio when I was a child, contains within its 'elementary' certainty, a lie – or at least, a curious contradiction. For whilst it might be true that couples (nowadays at least) fall in love, and therefore marry, the fact is that love and marriage have been seen to be in *opposition* to each other for centuries.

This is not just a device of medieval literature, in which 'courtly love' places another man's wife upon a pedestal, singing to her of illicit passion. No, it is the background to much writing, from the legend of Tristan and Isolde, through Madame Bovary and Anna Karenina, to popular songs through the ages which have crooned and mooned of 'lurve', not domesticity. For love is seen as immediate, involuntary and passionate, whilst marriage is planned and involves a sober legal contract, not to mention subsequent mundane domesticity. Once the first fine frenzy is over, love and marriage, far from going together like the horse and carriage, are seen as pulling in opposite directions, sometimes tearing human happiness limb from limb.

'The romance has gone', complains the young wife, writing to the magazine agony aunt – and she is right. Soon she may be seeking advice about a love affair – for the conflict between conjugal and

1

illicit love exists in all centuries. In the ancient world they understood the distinction between sexual-love and friendship-love, and
that though both are necessary within a marriage, the blossoming
of the latter can make the loss of the former irrelevant. But somewhere the romantic lie creeps in: the notion that in matrimony men
and women should be able to perpetuate that bliss of early days
when the loved object has no faults, and the flesh sings out its
longing, and the whispered 'forever and ever' defies time itself. In
the late twentieth century it is probably harder than ever for us to
resolve the conflict between love and marriage – simply because the
illusions of romantic love and the expectations of marriage being
'sold' each day in the mass media are probably more closely identified
than ever before, with widespread disappointment bound to result.

Once, love was the province of poets, but marriage that of
parents: marriages were arranged and few young people thought to
question that *status quo*. First, marriages (in most classes) were
arranged by parents with little reference to the will of the children.
Then, in the sixteenth and seventeenth centuries, young people
started to be granted a right of veto, even though marriages were
still arranged. The next shift, from the seventeenth to the eighteenth
century, gave parents the right of veto, whilst the children started
to choose for themselves. By the time we reach this century (but
not before) children arrange their own marriages without obvious
reference to the will of their parents – although in practice, of
course, most do care what their families think of a chosen partner.
Most young people in Western society shudder at the idea of
arranged marriages – as practised, perhaps in the next street, by
their Muslim neighbours. Yet happiness *can* be found in an arranged
marriage (or peaceful cohabitation at least) whilst our divorce rate
goes up and up . . .

The divorce rate seems to make a mockery of marriage. Yet are
not the re-marriage figures proof, not so much of the failure of love,
as a determination not to live without it? Dr Johnson quipped, with
some truth, that re-marriage showed the triumph of hope over
experience; but that hope thus survives shows that the institution
of marriage has, paradoxically, lost none of its power. Triumph it
is.

But what is marriage *for*? Personally, I would agree with Milton and settle for 'a meet and happy conversation', but nothing can be so simple. Within the concept of 'marriage' we find a cluster of ideas, some of them contradictory. Is it a human institution, to be regulated by civil law and moral custom? Or a religious sacrament? Or a contract under natural law, since men and women will, under any circumstances be drawn together to couple, but more than that to *be* a couple? Whether you view marriage as civil, divine or natural will obviously affect your attitude to monogamy, adultery and divorce.

Even within the Christian tradition thinkers differ. Locke and Milton, for example, admitted the necessity for separation. In contrast, Dr Johnson argued that, 'to the contract of marriage, besides the man and wife, there is a third party – society; and if it be considered as a vow – God; and therefore it cannot be dissolved by their consent alone.' Marriage is clearly 'for' a number of things – the most important being, according to the Book of Common Prayer, the procreation of children and the avoidance of fornication. In other words, safe sex – with 'help and comfort' for good measure. Even those who have no faith, will probably agree with the female in T. S. Eliot's *The Waste Land* who asks, 'What you get married for if you don't want children?'

Leaving aside social custom, religion and law for the philosophers and historians to ponder, let us repeat: What is marriage *for*? I offer one answer: people marry because of the loneliness at the heart of love. Someone else might say people marry for a home and companionship – which comes to almost (but not quite) the same thing. And yes, oh dear yes, people marry for love, which returns us to the conflict ...

For it is the concept of love (Mills and Boon romances elevated far beyond their station) that has made the perceived conflict inevitable: love as the sublime, the totally fulfilling passion, which makes one little room an everywhere, and which should, no matter how miraculously, transform the everyday into a permanent, shuddering ecstasy. Were it possible, it would be exhausting.

A popular newspaper once quoted a young woman who said that her proudest moment came when, in her wedding finery, coiffed and made-up, she joined her boyfriend at the altar, to find that he literally did not recognise her, did not 'know' her. It is a fitting metaphor for the potential destructiveness of such illusions. Will he come to 'know' her afterwards, when the wedding roses have wilted? What *help* is given by all the display? The rite of passage being ritually celebrated transforms the girl from single woman to wife, and she may come to look back and see it as a sacrifice upon an altar. But so might her husband.

It is because I *know* marriage contains great potential for lasting joy that I would snatch the veil from the young bride's face, and show her how difficult it is. Marriage means far more than a ceremony and a ring: 'from this day forward' signals a pathway into a maze. Marriage is crises and tensions and boredom and disappointment. It can involve conflict between love and duty, between reason and passion, between expectation and reality. I would also tell the expectant young couple that most successful marriages end up as unions of affectionate friends, who live together in mutual sympathy – knowing that young romantics might find such a prosaic idea harder to take than the thought of drama.

The double bed can be comforting and companionable, or lonely. We know that some marriages will end in bitterness, or even in tragedy; others just fizzle out. Some will seem so happy as to excite envy, although the outsider cannot know what goes on beneath the apparently smooth surface. We may call marriage the bedrock of society, the firm foundation, not only of individual happiness, but of social harmony too. But we also know that it can be the savage rock on which lives are wrecked.

Either way, people will be shaken and shaped by one of the greatest tests of character any of us have to face. That is the testimony of this book. Yet it is conceived in celebration too – an answer to the common assumption that passion and unrequited love inspire literature, but not enduring married love. I began by noting down, commonplace-book fashion, poems and passages I liked that praised the state of wedlock. But that would not do; the harsher realities of domesticity and disappointment had to be included too. Although I include pain and infidelity and disillusion, I do not include divorce. Why? Because the book is 'about' marriage, not its dissolving.

Within these pages we pull back from that brink, clinging on for survival.

Moreover, it is not relevant to the words on the page whether this poet left his wife, or that historian in fact had a difficult marriage. Each extract is its own reality as it appears on the page. I include biographical detail and plot 'explanation' only when I deem it necessary. Like any commonplace-book selection it is highly personal, and mixes diaries and letters with prose and verse, fact (in other words) with fiction. Some extracts will be familiar, like Mr Rochester's passionate proposal to Jane Eyre; some will be unfamiliar, like the sexual problems of the hapless husband of Margery Kempe. To keep the anthology to a managable length I had to jettison much of what I found: the seam is rich. Although there are many 'stories' in this collection, and the selection is varied, there is an overall narrative which is, I believe, universal. It will speak to all those who are considering marriage, or who are married, or who have been married – and provide comfort, as well as confirmation.

A NOTE ON THE TEXT

Where possible I have given the date of composition, or of first publication of each extract; failing that, the author's dates. In one or two cases this proved harder than I had anticipated and the entry in my notebook remains a mystery.

QUESTIONS

'.. an honourable estate'?

IT MAY NOT BE A TRUTH universally acknowledged, but marriage terrifies. The young girls may dream of it, and the young men approach it reluctantly – as the stereotypes go. Nevertheless, for centuries men and women have asked themselves crucial questions before locking themselves for life into this 'honourable estate'. Philosophers have theorised about marriage in the ideal society, whilst marriages were arranged as matters of convenience, in the un-ideal world.

Charles Darwin cannot be the only person to have taken a sheet of paper and made two lists – the *pros* and *cons* of matrimony. But unwritten, unspoken even, the anxious questions can usually be reduced to a similar, largely self-centred, set of formulae: Who are you really? Will you make me happy? Will I become bored? Can we possibly stay together until we grow old? What if you are unfaithful to me? Do you really know me? Do you really love me? Can you accept me with all my faults? Will you ever truly know me? Who *are* you? What *is* this thing called marriage?

The answer to all those questions can only be another question – Who knows? And that is the most terrifying thing of all. Yet we *will* marry, most of us ... or will we?

(*The philosopher enquires, 'What is a rose? ...'*)

7

SOME MAXIMS

Benedick. The world must be peopled. When I said I would die a bachelor, I did not think I should live till I were married.

William Shakespeare, *Much Ado About Nothing*, Act II,
scene iii

There is no greater risk, perhaps, than matrimony, but there is nothing happier than a happy marriage.

Benjamin Disraeli, writing to Princess Louise on her
engagement to the Marquess of Lorne, 1870

Did you ever hear my definition of marriage? It is, that it resembles a pair of shears, so joined that they cannot be separated; often moving in opposite directions, yet always punishing any one who comes between them.

Reverend Sydney Smith (1771–1845)

Marriage is popular because it combines the maximum of temptation with the maximum of opportunity.

George Bernard Shaw, *Man and Superman*,
Maxims for Revolutionists (1903)

Rosalind. Men are April when they woo, December when they wed: maids are May when they are maids, but the sky changes when they are wives.

William Shakespeare, *As You Like It*, Act IV, scene i

It is a truth universally acknowledged, that a single man in possession of a good fortune must be in want of a wife.

Jane Austen, *Pride and Prejudice* (1813)

Who can be in doubt of what followed? When any two young people take it into their heads to marry, they are pretty sure by perseverance to carry their point, be they ever so poor, or ever so imprudent, or ever so little likely to be necessary to each other's ultimate comfort.

Jane Austen, *Persuasion* (1818)

GOD IN THE FIRST ORDAINING of marriage taught us to what end he did it, in words expressly implying the apt and cheerful conversation of man with woman, to comfort and refresh him against the evil of solitary life, not mentioning the purpose of generation till afterwards, as being but a secondary end in dignity, though not in necessity.

John Milton, *The Doctrine and Discipline of Divorce* (1643)

JOHN LOCKE ON MARRIAGE

CONJUGAL SOCIETY IS MADE by a voluntary compact between man and woman, and though it consists chiefly in such a communion and right in one another's bodies as is necessary to its chief end, procreation, yet it draws with it mutual support and assistance, and a communion of interests too, as necessary not only to unite their care and affection, but also necessary to their common offspring, who have a right to be nourished and maintained by them till they are able to provide for themselves.

John Locke, *Concerning Civil Government* (1690)

THE VOICE OF REALISM

NOW CONCERNING THE THINGS whereof ye wrote unto me: It is good for a man not to touch a woman.

Nevertheless, to avoid fornication, let every man have his own wife, and let every woman have her own husband.

Let the husband render unto the wife due benevolence: and likewise also the wife unto her husband.

The wife hath not power of her own body, but the husband: and likewise also the husband hath not power of his own body, but the wife.

Defraud ye not one the other, except it be with consent for a time, that ye may give yourselves to fasting and prayer; and come together again, that Satan tempt you not for your incontinency.

But I speak this by permission, and not of commandment.

For I would that all men were even as I myself. But every man hath his proper gift of God, one after this manner, and another after that.

10

I say therefore to the unmarried and widows, It is good for them if they abide even as I.

But if they cannot contain, let them marry: for it is better to marry than to burn.

I Corinthians 7:1–9

THEIR [THE LILLIPUTIANS'] MAXIM IS, that among people of quality, a wife should be always a reasonable and agreeable companion, because she cannot always be young.

Jonathan Swift, *Gulliver's Travels* (1726)

WELL, QUOTH *SANCHO*, who had been silent, and list'ning all the while, my Wife us'd to tell me, she would have every one marry with their Match. Like to like, quoth the Devil to the Collier, and every Sow to her own Trough, as t'other Saying is. . . . A Murrain seize those that will spoil a good Match between those that love one another! Nay, said Don *Quixote*, if Marriage should be always the Consequence of mutual Love, what would become of the Prerogative of Parents, and their Authority over their Children? If young Girls might always chuse their own Husbands, we should have the best Families intermarry with Coachmen and Grooms; and your Heiresses would throw themselves away upon the first wild young Fellows, whose promising Out-sides and Assurance makes 'em set up for Fortunes, though all their Stock consists in Impudence. For the Understanding which alone should distinguish and chuse in these Cases as in all others, is apt to be blinded or bias'd by Love and Affection; and Matrimony is so nice and critical a Point, that it requires not only our own cautious Management, but even the Direction of a superior Power to chuse right. Whoever undertakes a long Journey, if he be wise, makes it his Business to find out an agreeable Companion. How cautious then should He be, who is to take a Journey for Life, whose Fellow-Traveller must not part with him but at the Grave; his Companion at Bed and Board and Sharer of all the Pleasures and Fatigues of his Journey; as the Wife must be to the Husband! She is no such Sort of Ware, that a Man can be rid of when he pleases: When once that's purchas'd, no Exchange, no Sale, no Alienation can be made: She is an inseparable Accident to Man: Marriage is a Noose, which, fasten'd about the Neck, runs the closer, and fits more uneasy by our struggling to get loose: 'Tis a *Gordian* Knot which none can unty, and being twisted with our Thread of Life, nothing but the Scythe of Death can cut it.

Miguel de Cervantes, *Don Quixote* (1615)

THE SECRET OF A HAPPY MARRIAGE

THOSE INDEED who begin this course of life without jars at their setting out, arrive within few months at a pitch of benevolence and affection, of which the most perfect friendship is but a faint resemblance.   As in the unfortunate marriage, the most minute and indifferent things are objects of the sharpest resentment; so in an happy one, they are occasions of the most exquisite satisfaction. For what does not oblige in one we love? What does not offend in one we dislike?   For these reasons I take it for a rule, that in marriage, the chief business is to acquire a prepossession in favour of each other. They should consider one another's words and actions with a secret indulgence. There should be always an inward fondness pleading for each other, such as may add new beauties to everything that is excellent, give charms to what is indifferent, and cover everything that is defective. For want of this kind propensity and bias of mind, the married pair often take things ill of each other, which no one else would take notice of in either of them.

Richard Steele, writing as the columnist Mr Bickerstaff
in *The Tatler* (1709/11)

ODYSSEUS TO NAUSICAA

MAY HEAVEN GRANT you in all things your heart's desire – husband, house and a happy peaceful home. For there is nothing better in this world than that a man and woman, sharing the same ideas, keep house together. It discomforts their enemies and makes the hearts of their friends glad – but they themselves know more about it than anyone.

Homer, *The Odyssey*, Book IV (8th century BC)

MONTAIGNE ON MARRIAGE

A MAN DOES NOT MARRY for himselfe, whatsoever he aleageth; but as much or more for his posteritie and familie. The use and interest of mariage concerneth our off-spring, a great way beyond us. Therefore doth this fashion please me, to guide it rather by a third hand, and by anothers sence, then our owne: All which, how much doth it dissent from amorous conventions? Nor is it other then a kinde of incest, in this reverent alliance and sacred bond, to employ the efforts and extravagant humor of an amorous licentiousnes, as I thinke to have said else-were. One should (saith *Aristotle*) touch his wife soberly,

13

discreetly and severely, least that tickling too lasciviously pleasure transport her beyond the bounds of reason. What he speaketh for conscience, Phisitions alledge for health: saying that pleasure excessively whotte, voluptuous and continuall, altereth the seede, and hindereth conception. Some other say, besides that to a languishing congression (as naturally that is) to store it with a convenient, and fertile heat, one must but seldome, and by moderate intermissions present himselfe unto it.

Quo rapiet sitiens venerem interjusque recondant.
—Virg. *Georg.* iii, 137.

Thirsting to snatch a fit,
And inly harbour it.

I see no mariages faile sooner, or more troubled, then such as are concluded for beauties sake, and hudled up for amorous desires. There are required more solide foundations, and more constant grounds, and a more warie marching to it: this earnest youthly heate serveth to no purpose. Those who thinke to honour marriage, by joyning love unto it, (in mine opinion) doe as those, who to doe vertue a favour, holde, that nobilitie is no other thing then Vertue ...

... A good marriage (if any there be) refuseth the company and conditions of love; it endevoureth to present those of amity. It is a sweete society of life, full of constancy, of trust, and an infinite number of profitable and solid offices, and mutuall obligations:

Montaigne, *Essays* (1580)

THE EQUAL MARRIAGE

A GOOD MARRIAGE, if such there be, rejects the company and conditions of love. It tries to reproduce those of friendship. It is a sweet association in life, full of constancy, trust, and an infinite number of useful and solid services and mutual obligations. No woman who savors the taste of it ... would want to have the place of a mistress or paramour to her husband. If she is lodged in his affection as a wife, she is lodged there much more honorably and securely. When he dances ardent and eager attention elsewhere, still let anyone ask him then on whom he would rather have some shame fall, on his wife or his mistress; whose misfortune would afflict him more; for whom he wishes more honor. These questions admit of no doubt in a sound marriage.

Montaigne, *Essays* (1580)

W HAT MARRIAGE MAY BE in the case of two persons of cultivated faculties, identical in opinions and purposes, between whom there exists that best kind of equality, similarity of powers and capacities with reciprocal superiority in them – so that each can enjoy the luxury of looking up to the other, and can have alternately the pleasure of leading and of being led in the path of development – I will not attempt to describe. To those who can conceive it, there is no need; to those who cannot, it would appear the dream of an enthusiast. But I maintain, with the profoundest conviction, that this, and this only, is the ideal of marriage; and that all opinions, customs, and institutions which favour any other notion of it, or turn the conceptions and aspirations connected with it into any other direction, by whatever pretences they may

15

be coloured, are relics of primitive barbarism. The moral regeneration of mankind will only really commence, when the most fundamental of the social relations is placed under the rule of equal justice, and when human beings learn to cultivate their strongest sympathy with an equal in rights and in cultivation.

John Stuart Mill, *Subjection of Women* (1869)

I T IS ... POSSIBLE for a civilized man and woman to be happy in marriage, although if this is to be the case a number of conditions must be fulfilled. There must be a feeling of complete equality on both sides; there must be no interference with mutual freedom; there must be the most complete physical and mental intimacy; and there must be a certain similarity in regard to standards of values. (It is fatal, for example, if one values only money while the other values only good work.) Given all these conditions, I believe marriage to be the best and most important relation that can exist between two human beings. If it has not often been realized hitherto, that is chiefly because husband and wife have regarded themselves as each other's policeman. If marriage is to achieve its possibilities, husbands and wives must learn to understand that whatever the law may say, in their private lives they must be free.

Bertrand Russell, *Marriage and Morals* (1929)

A GOOD WIFE

(SHE) IS A MAN'S BEST MOVABLE, a scion incorporate with his stock, bringing sweet fruit; one that to her husband is more than a friend, less than trouble; an equal with him in the yoke. Calamities and troubles she

16

shares alike, nothing pleases her that doth not him. She is relative in all, and he without her but half himself. She is his absent hands, eyes, ears and mouth; his present and absent all ... a husband without her is a misery to man's apparel: none but she hath an aged husband to whom she is both a staff and a chair.

Sir Thomas Overbury, *Characters* (1641)

THE PROS AND CONS ACCORDING TO DARWIN

This is the question

Marry   Not Marry

Marry
Children – (if it please God) – constant companion, who will feel interested in one (a friend in old age) – object to be beloved and played with – better than a dog anyhow – Home, and someone to take care of the house – Classics of Music and female Chit Chat – These things good for one's health – (forced to visit and receive relations – crossed out) but terrible loss of time – My God, it is unthinkable to think of spending one's whole life, like a neuter bee, working, working, and nothing after all – No, no won't do – Imagine living all one's days solitarily in smoky dirty London House – Only picture to yourself a nice soft wife on a sofa with good fire, and books and music perhaps – compare this vision with dingy reality of Grt. Marlb. Str.
Marry. Marry. Marry. Q.E.D.

Not Marry
No children (no second life) – no one to care for one in old age – what is the use of working without sympathy from near and dear friends – who are near and dear friends

17

to the old except relatives – Freedom to go where one liked – choice of Society and little of it. Conversation with clever men at clubs – Not forced to visit relatives, and to bend in every trifle – to have the expense and anxiety of children – perhaps quarrelling – Loss of time – cannot read in the Evenings – fatness and idleness – anxiety and responsibility – less money for books etc – if many children forced to gain one's bread (But then it is very bad for one's health to work too much). Perhaps my wife won't like London, then the sentence is punishment and degradation with indolent, idle fool.

It being proved necessary to Marry. When? Soon or Late. The Governor says soon for otherwise bad if one has children – one's character is more flexible – one's feelings more lively and if one does not marry soon, one misses so much good pure happiness – But then if I married tomorrow: there would be an infinity of troubles and expense in getting and furnishing a house – insisting about no Society – morning calls – awkwardness – loss of time every day (without one's wife was an angel and made one keep indentures) – Then how should I manage all my business if I were obliged to go every day walking with my wife – Ehem!! I never should no French, or see the continent, or go to America, or go up in a Balloon, or take solitary trips in Wales – poor slave – you will be worse than a negro – And then horrid poverty (without one's wife was better than an angel and had money) Never mind my boy – Cheer Up – one cannot live this solitary life, with growing old age, friendless and cold, and childless staring in one's face, already beginning to wrinkle – Never mind, trust to chance – Keep a sharp look out – There is many a happy slave –

[Charles Darwin wrote this appraisal of marriage on a sheet of paper in 1838. In January 1839, just before his thirtieth birthday, he married his cousin Emma Wedgewood.]

M AN SCANS WITH SCRUPULOUS CARE the character and pedigree of his horses, cattle, and dogs before he matches them; but when he comes to his own marriage he rarely, or never, takes any such care. He is impelled by nearly the same motives as the lower animals, when they are left to their own free choice, though he is in so far superior to them that he highly values mental charms and virtues. On the other hand he is strongly attracted by mere wealth or rank. Yet he might by selection do something not only for the bodily constitution and frame of his offspring, but for their intellectual and moral qualities. Both sexes ought to refrain from marriage if they are in any marked degree inferior in body or mind; but such hopes are Utopian and will never be even partially realised until the laws of inheritance are thoroughly known. Everyone does good service, who aids towards this end.

Charles Darwin, *Descent of Man* (1871)

MARIANNE ON MARRIAGE

M RS JENNINGS was remarkably quick in the discovery of attachments, and had enjoyed the advantage of raising the blushes and the vanity of many a young lady by insinuations of her power over a young man; and this kind of discernment enabled her soon after her arrival at Barton decisively to pronounce that Colonel Brandon was very much in love with Marianne Dashwood.

'It is too ridiculous!' [said Marianne to her mother, and her sister] 'When is a man to be safe from such wit, if age and infirmity will not protect him?'

'Infirmity!' said Elinor. 'Do you call Colonel Brandon infirm? I can easily suppose that his age may appear much greater to you than to my mother; but you can hardly deceive yourself as to his having the use of his limbs!'

'Did not you hear him complain of the rheumatism? and is not that the commonest infirmity of declining life?'

'My dearest child,' said her mother laughing, 'at this rate you must be in a continual terror of *my* decay; and it must seem to you a miracle that my life has been extended to the advanced age of forty.'

'Mama, you are not doing me justice. I know very well that Colonel Brandon is not old enough to make his friends yet apprehensive of losing him in the course of nature. He may live twenty years longer. But thirty-five has nothing to do with matrimony.'

'Perhaps,' said Elinor, 'thirty-five and seventeen had better not have anything to do with matrimony together. But if there should by any chance happen to be a woman who is single at seven and twenty, I should not think Colonel Brandon's being thirty-five any objection to his marrying *her*.'

'A woman of seven and twenty,' said Marianne, after pausing a moment, 'can never hope to feel or inspire affection again, and if her home be uncomfortable, or her fortune small, I can suppose that she might bring herself to submit to the offices of a nurse, for the sake of the provision and security of a wife. In his marrying such a woman therefore there would be nothing unsuitable. It would be a compact of convenience, and the world would be satisfied. In my eyes it would be no marriage at all, but that would be nothing. To me it would seem only a commercial exchange, in which each wished to be benefited at the expense of the other.'

Jane Austen, *Sense and Sensibility* (1811)

REASONS FOR MARRIAGE

Though marriage by some folks
Be reckoned a curse,
Three wives I did marry
For better or worse —
The first for her person,
The next for her purse,
Third for a warming-pan,
Doctress and nurse.

Anon.

A man that's looking for a wife,
Here's a face that will keep for life!
Hand and arm and neck and breast,
Each is better than the rest.
Look at that waist! my legs are long,
Limber as willows and light and strong,
There's bottom and belly that claim attention
And the best concealed that I needn't mention.

Bryan Merriman, *The Midnight Court*
(1780)

There once was an old man of Lyme
Who married three wives at a time;
When asked, 'Why a third?'
He replied, 'One's absurd!
And bigamy, sir, is a crime.'

William Cosmo Monkhouse
(1840–1901)

21

'MARRY! MADNESS!'

W E WERE SITTING – Miss Matty and I – much as usual; she in the blue chintz easy-chair, with her back to the light, and her knitting in her hand – I reading aloud the *St James's Chronicle*. A few minutes more, and we should have gone to make the little alterations in dress usual before calling time (twelve o'clock) in Cranford. I remember the scene and the date well. We had been talking of the Signor's rapid recovery since the warmer weather had set in, and praising Mr Hoggins's skill, and lamenting his want of refinement and manner – (it seems a curious coincidence that this should have been our subject, but so it was) – when a knock was heard; a caller's knock – three distinct taps – and we were flying (that is to say, Miss Matty could not walk very fast, having had a touch of rheumatism) to our rooms, to change cap and collars, when Miss Pole arrested us by calling out as she came up the stairs, 'Don't go – I can't wait – it is not twelve, I know – but never mind your dress – I must speak to you.' We did our best to look as if it was not we who had made the hurried movement, the sound of which she had heard; for, of course, we did not like to have it supposed that we had any old clothes that it was convenient to wear out in the 'sanctuary of home,' as Miss Jenkyns once prettily called the back parlour, where she was tying up preserves. So we threw our gentility with double force into our manners, and very genteel we were for two minutes while Miss Pole recovered breath, and excited our curiosity strongly by lifting up her hands in amazement, and bringing them down in silence, as if what she had to say was too big for words, and could only be expressed by pantomime.

'What do you think, Miss Matty? What *do* you think? Lady Glenmire is to marry – is to be married, I mean – Lady Glenmire – Mr Hoggins – Mr Hoggins is going to marry Lady Glenmire!'

'Marry!' said we. 'Marry! Madness!'

'Marry!' said Miss Pole, with the decision that belonged to her character. '*I* said marry! as you do; and I also said, "What a fool my lady is going to make of herself!" I could have said "Madness!" but I controlled myself, for it was in a public shop that I heard of it. Where feminine delicacy is gone to, I don't know! You and I, Miss Matty, would have been ashamed to have known that our marriage was spoken of in a grocer's shop, in the hearing of shopmen!'

'But,' said Miss Matty, sighing as one recovering from a blow, 'perhaps it is not true. Perhaps we are doing her injustice.'

'No,' said Miss Pole. 'I have taken care to ascertain that. I went straight to Mrs Fitz-Adam, to borrow a cookery book which I knew she had; and I introduced my congratulations *à propos* of the difficulty gentlemen must have in housekeeping; and Mrs Fitz-Adam bridled up, and said that she believed it was true, though how and where I could have heard it she did not know. She said her brother and Lady Glenmire had come to an understanding at last. "Understanding!" such a coarse word! But my lady will have to come down to many a want of refinement. I have reason to believe Mr Hoggins sups on bread-and-cheese and beer every night!'

'Marry!' said Miss Matty once again. 'Well! I never thought of it. Two people that we know going to be married. It's coming very near!'

'So near that my heart stopped beating, when I heard of it, while you might have counted twelve,' said Miss Pole.

'One does not know whose turn may come next. Here, in Cranford, poor Lady Glenmire might have thought herself safe,' said Miss Matty, with a gentle pity in her tones.

Elizabeth Gaskell, *Cranford* (1853)

A SLICE OF WEDDING CAKE

Why have such scores of lovely, gifted girls
  Married impossible men?
Simple self-sacrifice may be ruled out,
  And missionary endeavour, nine times out of ten.

Repeat 'impossible men': not merely rustic,
  Foul-tempered or depraved
(Dramatic foils chosen to show the world
  How well women behave, and always have
  behaved).

Impossible men: idle, illiterate,
  Self-pitying, dirty, sly,
For whose appearance even in City parks
  Excuses must be made to casual passers-by.

Has God's supply of tolerable husbands
  Fallen, in fact, so low?
Or do I always over-value woman
  At the expense of man?
          Do I?
              It might be so.

Robert Graves (1967)

KANT ON MARRIAGE

THE DOMESTIC RELATIONS are founded on marriage, and marriage is founded upon the natural reciprocity or intercommunity ... of the sexes. This natural union of the sexes proceeds according to the mere animal nature ... or according to the law. The latter is marriage ... which is the union of two persons of different sex for life-long reciprocal possession of their sexual faculties. The end of producing and educating children may be regarded as always the end of nature in implanting mutual desire and inclination in the sexes; but it is not necessary for the rightfulness of marriage that those who marry should set this before themselves as the end of their union, otherwise the marriage would be dissolved of itself when the production of children ceased.

Immanuel Kant, *The Science of Right* (c. 1788)

MARRIAGE OR NOT

THE BRANGWEN FAMILY was going to move from Beldover. It was necessary now for the father to be in town.

Birkin had taken out a marriage license, yet Ursula deferred from day to day. She would not fix any definite time – she still wavered. Her month's notice to leave the Grammar School was in its third week. Christmas was not far off.

Gerald waited for the Ursula-Birkin marriage. It was something crucial to him.

'Shall we make it a double-barrelled affair?' he said to Birkin one day.

'Who for the second shot?' asked Birkin.

'Gudrun and me,' said Gerald, the venturesome twinkle in his eyes.

Birkin looked at him steadily, as if somewhat taken aback.

'Serious – or joking?' he asked.

'Oh, serious. – Shall I? Shall Gudrun and I rush in along with you?'

'Do by all means,' said Birkin. 'I didn't know you'd got that length.'

'What length?' said Gerald, looking at the other man, and laughing.

'Oh yes, we've gone all the lengths.'

'There remains to put it on a broad social basis, and to achieve a high moral purpose,' said Birkin.

'Something like that: the length and breadth and height of it,' replied Gerald, smiling.

'Oh well,' said Birkin, 'it's a very admirable step to take, I should say.'

Gerald looked at him closely.

'Why aren't you enthusiastic?' he asked. 'I thought you were such dead nuts on marriage.'

Birkin lifted his shoulders.

'One might as well be dead nuts on noses. – There are all sorts of noses, snub and otherwise. –'

Gerald laughed.

'And all sorts of marriage, also snub and otherwise?' he said.

'That's it.'

'And you think if I marry, it will be snub?' asked Gerald quizzically, his head a little on one side.

Birkin laughed quickly.

'How do I know what it will be!' he said. 'Don't lambaste me with my own parallels –'

Gerald pondered a while.

'But I should like to know your opinion, exactly,' he said.

'On your marriage? – or marrying? – Why should you

26

want my opinion? I've got no opinions. I'm not interested in legal marriage, one way or another. – It's a mere question of convenience.'

Still Gerald watched him closely.

'More than that, I think,' he said seriously. 'However you may be bored by the ethics of marriage, yet really to marry, in one's own personal case, is something critical, final –'

'You mean there is something final in going to the registrar with a woman?'

'If you're coming back with her, I do,' said Gerald. 'It is in some way irrevocable.'

'Yes, I agree,' said Birkin.

'No matter how one regards legal marriage, yet to enter into the married state, in one's own personal instance, is final –'

'I believe it is,' said Birkin, 'somewhere.'

'The question remains then, should one do it,' said Gerald.

Birkin watched him narrowly, with amused eyes.

'You are like Lord Bacon, Gerald,' he said. 'You argue it like a lawyer – or like Hamlet's to-be-or-not-to-be. – If I were you I would *not* marry: but ask Gudrun, not me. You're not marrying me, are you?'

Gerald did not heed the latter part of this speech.

'Yes,' he said, 'one must consider it coldly. – It is something critical. – One comes to the point where one must take a step in one direction or another. And marriage is in one direction – '

'And what is the other?' asked Birkin quickly.

Gerald looked up at him with hot, strangely-conscious eyes, that the other man could not understand.

'I can't say,' he replied. 'If I knew *that* –.' He moved uneasily on his feet, and did not finish.

'You mean if you knew the alternative?' asked Birkin. 'And since you don't know it, marriage is a *pis aller*.'

27

Gerald looked up at Birkin with the same hot, constrained eyes.

'One does have the feeling that marriage is a *pis aller*,' he admitted.

'Then don't do it,' said Birkin. 'I tell you,' he went on, 'the same as I've said before, marriage in the old sense seems to me repulsive. *Egoïsme à deux* is nothing to it. It's a sort of tacit hunting in couples: the world all in couples, each couple in its own little house, watching its own little interests, and stewing in its own little privacy – it's the most repulsive thing on earth.'

'I quite agree,' said Gerald. 'There's something inferior about it. But as I say, what's the alternative.'

'One should avoid this *home* instinct. It's not an instinct, it's a habit of cowardliness. One should never have a *home*.'

'I agree really,' said Gerald. 'But there's no alternative.'

'We've got to find one. – I do believe in a permanent union between a man and a woman. Chopping about is merely an exhaustive process. – But a permanent relation between a man and a woman isn't the last word – it certainly isn't.'

'Quite,' said Gerald.

'In fact,' said Birkin, 'because the relation between man and woman is made the supreme and exclusive relationship, that's where all the tightness and meanness and insufficiency comes in.'

'Yes, I believe you,' said Gerald.

'You've got to take down the love-and-marriage ideal from its pedestal. We want something broader. – I believe in the *additional* perfect relationship between man and man – additional to marriage.'

'I can never see how they can be the same,' said Gerald.

'Not the same – but equally important, equally creative, equally sacred, if you like.'

Gerald moved uneasily. – 'You know, I can't feel that,' said he. 'Surely there can never be anything as strong

28

between man and man as sex love is between man and woman. Nature doesn't provide the basis.'

'Well, of course, I think she does. And I don't think we shall ever be happy till we establish ourselves on this ·basis. You've got to get rid of the *exclusiveness* of married love. And you've got to admit the unadmitted love of man for man. It makes for a greater freedom for everybody, a greater power of individuality both in men and women.'

'I know,' said Gerald, 'you believe something like that. Only I can't *feel* it, you see.' He put his hand on Birkin's arm, with a sort of deprecating affection. And he smiled as if triumphantly.

He was ready to be doomed. Marriage was like a doom to him. He was willing to condemn himself in marriage, to become like a convict condemned to the mines of the underworld, living no life in the sun, but having a dreadful subterranean activity. He was willing to accept this. And marriage was the seal of his condemnation. He was willing to be sealed thus in the underworld, like a soul damned but living forever in damnation. – But he would not make any pure relationship with any other soul. He could not. Marriage was not the committing of himself into a relationship with Gudrun. It was a committing of himself in acceptance of the established world, he would accept the established order, in which he did not livingly believe, and then he would retreat to the underworld for his life. This he would do.

The other way was to accept Rupert's offer of love, to enter into the bond of pure trust and love with the other man, and then subsequently with the woman. If he pledged himself with the man he would later be able to pledge himself with the woman: not merely in legal marriage, but in absolute, mystic marriage.

D. H. Lawrence, *Women in Love* (1921)

SONNET 116

Let me not to the marriage of true minds
Admit impediments. Love is not love
Which alters when it alteration finds,
Or bends with the remover to remove:
O, no! It is an ever fixed mark,
That looks on tempests and is never shaken,
It is the star to every wandering bark,
Whose worth's unknown, although his height be taken
Love's not Time's fool, though rosy lips and cheeks
Within his bending sickle's compass come;
Love alters not, with his brief hours and weeks,
But bears it out even to the edge of doom.
If this be error and upon me proved,
I never writ, nor no man ever loved.

William Shakespeare (1609)

MONTESQUIEU ON MARRIAGE

THE NATURAL OBLIGATION of the father to provide for his children has established marriage, which makes known the person who ought to fulfil this obligation ... Among civilised nations, the father is that person on whom the laws, by the ceremony of marriage, have fixed this duty, because they find in him the man they want ... Illicit conjunctions contribute but little to the propagation of the species. The father, who is under a natural obligation to nourish his children, is not then fixed; and the mother, with whom the obligation remains, finds a thousand obstacles from shame, remorse, the constraint of her sex, and the rigour of laws; and besides, she generally wants the means ...

30

QUESTIONS

Of The Father's Consent To Marriage

The consent of fathers is founded on their authority, that is, on the right of property. It is also founded on their love, on their reason, and on the uncertainty of that of their children, whom youth confines in a state of ignorance and passion in a state of ebriety ...

In England the law is frequently abused by the daughters marrying according to their own fancy without consulting their parents. This custom is, I am apt to imagine, more tolerated there than anywhere else from a consideration that as the laws have not established a monastic celibacy, the daughters have no other state to choose but that of marriage, and this they cannot refuse. In France, on the contrary, young women have always the resource of celibacy; and therefore the law which ordains they shall wait for the consent of their fathers may be more agreeable. In this light the custom of Italy and Spain must be less rational; convents are there established, and yet they may marry without the consent of their fathers ...

Of Young Women

Young women who are conducted by marriage alone to liberty and pleasure, who have a mind which dares not think, a heart which dares not feel, eyes which dare not see, ears which dare not hear, who appear only to show themselves silly, condemned without intermission to trifles and precepts, have sufficient inducements to lead them on to marriage: it is the young men that want to be encouraged.

What It Is That Determines Marriage

Wherever a place is found in which two persons can live commodiously, there they enter into marriage ...

Baron de Montesquieu, *The Spirit of Laws* (1748)

31

JOHN STUART MILL'S MARRIAGE 'CONTRACT'

John Stuart Mill caused a sensation in London by being seen openly with Harriet Taylor, wife of John Taylor. Taylor himself did his best to accommodate their relationship, believing that tolerance would enable him to keep her. When Taylor became terminally ill, Harriet nursed him devotedly: 'There is nothing on earth I would not do for him and there is nothing on earth which *can* be done.' He died in 1849; by 1852 Harriet and Mill realised that although both disapproved of marriage as an institution, they wanted to live together and therefore must marry. So Mill produced this formal disclaimer:

BEING ABOUT, IF I AM so happy as to obtain her consent, to enter into the marriage relation with the only woman I have ever known, with whom I would have entered into that state; and the whole character of the marriage relation as constituted by law being such as both she and I entirely and conscientiously disapprove, for this amongst other reasons, that it confers upon one of the parties to the contract, legal power and control over the person, property, and freedom of action of the other party, independent of her own wishes and will; I, having no means of legally divesting myself of these odious powers ... feel it my duty to put on record a formal protest against the existing law of marriage, in so far as conferring such powers; and a solemn promise never in any case or under any circumstances to use them. And in the event of marriage between Mrs. Taylor and me I declare it to be my will and intention, and the condition of the engagement between us, that she retains in all respects whatever the same absolute freedom of action, and freedom of disposal of herself and of all that does or may at any time belong to her, as if no such marriage had taken place; and I absolutely disclaim and repudiate all pretension to have acquired any *rights* whatever by virtue of such marriage.

John Stuart Mill, *Autobiography* (1873)

THE PROPHET

Then Almitra spoke again and said, And what of Marriage, master?
And he answered saying:
You were born together, and together you shall be for evermore.
You shall be together when the white wings of death scatter your days.
Aye, you shall be together even in the silent memory of God.
But let there be spaces in your togetherness.
And let the winds of the heavens dance between you.

Love one another, but make not a bond of love:
Let it rather be a moving sea between the shores of your souls.
Fill each other's cup but drink not from one cup.
Give one another of your bread but eat not from the same loaf.
Sing and dance together and be joyous, but let each one of you be alone,
Even as the strings of a lute are alone though they quiver with the same
*   music.*
Give your hearts, but not into each other's keeping.
For only the hand of Life can contain your hearts.
And stand together yet not too near together:
For the pillars of the temple stand apart,
And the oak tree and the cypress grow not in each other's shadow.

Kahlil Gibran (1926)

DR JOHNSON ON MARRIAGE

WE ALL MET AT DINNER at Mr Lloyd's, where we were entertained with great hospitality. Mr and Mrs Lloyd had been married the same year with their Majesties, and like them, had been blessed with a numerous family of fine children, their numbers being exactly the same. Johnson said, 'Marriage is the best state for a man in general; and every man is a worse man, in proportion as he is unfit for the married state' ...

... When he again talked on Mrs Careless tonight, he seemed to have had his affection revived, for he said, 'If I had married her, it might have been as happy for me.' BOSWELL. 'Pray, Sir, do you not suppose that there are fifty women in the world, with any one of whom a man may be as happy, as with any one woman in particular?' JOHNSON. 'Ay, Sir, fifty thousand.' BOSWELL 'Then, Sir, you are not of opinion with some who imagine that certain men and certain women are made for each other; and that they cannot be happy if they miss their counterparts?' JOHNSON. 'To be sure not, Sir. I believe marriages would in general be as happy, and often more so, if they were all made by the Lord Chancellor, upon a due consideration of characters and circumstances, without the parties having any choice in the matter.'

James Boswell, *Life of Samuel Johnson* (1791)

I DO, I WILL, I HAVE

*How wise I am to have instructed the butler to instruct
the first footman to instruct the second footman to
instruct the doorman to order my carriage;
I am about to volunteer a definition of marriage.
Just as I know that there are two Hagens, Walter and
Copen,
I know that marriage is a legal and religious alliance
entered into by a man who can't sleep with the window
shut and a woman who can't sleep with the window open.
Moreover, just as I am unsure of the difference between
flora and fauna and flotsam and jetsam,
I am quite sure that marriage is the alliance of two people
one of whom never remembers birthdays and the other
never forgetsam,*

*And he refuses to believe there is a leak in the water pipe
or the gas pipe and she is convinced she is about to
asphyxiate or drown,
And she says Quick get up and get my hairbrushes off the
windowsill, it's raining in, and he replies Oh they're all
right, it's only raining straight down.
That is why marriage is so much more interesting than
divorce,
Because it's the only known example of the happy
meeting of the immovable object and the irresistible force.
So I hope husbands and wives will continue to debate and
combat over everything debatable and combatable,
Because I believe a little incompatibility is the spice of life,
particularly if he has income and she is pattable.*

Ogden Nash (1948)

OF MARRIAGE AND SINGLE LIFE

HE THAT HATH WIFE and children hath given
hostages to fortune, for they are impediments to
great enterprises, either of virtue or mischief. Certainly
the best works, and of greatest merit for the public, have
proceeded from the unmarried or childless men, which
both in affection and means have married and endowed
the public. Yet it were great reason that those that have
children should have greatest care of future times, unto
which they know they must transmit their dearest pledges.
Some there are who, though they lead a single life, yet
their thoughts do end with themselves, and account future
times impertinences. Nay, there are some other that
account wife and children but as bills of charges. Nay
more, there are some foolish rich covetous men that take
a pride in having no children, because they may be thought
so much the richer. For perhaps they have heard some
talk, *Such an one is a great rich man,* and another except to

35

it, *Yea, but he hath a great charge of children,* as if it were an abatement to his riches. But the most ordinary cause of a single life is liberty, especially in certain self-pleasing and humorous minds, which are so sensible of every restraint as they will go near to think their girdles and garters to be bonds and shackles. Unmarried men are best friends, best masters, best servants; but not always best subjects, for they are light to run away; and almost all fugitives are of that condition. ... Certainly wife and children are a kind of discipline of humanity; and single men, though they be many times more charitable, because their means are less exhaust, yet, on the other side, they are more cruel and hard-hearted (good to make severe inquisitors), because their tenderness is not so oft called upon. Grave natures, led by custom, and therefore constant, are commonly loving husbands, as was said of Ulysses, *Vetulam suam praetulit immortalitati.* Chaste women are often proud and forward, as presuming upon the merit of their chastity. It is one of the best bonds both of chastity and obedience in the wife if she think her husband wise, which she will never do if she find him jealous. Wives are young men's mistresses, companions for middle age, and old men's nurses. So as a man may have a quarrel to marry when he will. But yet he was reputed one of the wise men that made answer to the question, when a man should marry: *A young man not yet, an elder man not at all.* It is often seen that bad husbands have very good wives; whether it be that it raiseth the price of their husband's kindness when it comes, or that the wives take a pride in their patience. But this never fails if the bad husbands were of their own choosing, against their friends' consent; for then they will be sure to make good their own folly.

Francis Bacon, *Essays* (1625)

36

'IT MAY BE BAD, IT MAY BE GOOD ...'

BUT WHAT DO I TROUBLE MYSELF to find arguments to persuade to, or commend marriage? behold a brief abstract of all that which I have said, and much more, succinctly, pithily, pathetically, perspicuously, and elegantly delivered in twelve motions to mitigate the miseries of marriage, by Jacobus de Voragine....

1. Hast thou means? thou hast one to keep and increase it. – 2. Hast none? thou hast one to help get it. – 3. Art in prosperity? thine happiness is doubled. – 4. Art in adversity? she'll comfort, assist, bear a part of thy burden to make it more tolerable. – 5. Art at home? she'll drive away melancholy. – 6. Art abroad? she looks after thee going from home, wishes for thee in thine absence, and joyfully welcomes thy return. – 7. There's nothing delightsome without society, no society so sweet as matrimony. – 8. The band of conjugal love is adamantine. – 9. The sweet company of kinsmen increaseth, the number of parents is doubled, of brothers, sisters, nephews. – 10. Thou art made a father by a fair and happy issue. – 11. Moses curseth the barrenness of matrimony, how much more a single life? – 12. If nature escape not punishment, surely thy will shall not avoid it.

All this is true, say you, and who knows it not? but how easy a matter is it to answer these motives, and to make an *Antiparodia* quite opposite unto it? To exercise myself I will essay:

1. Hast thou means? thou hast one to spend it. – 2. Hast none? thy beggary is increased. – 3. Art in prosperity? thy happiness is ended. – 4. Art in adversity? like Job's wife she'll aggravate thy misery, vex thy soul, make thy burden intolerable. – 5. Art at home? she'll scold thee out of doors. – 6. Art abroad? If thou be wise, keep thee so, she'll perhaps graft horns in thy absence, scowl on thee coming home. – 7. Nothing gives more content than

37

solitariness, no solitariness like this of a single life. – 8. The band of marriage is adamantine, no hope of loosing it, thou art undone. – 9. Thy number increaseth, thou shalt be devoured by thy wife's friends. – 10. Thou art made a cornuto by an unchaste wife, and shalt bring up other folk's children, instead of thine own. – 11. Paul commends marriage, yet he prefers a single life. – 12. Is marriage honourable? What an immortal crown belongs to virginity!

So Siracides himself speaks as much as may be for and against women, so doth almost every philosopher plead *pro* and *con*, every poet thus argues the case: (though what cares *vulgus hominum* what they say?) so can I conceive peradventure, and so canst thou. . . . 'Tis a hazard both ways I confess, to live single or to marry, *Nam et uxorem ducere, et non ducere malum est,* it may be bad, it may be good, as it is a cross and calamity on the one side, so 'tis a sweet delight, an incomparable happiness, a most unspeakable benefit, a sole content, on the other, 'tis all in the proof. Be not then so wayward, so covetous, so distrustful, so curious and nice, but let's all marry, *mutuos foventes amplexus*; 'Take me to thee, and thee to me', tomorrow is St. Valentine's day, let's keep it holiday for Cupid's sake, for that great god Love's sake, for Hymen's sake, and celebrate Venus's vigil with our ancestors for company together, singing as they did . . .

> *Let those love now who never loved before,*
> *And those who always loved now love the more,*
> *Sweet loves are born with every opening spring;*
> *Birds from the tender boughs their pledges sing, etc.* . . . .

Robert Burton, *The Anatomy of Melancholy* (1621)

'THE DESIRE FOR A WIFE . . .'

HE REALISED THAT HE HAD deceived himself; it was no self-sacrifice that had driven him to think of marrying, but the desire for a wife and a home and love; and now that it all seemed to slip through his fingers he was seized with despair. He wanted all that more than anything in the world. What did he care for Spain and its cities, Cordova, Toledo, Leon; what to him were the pagodas of Burmah and the lagoons of South Sea Islands? America was here and now. It seemed to him that all his life he had followed the ideals that other people, by their words or their writings, had instilled into him, and never the desires of his own heart. Always his course had been swayed by what he thought he should do and never by what he wanted with his whole soul to do. He put all that aside now with a gesture of impatience. He had lived always in the future, and the present always, always had slipped through his fingers. His ideals? He thought of his desire to make a design, intricate and beautiful, out of the myriad, meaningless facts of life: had he not seen also that the simplest pattern, that in which a man was born, worked, married, had children, and died, was likewise the most perfect? It might be that to surrender to happiness was to accept defeat, but it was a defeat better than many victories. He glanced quickly at Sally, he wondered what she was thinking, and then looked away again.

'I was going to ask you to marry me,' he said.

'I thought p'raps you might, but I shouldn't have liked to stand in your way.'

'You wouldn't have done that.'

'How about your travels, Spain and all that?'

'How d'you know I want to travel?'

'I ought to know something about it. I've heard you and Dad talk about it till you were blue in the face.'

'I don't care a damn about all that.' He paused for an instant and then spoke in a low, hoarse whisper. 'I don't want to leave you! I can't leave you.'

She did not answer. He could not tell what she thought.

'I wonder if you'll marry me, Sally.'

She did not move and there was no flicker of emotion on her face, but she did not look at him when she answered.

'If you like.'

'Don't you want to?'

'Oh, of course I'd like to have a house of my own, and it's about time I was settling down.'

He smiled a little. He knew her pretty well by now, and her manner did not surprise him.

'But don't you want to marry *me*?'

'There's no one else I would marry.'

'Then that settles it.'

'Mother and Dad will be surprised, won't they?'

'I'm so happy.'

'I want my lunch,' she said

'Dear!'

He smiled and took her hand and pressed it. They got up and walked out of the gallery. They stood for a moment at the balustrade and looked at Trafalgar Square. Cabs and omnibuses hurried to and fro, and crowds passed, hastening in every direction, and the sun was shining.

W. Somerset Maugham, *Of Human Bondage* (1915)

'WOMEN WHO CANNOT GROW ALONE ...'

THERE ARE SOME WOMEN who cannot grow alone as standard trees – for whom the support and warmth of some wall, some paling, some post, is absolutely necessary; – who, in their growth, will bend and incline themselves towards some prop for their life, creeping with their tendrils along the ground till they reach it, when the circumstances of life have brought no such prop within their natural and immediate reach. Of most women it may be said that it would be well for them that they should marry, – as indeed of most men also, seeing that man and wife will lend each other strength, and yet in lending lose none; but to the women of whom I now speak some kind of marriage is quite indispensable, and by them some kind of marriage is always made ...

Anthony Trollope, Rachel Ray (1862)

ADVICE TO YOUNG MEN

THE THINGS WHICH YOU OUGHT to desire in a wife are, 1. Chastity; 2. Sobriety; 3. Industry; 4. Frugality; 5. Cleanliness; 6. Knowledge of domestic affairs; 7. Good temper; 8. Beauty....

Though I have reserved beauty to the last ... I by no means think it the last in point of importance. The less favoured part of the sex say, that 'beauty is but skin deep'; and this is very true; but it is very agreeable, though, for all that.... 'Handsome is that handsome does', used to say to me an old man, who had marked me out for his not overhandsome daughter. 'Please your eye and plague your heart,' is an adage the want of beauty invented, I dare say, more than a thousand years ago. These adages would say, if they had but the courage, that beauty is inconsistent with chastity, with sobriety of conduct, and with all the female virtues. The argument is that beauty exposes the possessor to greater temptation than women not beautiful are exposed to; and that, therefore, their fall is more probable....

It is certainly true that pretty girls will have more, and more ardent admirers than ugly ones; but as to the temptation when in their unmarried state, there are few so very ugly as to be exposed to no temptation at all; and which is the most likely to resist; she who has a choice of lovers, or she, who, if she let the occasion slip, may never have it again? ... And as to women in the married state ... conjugal infidelity is, in so many cases, caused by the want of affection and due attention to the husband ... that it must more frequently happen in the case of ugly than in that of handsome women....

But the great use of female beauty, the great practical advantage of it is, that it naturally and unavoidably tends to keep the husband in good humour with himself, to make him, to use the dealer's phrase, pleased with his bargain. When old age approaches, and the parties have become endeared to each other by a long series of joint cares and interests, and when children have come and bound them together by the strongest ties that nature has in store, at this age the features and the person are of less consequence; but in the young days of matrimony, when the roving eye of the bachelor is scarcely become steady in the head of the husband, it is dangerous for him to see, every time he stirs out, a face more captivating than that of the person to whom he is bound for life. Beauty is, in some degree, a matter of taste: what one man admires, another does not; and it is fortunate for us that it is thus. But still there are certain things that all men admire; and a husband is always pleased when he perceives that a portion, at least, of these things are in his own possession: he takes this possession as a compliment to himself: there must, he will think the world will believe, have been some merit in him, some charm, seen or unseen, to have caused him to be blessed with the acquisition.

And then there arise so many things, sickness, misfortune in business, losses, many, many things, wholly unexpected; and there are so many circumstances, perfectly nameless, to communicate to the new-married man the fact, that it is not a real angel of whom he has got the possession; there are so many things of this sort, so many and such powerful dampers of the passions, and so many incentives to cool reflection, that it requires something, and a good deal too, to keep the husband in countenance in this his altered and enlightened state. The passion of women does not cool so soon; the lamp of their love burns more steadily, and even brightens as it burns; and there is, the young man may be assured, a vast difference in the effect of the fondness of a pretty woman and that of one of a different description; and let reason and philosophy say what they will, a man will come downstairs of a morning better pleased after seeing the former, than he would after seeing the latter, in her nightcap. . . .

William Cobbett, *Advice to Young Men and (Incidentally) to Young Women* (1829)

HEGEL ON MARRIAGE

MARRIAGE, AS THE IMMEDIATE type of ethical relationship, contains first, the moment of physical life; and since marriage is a *substantial* tie, the life involved in it is life in its totality, i.e. as the actuality of the race and its life process. But secondly, in self-consciousness the natural sexual union . . . is changed into a union on the level of mind, into self-conscious love.

On the subjective side, marriage may have a more obvious source in the particular inclination of the two persons who are entering upon the marriage tie, or in the foresight and contrivance of the parents, and so forth. But its objective source lies in the free consent of the persons, especially in their consent to make themselves one person, to renounce their natural and individual personality to this unity of one with the other. From this point of view their union is a self-restriction, but in fact it is their liberation, because in it they attain their substantive self-consciousness.

G. W. F. Hegel, *The Philosophy of Right* (1821)

FOR BETTER FOR WORSE

IT WOULD BE HARD to find any document in practical daily use in which these obvious truths seem so stupidly overlooked as they are in the marriage service. As we have seen, the stupidity is only apparent: the service was really only an honest attempt to make the best of a commercial contract of property and slavery by subjecting it to some religious restraint and elevating it by some touch of poetry. But the actual result is that when two people are under the influence of the most violent, most insane, most delusive, and most transient of passions, they are required to swear that they will remain in that excited, abnormal, and exhausting condition continuously until death do them part. And though of course nobody expects them to do anything so impossible and so unwholesome, yet the law that regulates their relations, and the public opinion that regulates that law, is actually founded on the assumption that the marriage vow is not only feasible but beautiful and holy, and that if they are false to it, they deserve no sympathy and no relief. If all married people really lived together, no doubt the mere force of facts would make an end to this inhuman nonsense in a month, if not sooner; but it is very seldom brought to that test. The typical British husband sees much less of his wife than he does of his business partner, his fellow clerk, or whoever works beside him day by day. Man and wife do not, as a rule, live together: they only breakfast together, dine together, and sleep in the same room. In most cases the woman knows nothing of the man's working life and he knows nothing of her working life (he calls it her home life). It is remarkable that the very people who romance most absurdly about the closeness and sacredness of the marriage tie are also those who are most convinced that the man's sphere and the woman's sphere are so entirely separate that only in their leisure moments can they ever be together . . .

Marriage As A Magic Spell

The truth which people seem to overlook in this matter
is that the marriage ceremony is quite useless as a magic
spell for changing in an instant the nature of the relations
of two human beings to one another. If a man marries a
woman after three weeks acquaintance, and the day after
meets a woman he has known for twenty years, he finds,
sometimes to his own irrational surprise and his wife's
equally irrational indignation, that his wife is a stranger
to him, and the other woman an old friend. Also, there is
no hocus pocus that can possibly be devized with rings
and veils and vows and benedictions that can fix either a
man's or woman's affection for twenty minutes, much less
twenty years. Even the most affectionate couples must
have moments during which they are far more conscious
of one another's faults than of one another's attractions.
There are couples who dislike one another furiously for
several hours at a time; there are couples who dislike one
another permanently; and there are couples who never
dislike one another; but these last are people who are
incapable of disliking anybody. If they do not quarrel, it
is not because they are married, but because they are not
quarrelsome. The people who are quarrelsome quarrel
with their husbands and wives just as easily as with their
servants and relatives and acquaintances: marriage makes
no difference. Those who talk and write and legislate as
if all this could be prevented by making solemn vows
that it shall not happen, are either insincere, insane, or
hopelessly stupid. There is some sense in a contract to
perform or abstain from actions that are reasonably within
voluntary control; but such contracts are only needed to
provide against the possibility of either party being no
longer desirous of the specified performance or abstention.
A person proposing or accepting a contract not only to
do something but to like doing it would be certified as
mad. Yet popular superstition credits the wedding rite

with the power of fixing our fancies or affections for life even under the most unnatural conditions.

George Bernard Shaw, Preface to *Getting Married* (1908)

LILY BRISCOE REFLECTS UPON MARRIAGE

ANYHOW, SAID LILY, tossing off her little insincerity, she would always go on painting, because it interested her. Yes, said Mr Bankes, he was sure she would, and as they reached the end of the lawn he was asking her whether she had difficulty in finding subjects in London when they turned and saw the Ramsays. So that is marriage, Lily thought, a man and a woman looking at a girl throwing a ball. That is what Mrs Ramsay tried to tell me the other night, she thought. For she was wearing a green shawl, and they were standing close together watching Prue and Jasper throwing catches. And suddenly the meaning which, for no reason at all, as perhaps they are stepping out of the Tube or ringing a doorbell, descends on people, making them symbolical, making them representative, came upon them, and made them in the dusk standing, looking, the symbols of marriage, husband and wife. Then, after an instant, the symbolical outline which transcended the real figures sank down again, and they became, as they met them, Mr and Mrs Ramsay watching the children throwing catches. But still for a moment, though Mrs Ramsay greeted them with her usual smile (oh, she's thinking we're going to get married, Lily thought) and said, 'I have triumphed tonight,' meaning that for once Mr Bankes had agreed to dine with them and not run off to his own lodging where his man cooked vegetables properly; still, for one moment, there was a sense of things having been blown apart, of space, of irresponsibility as the ball soared high, and they followed it and lost it and saw the one star and the draped branches. In the failing light they all looked sharp-edged and ethereal and divided by great distances. Then, darting backwards over the vast space (for it seemed as if solidity had vanished altogether), Prue ran full tilt into them and caught the ball brilliantly high up in her left hand, and her mother said, 'Haven't they come back yet?' whereupon the spell was broken.

Virginia Woolf, *To the Lighthouse* (1927)

SIX RULES FOR A PERFECT MARRIAGE

1. Be the Perfect Man or Woman
2. Be the Perfect Gentleman or Lady
3. Share Purses and ALL Interests Together
4. Improve and Be Improved By Each Other
5. Promote Each Other's Happiness
6. Redouble Love by Redeclaring it

Professor Fowler, *Private Lectures on Perfect Men, Women and Children, in Happy Families, including Gender, Love, Matings, Married Life and Reproduction Etc.* (1883)

PROPOSALS

'Wilt thou ...'?

The celebrated pianist Artur Rubinstein once said, 'It took a great deal of courage to ask a beautiful girl to marry me. Believe me, it is easier to play the whole of "Petrushka" on the piano.' Most people would find that strange; in fact proposals come as no surprise in the majority of relationships. The couples meet and court and become more serious, and slip, or slide inevitably towards marriage.

Wilt thou ...?
Will you ...?
Shall we ...?
What if ...?
Should we ...?
Might you consider ...?
And – often, perhaps said with resignation – *We'll have to ...*

Not long ago a young man came to see me, eyes shining, and told me that he had proposed to his lady, on one knee, as the candles flickered, in the old-fashioned way. He spoke the language of romantic fiction, yet this was reality, in England, in the 1980s. My own proposal came in a cheap burger bar, couched in cautious terms: '*Would* you marry me?' The unspoken 'if' was never particularised. That was also reality, in England, in the 1960s. And so two marriages got under way, different yet sharing one thing – the euphoria of acceptance: the defiant YES that keeps loneliness at bay, at least for a while.

(*A rosebud is offered, and taken ...*)

ONE WAY OF CHOOSING ...

A FTER WHICH TIME he gave himself to devotion and prayer in the Charterhouse of London, religiously living there, without vow, about four years. Until he resorted to the house of one Master Colt, a gentleman of Eassex, that had oft invited him thither, having three daughters, whose honest conversation and virtuous education provoked him there especially to set his affections. And albeit his mind most served him to the second daughter, for that he thought her the fairest and best favoured – yet when he considered that it would be both grief and some shame also to the eldest to see her younger sister in marriage preferred before her, he then of certain pity framed his fancy towards her. And soon afterwards married her ...

William Roper, *Life of Sir Thomas More* (1626)

... AND ANOTHER

I N HIS UTOPIA (Sir Thomas More's) his lawe is that the young people are to see each other stark naked before marriage.

Sir William Roper, of Eltham, in Kent, came one morning pretty early, to my lord, with a proposall to marry one of his daughters. My lord's daughters were then both together abed in a truckle-bed in their father's chamber asleep. He carries Sir William into the chamber and takes the sheete by the corner and suddenly whippes it off. They lay on their backs and their Smocks up as high as their armpitts. This awakened them, and immediately they turned on their Bellies. Quoth Roper, 'I have seen both sides,' and so gave a patt on her Buttock, he made choice (of Margaret) sayeing, 'Thou art mine.'

John Aubrey, *Brief Lives* (1693)

'THAT'S THE GIRL FOR ME ...'

WHEN I FIRST SAW MY WIFE, she was thirteen years old, and I was within about a month of twenty-one. She was the daughter of a sergeant of artillery, and I was the sergeant-major of a regiment of foot, both stationed in forts near the city of St. John, in the province of New Brunswick. I sat in the same room with her for about an hour, in company with others, and I made up my mind that she was the very girl for me. That I thought her beautiful is certain, for that I had always said should be an indispensable qualification; but I saw in her what I deemed marks of that sobriety of conduct of which I have said so much, which has been by far the greatest blessing of my life. It was now dead of winter, and, of course, the snow several feet deep on the ground, and the weather piercing cold. It was my habit, when I had done my morning's writing, to go out at break of day to take a walk on a hill at the foot of which our barracks lay. In about three mornings after I had first seen her, I had, by an invitation to breakfast with me, got up two young men to join me in my walk; and our road lay by the house of her father and mother. It was hardly light, but she was out on the snow, scrubbing out a washing-tub. 'That's the girl for me,' said I, when we had got out of her hearing ...

From the day that I first spoke to her, I never had a thought of her ever being the wife of any other man, more than I had a thought of her being transformed into a chest of drawers; and I formed my resolution at once, to marry her as soon as we could get permission, and to get out of the army as soon as I could. So that this matter was at once settled as firmly as if written in the book of fate. At the end of about six months, my regiment, and I along with it, were removed to Frederickton, a distance of a hundred miles up the river of St. John; and, which was worse, the artillery were expected to go off to England a year or two before our regiment! The artillery went, and she along with them; and now it was that I acted a part becoming a real and sensible lover. I was aware that, when she got to that gay place Woolwich, the house of her father and mother, necessarily visited by numerous persons not the most select, might become unpleasant to her, and I did not like, besides, that she should continue to work hard. I had saved a hundred and fifty guineas, the earnings of my early hours, in writing for the paymaster, the quartermaster, and others, in addition to the savings of my own pay. I sent her all my money before she sailed; and wrote to her, to beg of her, if she found her home uncomfortable, to hire a lodging with respectable people: and, at any rate, not to spare the money, by any means, but to buy herself good clothes, and to live without hard work, until I arrived in England; and I, in order to induce her to lay out the money, told her that I should get plenty more before I came home.

As the malignity of the devil would have it, we were kept abroad two years longer than our time, Mr. Pitt (England not being so tame then as she is now) having knocked up a dust with Spain about Nootka Sound. Oh how I cursed Nootka Sound, and poor brawling Pitt too, I am afraid! At the end of four years, however, home I came, landed at Portsmouth, and got my discharge from the army by the great kindness of poor Lord Edward Fitzgerald, who was then the major of my regiment. I found my little girl a servant of all work (and hard work it was), at five pounds a year, in the house of a Captain Brisac; and, without hardly saying a word about the matter, she put into my hands the whole of my hundred and fifty guineas unbroken!

Need I tell the reader what my feelings were? ...

William Cobbett, *Advice to Young Men and (Incidentally) to Young Women* (1829)

51

THE WRITTEN PROPOSAL AND ACCEPTANCE

Professor Fowler, in his *Private Lectures on Perfect Men, Women and Children, in Happy Families, including Gender, Love, Mating, Married Life and Reproduction Etc,* published in New York in 1883, suggests the following ideal forms for the formal written proposal and acceptance:

Much Esteemed Friend.
Allow me to bring our mutual agreement to canvass our marital adaptations to this distinct issue. I hereby offer you my hand, heart and whole being in marriage, on this sole condition, that you *reciprocate* with yours. I will bestow my whole souled love and affection on you, if you can and will bestow yours on me; but not otherwise. Do you accord me this privilege, on this condition? If yes, please say wherein I can improve myself in your estimation and I will do my utmost to please you.

I wish you had better health, rose earlier, knew more about housekeeping &c., yet these are minor matters compared with your many conjugal excellencies. Deliberate fully, and if you wish to know more of me in order to decide, ask – or –. Your answer, as soon as you can fully decide upon this life affair, will much oblige,
Yours truly, AB.

Dear Sir:
I accept your proffer of your hand and heart in marriage and on its only condition, that I return my own; which I now do by consecrating my whole existence to you alone. Since you are mine, *let me make the most of you* by obviating your faults and developing your excellencies, that I may love you the better. Abstaining from tobacco will enhance

my affection for you, yet do as you please I will try to correct the faults you mention.

Thank Heaven that you are finally mine, and I yours, to love and live with and for, and be loved and lived with and for, and that my gushing affections can now rest on one so every way worthy of my complete devotion. We will arrange preliminaries when we meet, which I hope may be soon and often. Meanwhile, I am wholly yours.

CD.

A PROPOSAL

'*Life is all very pleasant for you,*'
    Said fair Chloe one night at a ball,
'*You men, you have plenty to do,*
    We poor women have nothing at all.'

I urged her to paint or to play
    To write or to knit or to sew,
To visit the poor and to pray,
    To each and to all she said, 'No'.

At last I exclaimed in despair,
    '*If you really are anxious to be*
Of some use, and for none of these care,
    You must marry! Why not marry me?'

Lord Robert Cecil (1888)

THE DUCHESS OF MALFI PROPOSES TO HER STEWARD ANTONIO

(Enter ANTONIO.)
    I sent for you: sit down;
Take pen and ink, and write: are you ready?
ANTONIO.   Yes.

53

DUCHESS.   What did I say?

ANTONIO.   That I should write somewhat.

DUCHESS.   Oh, I remember.
After these triumphs and this large expense,
It's fit, like thrifty husbands, we inquire
What's laid up for to-morrow.

ANTONIO.   So please your beauteous excellence.

DUCHESS.   Beauteous?
Indeed, I thank you: I look young for your
     sake;
You have ta'en my cares upon you.

ANTONIO.   I'll fetch your grace
The particulars of your revenue and expense.

DUCHESS.   Oh, you are an upright treasurer:
     but you mistook;
For when I said I meant to make inquiry
What's laid up for to-morrow, I did mean
What's laid up yonder for me.

ANTONIO.   Where?

DUCHESS.   In heaven.
I am making my will (as 'tis fit princes should,
In perfect memory), and, I pray, sir, tell me,
Were not one better make it smiling, thus,
Than in deep groans and terrible ghastly looks,
As if the gifts we parted with procur'd
That violent distraction?

ANTONIO.   Oh, much better.

DUCHESS.   If I had a husband now, this care
     were quit:
But I intend to make you overseer.
What good deed shall we first remember? say.

ANTONIO.   Begin with that first good deed began
     i' th' world
After man's creation, the sacrament of marriage:
I'd have you first provide for a good husband;
Give him all.

DUCHESS.   All?

ANTONIO.   Yes, your excellent self.
DUCHESS.   In a winding-sheet?
ANTONIO.   In a couple.
DUCHESS.   Saint Winfred,
That were a strange will!
ANTONIO.   'Twere strange[r] if there were no will in
    you
To marry again.
DUCHESS.   What do you think of marriage?
ANTONIO.   I take't, as those that deny purgatory;
It locally contains or Heaven or hell;
There's no third place in 't.
DUCHESS.   How do you affect it?
ANTONIO.   My banishment, feeding my melancholy,
Would often reason thus.
DUCHESS.   Pray, let's hear it.
ANTONIO.   Say a man never marry, nor have
    children,
What takes that from him? only the bare name
Of being a father, or the weak delight
To see the little wanton ride a-cock-horse
Upon a painted stick, or hear him chatter
Like a taught starling.
DUCHESS.   Fie, fie, what's all this?
One of your eyes is blood-shot; use my ring to 't,
They say 'tis very sovereign: 'twas my wedding-
    ring,
And I did vow never to part with it
But to my second husband.
ANTONIO.   You have parted with it now.
DUCHESS.   Yes, to help your eyesight.
ANTONIO.   You have made me stark blind.
DUCHESS.   How?
ANTONIO.   There is a saucy and ambitious devil
Is dancing in this circle.
DUCHESS.   Remove him.
ANTONIO.   How?

55

DUCHESS.   There needs small conjuration, when
    your finger
May do it: thus; is it fit?
       (She puts the ring upon his finger: he kneels.)
ANTONIO.   What said you?
DUCHESS.   Sir,
This goodly roof of yours is too low built;
I cannot stand upright in't nor discourse,
Without I raise it higher: raise yourself;
Or, if you please, my hand to help you: so.
                      (Raises him.)
ANTONIO.   Ambition, madam, is a great man's
    madness,
That is not kept in chains and close-pent rooms,
But in fair lightsome lodgings, and is girt
With the wild noise of prattling visitants,
Which makes it lunatic beyond all cure.
Conceive not I am so stupid but I aim
Whereto your favours tend: but he's a fool
That, being a-cold, would thrust his hands i' th'
    fire
To warm them.
DUCHESS.   So, now the ground's broke,
You may discover what a wealthy mine
I make you lord of.
ANTONIO.   O my unworthiness!
DUCHESS.   You were ill to sell yourself:
This darkening of your worth is not like that
Which tradesmen use i' th' city; their false lights
Are to rid bad wares off: and I must tell you,
If you will know where breathes a complete man
(I speak it without flattery), turn your eyes,
And progress through yourself.
ANTONIO.   Were there nor heaven
Nor hell, I should be honest: I have long serv'd
    virtue,
And ne'er ta'en wages of her.

56

DUCHESS.   Now she pays it.
The misery of us that are born great!
We are forc'd to woo, because none dare woo us;
And as a tyrant doubles with his words,
And fearfully equivocates, so we
Are forc'd to express our violent passions
In riddles and in dreams, and leave the path
Of simple virtue, which was never made
To seem the thing it is not. Go, go brag
You have left me heartless; mine is in your
          bosom:
I hope 'twill multiply love there. You do tremble:
Make not your heart so dead a piece of flesh,
To fear more than to love me. Sir, be confident:
What is't distracts you? This is flesh and blood,
          sir;
'Tis not the figure cut in alabaster
Kneels at my husband's tomb. Awake, awake,
          man!
I do here put off all vain ceremony,
And only do appear to you a young widow
That claims you for her husband, and, like a
          widow,
I use but half a blush in't.

John Webster, *The Duchess of Malfi*, Act I, scene ii (1613)

CATHERINE ARROWPOINT 'PROPOSES' TO HERR KLESMER, HER PIANO-TEACHER

"YOU AGREE WITH ME that I had better go?" said Klesmer, with some irritation.

"Certainly; if that is what your business and feeling prompt. I have only to wonder that you have consented to give us so much of your time in the last year. There must be treble the interest to you anywhere else. I have

never thought of your consenting to come here as anything else than a sacrifice."

"Why should I make the sacrifice?" said Klesmer, going
to seat himself at the piano, and touching the keys so as
to give with the delicacy of an echo in the far distance a
melody which he had set to Heine's "Ich hab' dich geliebet
und liebe dich noch."

"That is the mystery," said Catherine, not wanting to
affect anything, but from mere agitation. From the same
cause she was tearing a piece of paper into minute morsels,
as if at a task of utmost multiplication imposed by a cruel
fairy.

"You can conceive no motive?" said Klesmer, folding
his arms.

"None that seems in the least probable."

"Then I shall tell you. It is because you are to me the
chief woman in the world — the throned lady whose
colours I carry between my heart and my armour."

Catherine's hands trembled so much that she could no
longer tear the paper: still less could her lips utter a
word. Klesmer went on —

"This would be the last impertinence in me, if I meant
to found anything upon it. That is out of the question.
I mean no such thing. But you once said it was
your doom to suspect every man who courted you
of being an adventurer, and what made you angriest
was men's imputing to you the folly of believing that
they courted you for your own sake. Did you not say
so?"

"Very likely," was the answer, in a low murmur.

"It was a bitter word. Well, at least one man who has
seen women as plenty as flowers in May has lingered about
you for your own sake. And since he is one whom
you can never marry, you will believe him. That is an
argument in favour of some other man. But don't give
yourself for a meal to a minotaur like Bult. I shall go now
and pack. I shall make my excuses to Mrs Arrowpoint."

Klesmer rose as he ended, and walked quickly towards the door.

"You must take this heap of manuscript, then," said Catherine, suddenly making a desperate effort. She had risen to fetch the heap from another table. Klesmer came back, and they had the length of the folio sheets between them.

"Why should I not marry the man who loves me, if I love him?" said Catherine. To her the effort was something like the leap of a woman from the deck into the lifeboat.

"It would be too hard – impossible – you could not carry it through. I am not worth what you would have to encounter. I will not accept the sacrifice. It would be thought a *mésalliance* for you, and I should be liable to the worst accusations."

"Is it the accusations you are afraid of? I am afraid of nothing but that we should miss the passing of our lives together."

The decisive word had been spoken: there was no doubt concerning the end willed by each: there only remained the way of arriving at it, and Catherine determined to take the straightest possible. She went to her father and mother in the library, and told them that she had promised to marry Klesmer.

George Eliot, *Daniel Deronda* (1876)

BE MARRIED

I FEEL SAD when I don't see you. Be married, why won't you? And come to live with me. I will make you as happy as I can. You shall not be obliged to work hard; and when you are tired; you may lie in my lap and I will sing you to rest ... I will play you a tune upon the violin as often as you ask and as well as I can; and leave off smoking, if you say so ... I would always be very kind to you, I think, because I love you so well. I will not make you bring in wood and water, or feed the pig, or milk the cow, or go to the neighbors to borrow milk. Will you be married?

Letter from an American suitor (19th century)

JEM'S 'PROPOSAL' TO MARTHA

WHILE I WAS GIVING but absent answers to the questions Miss Matty was putting – almost as absently – we heard a clumping sound on the stairs, and a whispering outside the door: which indeed once opened and shut as if by some invisible agency. After a little while, Martha came in, dragging after her a great tall young man, all crimson with shyness, and finding his only relief in perpetually sleeking down his hair.

'Please, ma'am, he's only Jem Hearn,' said Martha, by way of introduction; and so out of breath was she, that I imagine she had had some bodily struggle before she could overcome his reluctance to be presented on the courtly scene of Miss Matilda Jenkyns's drawing-room.

'And please, ma'am, he wants to marry me off-hand. And please, ma'am, we want to take a lodger – just one quiet lodger, to make our two ends meet; and we'd take any house conformable; and, oh dear Miss Matty, if I may be so bold, would you have any objections to lodging with us? Jem wants it as much as I do.' [To Jem:] 'You great oaf! why can't you back me? – But he does want it, all the same, very bad – don't you, Jem? – only, you see, he's dazed at being called on to speak before quality.'

'It's not that,' broke in Jem. 'It's that you've taken me all on a sudden, and I didn't think for to get married so soon – and such quick work does flabbergast a man. It's not that I'm against it, ma'am' (addressing Miss Matty), 'only Martha has such quick ways with her, when once she takes a thing into her head; and marriage, ma'am – marriage nails a man, as one may say. I dare say I shan't mind it after it's once over.'

'Please, ma'am,' said Martha – who had plucked at his sleeve, and nudged him with her elbow, and otherwise tried to interrupt him all the time he had been speaking – 'don't mind him, he'll come to; 'twas only last night he was an-axing me, and an-axing me, and all the more because I said I could not think of it for years to come, and now he's only taken aback with the suddenness of the joy; but you know, Jem, you are just as full as me about wanting a lodger.' (Another great nudge.)

'Ay! If Miss Matty would lodge with us – otherwise I've no mind to be cumbered with strange folk in the house,' said Jem, with a want of tact which I could see enraged Martha, who was trying to represent a lodger as the great object they wished to obtain, and that, in fact, Miss Matty would be smoothing their path, and conferring a favour, if she would only come and live with them.

Miss Matty herself was bewildered by the pair; their, or rather Martha's sudden resolution in favour of matrimony staggered her, and stood between her and the contemplation of the plan which Martha had at heart. Miss Matty began:

'Marriage is a very solemn thing, Martha.'

'It is indeed, ma'am,' quoth Jem. 'Not that I've no objections to Martha.'

'You've never let me a-be for asking me for to fix when I would be married,' said Martha – her face all afire, and ready to cry with vexation – 'and now you're shaming me before my missus and all.'

'Nay, now! Martha, don't ee! don't ee! only a man likes to have breathing-time,' said Jem, trying to possess himself of her hand, but in vain. Then seeing that she was more seriously hurt than he had imagined, he seemed to try to rally his scattered faculties, and with more straightforward dignity than, ten minutes before, I should have thought it possible for him to assume, he turned to Miss Matty, and said, 'I hope, ma'am, you know that I am bound to respect every one who has been kind to Martha. I always looked on her as to be my wife – some time; and she has often and often spoke of you as the kindest lady that ever was; and though the plain truth is I would not like to be troubled with lodgers of the common run, yet if, ma'am, you'd honour us by living with us, I'm sure Martha would do her best to make you comfortable; and I'd keep out of your way as much as I could, which I reckon would be the best kindness such an awkward chap as me could do.'

Miss Matty had been very busy with taking off her spectacles, wiping them, and replacing them; but all she could say was, 'Don't let any thought of me hurry you into marriage: pray don't! Marriage is such a very solemn thing!'

'But Miss Matilda will think of your plan, Martha,' said I, struck with the advantages that it offered, and unwilling to lose the opportunity of considering about it. 'And I'm sure neither she nor I can ever forget your kindness; nor yours either, Jem.'

'Why, yes, ma'am! I'm sure I mean kindly, though I'm a bit fluttered by being pushed straight a-head into matrimony, as it were, and mayn't express myself conformable. But I'm sure I'm willing enough, and give me time to get accustomed; so, Martha, wench, what's the use of crying so, and slapping me if I come near?'

This last was *sotto voce*, and had the effect of making Martha bounce out of the room, to be followed and soothed by her lover. Whereupon Miss Matty sat down and cried very heartily, and accounted for it by saying that the thought of Martha being married so soon gave her quite a shock, and that she should never forgive herself if she thought she was hurrying the poor creature. I think my pity was more for Jem, of the two; but both Miss

Matty and I appreciated to the full the kindness of the honest couple, although we said little about this, and a good deal about the chances and dangers of matrimony.

Elizabeth Gaskell, *Cranford* (1853)

AUTUMN

He told his life story to Mrs Courtly
Who was a widow. 'Let us get married shortly',
He said. 'I am no longer passionate,
But we can have some conversation before it is too late.'

Stevie Smith (1942)

VICTORIA AND ALBERT

TUESDAY, 15TH OCTOBER – Saw my dear Cousins come home quite safe from the Hunt, and charge up the hill at an immense pace. Saw Esterhazy. At about $\frac{1}{2}$ p. 12 I sent for Albert; he came to the Closet where I was alone, and after a few minutes I said to him, that I thought he must be aware *why* I wished them to come here, – and that it would make me *too happy* if he would consent to what I wished (to marry me). We embraced each other, and he was *so* kind, *so* affectionate. I told him I was quite unworthy of him, – he said he would be very happy 'das Leben mit dir zu zubringen,' and was so kind, and seemed so happy, that I really felt it was the happiest brightest moment in my life. I told him it was a great sacrifice, – which he wouldn't allow; I then told him of the necessity of keeping it a secret, except to his father and Uncle Leopold and Stockmar, to whom he said he would send a Courier next day, – and also that it was to be as early as the beginning of February. I then told him to fetch Ernest,

63

which he did and he congratulated us both and seemed very happy. I feel the happiest of human beings.

Queen Victoria's journal, 1839

THE ENGLISH KING AND THE FRENCH PRINCESS

KING HENRY. Marry, if you would put me to verses or to dance for your sake, Kate, why you undid me: for the one, I have neither words nor measure, and for the other, I have no strength in measure, yet a reasonable measure in strength. If I could win a lady at leap-frog, or by vaulting into my saddle with my armour on my back, under the correction of bragging be it spoken, I should quickly leap into a wife. Or if I might buffet for my love, or bound my horse for her favours, I could lay on like a butcher and sit like a jack-an-apes, never off. But before God, Kate, I cannot look greenly nor gasp out my eloquence, nor I have no cunning in protestation; only downright oaths, which I never use till urged, nor never break for urging. If thou canst love a fellow of this temper, Kate, whose face is not worth sun-burning, that never looks in his glass for love of any thing he sees there, let thine eye be thy cook. I speak to thee plain soldier: if thou canst love me for this, take me; if not, to say to thee that I shall die, is true; but for thy love, by the Lord, no; yet I love thee too. And while thou livest, dear Kate, take a fellow of plain and uncoined constancy, for he perforce must do thee right, because he hath not the gift to woo in other places; for these fellows of infinite tongue, that can rhyme themselves into ladies' favours, they do always reason themselves out again. What! a speaker is but a prater; a rhyme is but a ballad. A good leg will fall, a straight back will stoop, a black beard will turn white, a curled pate will grow bald, a fair face will wither, a full

64

eye will wax hollow, but a good heart, Kate, is the sun and the moon; or, rather, the sun, and not the moon; for it shines bright and never changes, but keeps his course truly. If thou would have such a one, take me; and take me, take a soldier; take a soldier, take a king. And what sayest thou then to my love? speak, my fair, and fairly, I pray thee.

Katharine. Is it possible dat I sould love de enemy of France?

King Henry. No; it is not possible you should love the enemy of France, Kate; but, in loving me, you should love the friend of France; for I love France so well that I will not part with a village of it; I will have it all mine: and, Kate, when France is mine and I am yours, then yours is France and you are mine....

William Shakespeare, *Henry V*, Act V, scene ii

HOLIDAY GOWN

In holiday gown, and my new-fangled hat,
  Last Monday I tripped to the fair;
I held up my head, and I'll tell you for what,
  Brisk Roger I guessed would be there:
He woos me to marry whenever we meet,
  There's honey sure dwells on his tongue!
He hugs me so close, and he kisses so sweet,
  I'd wed – if I were not too young.

Fond Sue, I'll assure you, laid hold on the boy,
  (The vixen would fain be his bride)
Some token she claimed, either ribbon or toy,
  And swore that she'd not be denied:
A top-knot he bought her, and garters of green,
  Pert Susan was cruelly stung;
I hate her so much, that, to kill her with spleen,
  I'd wed – if I were not too young.

He whispered such soft pretty things in mine ear!
    He flattered, he promised, and swore!
Such trinkets he gave me, such laces and gear,
    That, trust me, – my pockets ran o'er:
Some ballads he bought me, the best he could find,
    And sweetly their burthen he sung;
Good faith! he's so handsome, so witty, and kind,
    I'd wed – if I were not too young.

The sun was just setting, 'twas time to retire,
    (Our cottage was distant a mile)
I rose to be gone – Roger bowed like a squire,
    And handed me over the stile:
His arms he threw round me – love laughed in his eye,
    He led me the meadows among,
There pressed me so close, I agreed, with a sigh,
    To wed – for I was not too young.

John Cunningham (1729–73)

MIRABELL AND MILLAMENT

MIRA. Like Daphne she, as lovely and as coy.
Do you lock yourself up from me, to make my search more curious? Or is this pretty artifice contrived, to signifie that here the chace must end, and my pursuit be crowned, for you can fly no further?

MILLA. Vanity! No – I'll fly and be followed to the last moment, though I am upon the very verge of matrimony, I expect you should sollicit me as much as if I were wavering at the grate of a monastery, with one foot over the threshold. I'll be sollicited to the very last, nay and afterwards.

MIRA. What, after the last?

MILLA. O, I should think I was poor and had nothing

66

to bestow, if I were reduced to an inglorious ease, and freed from the agreeable fatigues of sollicitation.

MIRA. But do not you know, that when favours are conferred upon instant and tedious sollicitation, that they diminish in their value, and that both the giver loses the grace, and the receiver lessens his pleasure?

MILLA. It may be in things of common application; but never sure in love.   O, I hate a lover that can dare to think he draws a moment's air, independent on the bounty of his mistress.   There is not so impudent a thing in nature, as the sawcy look of an assured man, confident of success.   The pedantick arrogance of a very husband has not so pragmatical an air.   Ah! I'll never marry, unless I am first made sure of my will and pleasure.

MIRA. Would you have 'em both before marriage?   Or will you be contented with the first now, and stay for the other 'till after grace?

MILLA. Ah, don't be impertinent – My dear liberty, shall I leave thee?   My faithful solitude, my darling contemplation, must I bid you then adieu?   Ay-h, adieu – my morning thoughts, agreeable wakings, indolent slumbers, all ye *douceurs*, ye *someils du matin,* adieu – I can't do't, 'tis more than impossible – Positively, Mirabell, I'll lye abed in a morning as long as I please.

MIRA. Then I'll get up in a morning as early as I please.

MILLA. Ah! Idle creature, get up when you will – And d'ye hear, I won't be called names after I'm married; positively I won't be called names.

MIRA. Names!

MILLA. Ay, as wife, spouse, my dear, joy, jewel, love, sweetheart, and the rest of that nauseous cant, in which men and their wives are so fulsomly familiar – I shall never bear that – Good Mirabell, don't let us be familiar or fond, nor kiss before folks, like my Lady Fadler and Sir Francis: nor go to Hide Park together the first Sunday in a new chariot, to provoke eyes and whispers; and then never be seen there together again; as if we were proud of one another the first week, and ashamed of one another ever after. Let us never visit together, nor go to a play together, but let us be very strange and well bred: let us be as strange as if we had been married a great while; and as well bred as if we were not married at all.

MIRA. Have you any more conditions to offer? Hitherto your demands are pretty reasonable.

MILLA. Trifles, – as liberty to pay and receive visits to and from whom I please; to write and receive letters, without interrogatories or wry faces on your part; to wear what I please; and chuse conversation with regard only to my own taste; to have no obligation upon me to converse with wits that I don't like, because they are your acquaintance; or to be intimate with fools because they may be your relations. Come to dinner when I please, dine in my dressing-room when I'm out of humour, without giving a reason. To have my closet inviolate; to be sole empress of my tea-table, which you must never presume to approach without first asking leave. And lastly, wherever I am, you shall always knock at the door before you come in. These articles subscribed, if I continue to endure you a little longer, I may by degrees dwindle into a wife.

MIRA. Your bill of fare is something advanced in this latter account. Well, have I liberty to offer conditions – that when you are dwindled into a wife, I may not be beyond measure enlarged into a husband?

MILLA. You have free leave, propose your utmost, speak and spare not.

MIRA. I thank you. *Inprimis* then, I covenant that your acquaintance be general; that you admit no sworn confident, or intimate of your own sex; no she friend to skreen her affairs under your countenance, and tempt you to make trial of a mutual secresie. No decoy-duck to wheadle you a *fop* – *scrambling* to the play in a mask – then bring you home in a pretended fright, when you think you shall be found out – and rail at me for missing the play, and disappointing the frolick which you had to pick me up and prove my constancy.

MILLA. Detestable *inprimis!* I go to the play in a mask!

MIRA. Item, I article, that you continue to like your own face as long as I shall: and while it passes currant with me, that you endeavour not to new coin it. To which end, together with all vizards for the day, I prohibit all masks for the night, made of oiled-skins and I know not what – hog's bones, hare's gall, pig water, and the marrow of a roasted cat. In short, I forbid all commerce with the gentlewoman in *what-d'ye-call-it* Court. *Item,* I shut my doors against all bauds with baskets, and pennyworths of *muslin, china, fans, atlasses,* etc. – *Item,* when you shall be breeding –

MILLA. Ah! name it not.

MIRA. Which may be presumed, with a blessing on our endeavours –

MILLA. Odious endeavours!

MIRA. I denounce against all strait lacing, squeezing for a shape, 'till you mould my boy's head like a sugar-loaf; and instead of a man-child, make me father to a crooked-billet. Lastly, to the dominion of the *tea-table* I submit. – But with *proviso,* that you exceed not in your province; but restrain yourself to native and simple *tea-table* drinks, as *tea, chocolate,* and *coffee.* As likewise to genuine and authorised *tea-table* talk – such as mending of fashions, spoiling reputations, railing at absent friends, and so forth – but that on no account you encroach upon the men's prerogative, and presume to drink healths, or toast fellows; for prevention of which, I banish all *foreign forces,* all auxiliaries to the *tea-table,* as *orange-brandy,* all *anniseed, cinamon, citron* and *Barbado's-waters,* together with *ratafia* and the most noble spirit of *clary.* But for *couslip-wine, poppy-water,* and all *dormitives,* those I allow. – These *provisos* admitted, in other things I may prove a tractable and complying husband.

MILLA. O horrid *provisos!* filthy strong waters! I toast fellows, odious men! I hate your odious *provisos.*

MIRA. Then we're agreed. Shall I kiss your hand upon the contract? and here comes one to be a witness to the sealing of the deed.

William Congreve, *The Way of the World,* Act IV, scene v (1700)

TWO MARRIAGES PROPOSED - WITHOUT PREJUDICE

The insufferable Mr Collins has been rejected by Elizabeth Bennet, so decides to switch his suit to her friend, Charlotte Lucas, who wants nothing more than to be married.

MISS LUCAS perceived him from an upper window as he walked towards the house, and instantly set out to meet him accidentally in the lane. But little had she dared to hope that so much love and eloquence awaited her there.

In as short a time as Mr. Collins's long speeches would allow, everything was settled between them to the satisfaction of both; and as they entered the house he earnestly entreated her to name the day that was to make him the happiest of men; and though such a solicitation must be waived for the present, the lady felt no inclination to trifle with his happiness. The stupidity with which he was favoured by nature must guard his courtship from any charm that could make a woman wish for its continuance; and Miss Lucas, who accepted him solely from the pure and disinterested desire of an establishment, cared not how soon that establishment were gained.

Sir William and Lady Lucas were speedily applied to for their consent; and it was bestowed with a most joyful alacrity. Mr. Collins's present circumstances made it a most eligible match for their daughter, to whom they could give little fortune; and his prospects of future wealth were exceedingly fair . . .

. . . Charlotte herself was tolerably composed. She had gained her point, and had time to consider of it. Her reflections were in general satisfactory. Mr. Collins, to be sure, was neither sensible nor agreeable; his society was irksome, and his attachment to her must be imaginary. But still he would be her husband. Without thinking highly either of men or of matrimony, marriage had always been her object; it was the only honourable provision for well-educated young women of small fortune, and however uncertain of giving happiness, must be their pleasantest preservative from want. This preservative she had now obtained; and at the age of twenty-seven, without having ever been handsome, she felt all the good luck of it.

[Elizabeth, of course, has always been loved by the proud Mr Darcy, but her prejudice has blinded her to his qualities. At last she realises her mistake.]

NOW WAS THE MOMENT for her resolution to be executed; and, while her courage was high, she immediately said –

'Mr. Darcy, I am a very selfish creature; and for the sake of giving relief to my own feelings, care not how much I may be wounding yours. I can no longer help thanking you for your unexampled kindness to my poor sister. Ever since I have known it, I have been most anxious to acknowledge to you how gratefully I feel it. Were it known to the rest of my family, I should not have merely my own gratitude to express.' . . .

71

... 'If you *will* thank me,' he replied, 'let it be for yourself alone. That the wish of giving happiness to you might add force to the other inducements which led me on, I shall not attempt to deny. But your *family* owe me nothing. Much as I respect them, I believe I thought only of *you*.'

Elizabeth was too much embarrassed to say a word. After a short pause, her companion added, 'You are too generous to trifle with me. If your feelings are still what they were last April, tell me so at once. *My* affections and wishes are unchanged; but one word from you will silence me on this subject for ever.'

Elizabeth, feeling all the more than common awkwardness and anxiety of his situation, now forced herself to speak; and immediately, though not very fluently, gave him to understand that her sentiments had undergone so material a change since the period to which he alluded, as to make her receive with gratitude and pleasure his present assurances. The happiness which this reply produced was such as he had probably never felt before, and he expressed himself on the occasion as sensibly and as warmly as a man violently in love can be supposed to do. Had Elizabeth been able to encounter his eyes, she might have seen how well the expression of heartfelt delight diffused over his face became him; but, though she could not look, she could listen, and he told her of feelings which, in proving of what importance she was to him, made his affection every moment more valuable.

They walked on, without knowing in what direction. There was too much to be thought, and felt, and said, for attention to any other objects.

Jane Austen, *Pride and Prejudice* (1813)

DR THORNE'S LOVE LETTER

HAVING FINISHED HIS TEA, which did not take place till near eleven, he went downstairs to an untidy little room which lay behind his dépôt of medicines, and in which he was wont to do his writing; and herein he did at last set himself down to his work.   Even at that moment he was in doubt.   But he would write his letter to Miss Dunstable and see how it looked.   He was almost determined not to send it; so, at least, he said to himself: but he could do no harm by writing it.   So he did write it, as follows: – 'Greshamsbury, June, 185–.   My dear Miss Dunstable –'   When he had got so far, he leaned back in his chair and looked at the paper.   How on earth was he to find words to say that which he now wished to have said?   He had never written such a letter in his life, or anything approaching to it, and now found himself overwhelmed with a difficulty of which he had not pre- viously thought.   He spent another half-hour in looking at the paper, and was at last nearly deterred by this new difficulty.   He would use the simplest, plainest language, he said to himself over and over again; but it is not always easy to use simple, plain language – by no means so easy as to mount on stilts, and to march along with sesquipedalian words, with pathos, spasms, and notes of interjection.   But the letter did at last get itself written, and there was not a note of interjection in it.

'MY DEAR MISS DUNSTABLE,

'I think it right to confess that I should not now be writing this letter to you, had I not been led to believe by other judgement than my own that the proposition which I am going to make would be regarded by you with favour.   Without such other judgement I should, I own, have feared that the great disparity between you and me in regard to money would have given to such a pro-

FROM THIS DAY FORWARD

position an appearance of being false and mercenary. All I ask of you now, with confidence, is to acquit me of such fault as that.

'When you have read so far you will understand what I mean. We have known each other now somewhat intimately, though indeed not very long, and I have some-times fancied that you were almost as well pleased to be with me as I have been to be with you. If I have been wrong in this, tell me so simply, and I will endeavour to let our friendship run on as though this letter had not been written. But if I have been right, and if it be possible that you can think that a union between us will make us both happier than we are single, I will plight you my word and troth with good faith, and will do what an old man may do to make the burden of the world lie light on your shoulders. Looking at my age I can hardly keep myself from thinking that I am an old fool: but I try to reconcile myself to that by remembering that you yourself are no longer a girl. You see that I pay you no com-pliments, and that you need expect none from me.

'I do not know that I could add anything to the truth of this, if I were to write three times as much. All that is necessary is, that you should know what I mean. If you do not believe me to be true and honest already, nothing that I can write will make you believe it.

'God bless you. I know you will not keep me long in suspense for an answer. – Affectionately your friend,

'THOMAS THORNE'

When he had finished he meditated again for another half-hour whether it would not be right that he should add something about her money. Would it not be well for him to tell her – it might be said in a postscript – that with regard to all her wealth she would be free to do what she chose? At any rate he owed no debts for her to pay, and would still have his own income, sufficient for his own purposes. But about one o'clock he came to the conclusion that it would be better to leave the matter alone. If she cared for him, and could trust him, and was worthy also that he should trust her, no omission of such a statement would deter her from coming to him: and if there were no such trust, it would not be created by any such assurance on his part. So he read the letter over twice, sealed it, and took it up, together with his bed candle, into his bedroom. Now that the letter was written it seemed to be a thing fixed by fate that it must go. He had written it that he might see how it looked when written; but now that it was written, there remained no doubt that it must be sent. So he went to bed, with the letter on the toilette-table beside him; and early in the morning – so early as to make it seem that the importance of the letter had disturbed his rest – he sent it off by a special messenger to Boxall Hill. 'I'se wait for an answer?' said the boy.

'No,' said the doctor: 'leave the letter, and come away.'

The breakfast hour was not very early at Boxall Hill in these summer months. Frank Gresham, no doubt, went round his farm before he came in for prayers, and his wife was probably looking to the butter in the dairy. At any rate, they did not meet till near ten, and therefore, though the ride from Greshamsbury to Boxall Hill was nearly two hours' work, Miss Dunstable had her letter in her own room before she came down. She read it in silence as she was dressing, while the maid was with her in the room; but she made no sign which could induce her Abigail to think that the epistle was more than ordinarily important. She read it, and then quietly refolding it and placing it in the envelope, she put it down on the table at which she was sitting. It was full fifteen minutes afterwards that she begged her servant to see if Mrs Gresham were still in her own room. 'Because I want to see her for five minutes, alone, before breakfast,' said Miss Dunstable.

'You traitor; you false, black traitor!' were the first

75

words which Miss Dunstable spoke when she found herself alone with her friend.

'Why, what's the matter?'

'I did not think there was so much mischief in you, nor so keen and commonplace a desire for match-making. Look here. Read the first four lines; not more, if you please; the rest is private. Whose is the other judgement of whom your uncle speaks in this letter?'

'Oh, Miss Dunstable! I must read it all.'

'Indeed you'll do no such thing. You think it's a love-letter, I dare say; but indeed there's not a word about love in it.'

'I know he has offered. I shall be so glad, for I know you like him.'

'He tells me that I am an old woman, and insinuates that I may probably be an old fool.'

'I am sure he does not say that.'

'Ah! but I'm sure that he does. The former is true enough, and I never complain of the truth. But as to the latter, I am by no means so certain that it is true – not in the sense that he means it.'

'Dear, dearest woman, don't go on in that way now. Do speak out to me, and speak without jesting.'

'Whose was the other judgement to whom he trusts so implicitly? Tell me that.'

'Mine, mine, of course. No one else can have spoken to him about it. Of course I talked to him.'

'And what did you tell him?'

'I told him –'

'Well, out with it. Let me have the real facts. Mind, I tell you fairly that you had no right to tell him anything. What passed between us, passed in confidence. But let us hear what you did say.'

'I told him that you would have him if he offered.' And Mrs Gresham, as she spoke, looked into her friend's face doubtingly, not knowing whether in very truth Miss Dunstable were pleased with her or displeased. If she were displeased, then how had her uncle been deceived!

'You told him that as a fact?'

'I told him that I thought so.'

'Then I suppose I am bound to have him,' said Miss Dunstable, dropping the letter on to the floor in mock despair.

'My dear, dear, dearest woman!' said Mrs Gresham, bursting into tears, and throwing herself on to her friend's neck.

'Mind you are a dutiful niece,' said Miss Dunstable. 'And now let me go and finish dressing.'

In the course of the afternoon, an answer was sent back to Greshamsbury, in these words: –

'DEAR DR THORNE,

'I do and will trust you in everything; and it shall be as you would have it. Mary writes to you; but do not believe a word she says. I never will again, for she has behaved so bad in this matter. – Yours affectionately and very truly,

'MARTHA DUNSTABLE'

'And so I am going to marry the richest woman in England,' said Dr Thorne to himself, as he sat down that day to his mutton-chop.

Anthony Trollope, *Framley Parsonage* (1861)

'WE MIGHT AS WELL ...'

THE OTHER PROBLEM with this is, when she's not here I find it very difficult to remember her and precisely how she would behave in any given situation. It's the thing I was talking through earlier. Ellen as Fictional Woman just doesn't seem real to me at all, probably because I don't understand her. Or don't want

77

to understand her. One of the essential features of a fictional character is that you (the author) have the power to determine exactly what they will do next, and one of the most important features of the Ellen/Me set-up is that I never have the faintest idea what's in store. I didn't really, from the day we met. I recall, unwillingly, the day we decided to get married. Early spring in Hyde Park – the two of us lying about six feet away from each other.

"Well." I said, "I don't know. We might as well –"

"What?"

"You know. I mean we might as *well* get –"

"Get what?"

"Get ... You know."

"Oh *that*."

She turned over on her stomach and looked at me, amused as usual. She rested her chin on her hands. I screwed my neck round painfully.

"Do you think?" I said.

"Fine," she said, and then she got to her feet. She crossed over to me and prodded me in the stomach with her toe. The sun was behind her and she looked very pretty. "But," she went on, "you said it first, little man. You said it first. Okey dokey?"

"Sure I said it first," I replied, "what's wrong with that?"

And then we looked at each other for quite a long time, like heavyweight wrestlers sizing each other up. And then I bought her a ring. And she said DIAMONDS MAKE IT PERFECT ESPECIALLY FROM BRAVINGTONS.

Nigel Williams, *My Life Closed Twice* (1986)

JANE DISBELIEVES

'JANE, BE STILL; don't struggle so, like a wild, frantic bird that is rending its own plumage in its desperation.'

'I am no bird; and no net ensnares me; I am a free human being with an independent will; which I now exert to leave you.'

Another effort set me at liberty, and I stood erect before him.

'And your will shall decide your destiny,' he said: 'I offer you my hand, my heart, and a share of all my possessions.'

'You play a farce, which I merely laugh at.'

'I ask you to pass through life at my side – to be my second self and best earthly companion.'

'For that fate you have already made your choice, and must abide by it.'

'Jane, be still a few moments: you are over-excited: I will be still too.'

A waft of wind came sweeping down the laurel-walk, and trembled through the boughs of the chestnut: it wandered away – away – to an indefinite distance – it died. The nightingale's song was then the only voice of the hour: in listening to it, I again wept. Mr Rochester sat quiet, looking at me gently and seriously. Some time passed before he spoke: he at last said: –

'Come to my side, Jane, and let us explain and understand one another.'

'I will never again come to your side: I am torn away now, and cannot return.'

'But, Jane, I summon you as my wife: it is you only I intend to marry.'

I was silent: I thought he mocked me.

'Come Jane – come hither.'

'Your bride stands between us.'

He rose, and with a stride reached me.

'My bride is here,' he said, again drawing me to him, 'because my equal is here, and my likeness. Jane, will you marry me?'

Still I did not answer, and still I writhed myself from his grasp: for I was still incredulous.

'Do you doubt me, Jane?'

'Entirely.'

'You have no faith in me?'

'Not a whit.'

'Am I a liar in your eyes?' he asked passionately. "Little sceptic, you *shall* be convinced. What love have I for Miss Ingram? None: and that you know. What love has she for me? None: as I have taken pains to prove: I caused a rumour to reach her that my fortune was not a third of what was supposed, and after that I presented myself to see the result, it was coldness both from her and her mother. I would not – I could not – marry Miss Ingram. You – you strange – you almost unearthly thing! – I love as my own flesh. You – poor and obscure, and small and plain as you are – I entreat to accept me as a husband.'

'What me!' I ejaculated: beginning in his earnestness – and especially in his incivility – to credit his sincerity: 'me who have not a friend in the world but you – if you are my friend: not a shilling but what you have given me?'

'You, Jane. I must have you for my own – entirely my own. Will you be mine? Say yes, quickly.'

'Mr Rochester, let me look at your face: turn to the moonlight.'

'Why?'

'Because I want to read your countenance; turn!'

'There: you will find it scarcely more legible than a crumpled, scratched page. Read on: only make haste, for I suffer.'

His face was very much agitated and very much flushed,

80

and there were strong workings in the features, and strange gleams in the features, and strange gleams in the eyes.

'Oh, Jane, you torture me!' he exclaimed. 'With that searching and yet faithful and generous look, you torture me!'

'How can I do that? If you are true and your offer real, my only feelings to you must be gratitude and devotion – they cannot torture.'

'Gratitude!' he ejaculated; and added wildly – 'Jane, accept me quickly. Say Edward – give me my name – Edward – I will marry you.'

'Are you in earnest? – Do you truly love me? – Do you sincerely wish me to be your wife?'

'I do; and if an oath is necessary to satisfy you, I swear it.'

'Then, sir, I will marry you.'

Charlotte Bronte, *Jane Eyre* (1847)

MARY LAWRIE ACCEPTS MR WHITTLESTAFF

Mr Whittlestaff is much older than Mary Lawrie. She has confessed to him her unrequited love for John Gordon . . .

'I THINK IT IS THREE YEARS since he went.'
'Three years is a long time. Has he never written?'

'Not to me. How should he write? There was nothing for him to write about.'

'It has been a fancy.'

'Yes; – a fancy.' He had made this excuse for her, and she had none stronger to make for herself.

He certainly did not think the better of her in that she had indulged in such a fancy; but in truth his love was sharpened by the opposition which this fancy made. It

81

had seemed to him that his possessing her would give a brightness to his life, and this brightness was not altogether obscured by the idea that she had ever thought that she had loved another person. As a woman she was as lovable as before, though perhaps less admirable. At any rate he wanted her, and now she seemed to be more within his reach than she had been. 'The week has passed by, Mary, and I suppose that now you can give me an answer.' Then she found that she was in his power. She had told him her story, as though with the understanding that if he would take her with her 'fancy,' she was ready to surrender herself. 'Am I not to have an answer now?'

'I suppose so.'

'What is it to be?'

'If you wish for me, I will be yours.'

'And you will cease to think of Mr. Gordon?'

'I shall think of him; but not in a way that you would begrudge me.'

'That will suffice. I know that you are honest, and I will not ask you to forget him altogether. But there had better be no speaking of him. It is well that he should be banished from your mind. And now, dearest, dearest love, give me your hand.' She put her hand at once into his. 'And a kiss.' She just turned herself a little round, with her eyes bent upon the ground. 'Nay; there must be a kiss.' Then he bent over her, and just touched her cheek. 'Mary, you are now all my own.' Yes; – she was now all his own, and she would do for him the best in her power. He had not asked for her love, and she certainly had not given it. She knew well how impossible it would be that she should give him her love. 'I know you are disturbed,' he said, 'I wish also for a few minutes to think of it all.' Then he turned away from her, and went up the garden walk by himself.

She, slowly loitering, went into the house alone, and seated herself by the open window in her bed-chamber. As she sat there she could see him up the long walk, going and returning. As he went his hands were folded behind his back, and she thought that he appeared older than she had ever remarked him to be before. What did it signify? She had undertaken her business in life, and the duties she thought would be within her power. She was sure that she would be true to him, as far as truth to his material interests was concerned. His comforts in life should be her first care. If he trusted her at all, he should not become poorer by reason of his confidence. And she would be as tender to him as the circumstances would admit. She would not begrudge him kisses if he cared for them. They were his by all the rights of contract. He certainly had the best of the bargain, but he should never know how much the best of it he had. He had told her that there had better be no speaking of John Gordon. There certainly should be none on her part. She had told him that she must continue to think of him. There at any rate she had been honest. But he should not see that she thought of him.

Then she endeavoured to assure herself that this think-ing would die out. Looking round the world, her small world, how many women there were who had not married the men they had loved first! How few, perhaps, had done so! Life was not good-natured enough for smoothness such as that. And yet did not they, as a rule, live well with their husbands? What right had she to expect anything better than their fate? Each poor insipid dame that she saw, toddling on with half-a-dozen children at her heels, might have had as good a John Gordon of her own as was hers. And each of them might have sat on a summer day, at an open window, looking out with something, oh, so far from love, at the punctual steps of him who was to be her husband.

Then her thoughts turned, would turn, could not be kept from turning, to John Gordon. He had been to her the personification of manliness. That which he resolved to do, he did with an iron will. But his manners to all women were soft, and to her seemed to have been suffused

83

with special tenderness. But he was chary of his words, – as he had even been to her. He had been the son of a banker at Norwich; but, just as she had become acquainted with him, the bank had broke, and he had left Oxford to come home and find himself a ruined man. But he had never said a word to her of the family misfortune. He had been six feet high, with dark hair cut very short, somewhat full of sport of the roughest kind, which, however, he had abandoned instantly. 'Things have so turned out,' he had once said to Mary, 'that I must earn something to eat instead of riding after foxes.' She could not boast that he was handsome. 'What does it signify?' she had once said to her step-mother, who had declared him to be stiff, upsetting, and ugly. 'A man is not like a poor girl, who has nothing but the softness of her skin to depend upon.' Then Mrs. Lawrie had declared to him that 'he did no good coming about the house,' – and he went away.

Why had he not spoken to her? He had said that one word, promising that if he returned he would come to Norwich. She had lived three years since that, and he had not come back. And her house had been broken up, and she, though she would have been prepared to wait for another three years, – though she would have waited till she had grown grey with waiting, – she had now fallen into the hands of one who had a right to demand from her that she should obey him. 'And it is not that I hate him,' she said to herself. 'I do love him. He is all good. But I am glad that he has not bade me not to think of John Gordon.'

Anthony Trollope, *An Old Man's Love* (1884)

A DRAPER MAD WITH LOVE

MR EDWARDS: Myfanwy Price!

MISS PRICE: Mr Mog Edwards!

MR EDWARDS: I am a draper mad with love. I love you
more than all the flannelette and calico, candlewick,
dimity, crash and merino, tussore, cretonne, crepon,
muslin, poplin, ticking and twill in the whole Cloth
Hall of the world. I have come to take you away to my
Emporium on the hill, where the change hums on
wires. Throw away your little bedsocks and your Welsh
wool knitted jacket, I will warm the sheets like an
electric toaster, I will lie by your side like the Sunday
roast.

MISS PRICE: I will knit you a wallet of forget-me-not blue,
for the money to be comfy. I will warm your heart by
the fire so that you can slip it in under your vest when
the shop is closed.

MR EDWARDS: Myfanwy, Myfanwy, before the mice gnaw
at your bottom drawer will you say

MISS PRICE: Yes, Mog, yes, Mog, yes, yes, yes.

MR EDWARDS: And all the bells of the tills of the town
shall ring for our wedding.

Dylan Thomas, *Under Milk Wood* (1954)

A COMFORTABLE COUPLE

Miss La Creevy is deeply moved to learn that Nicholas and Kate
Nickleby are both to be married to their chosen partners. She is –
accidentally on purpose – left alone with Tim Linkinwater.

NOW, TIM AND MISS La Creevy had met very
often, and had always been very chatty and pleasant
together – had always been great friends – and conse-

quently it was the most natural thing in the world that
Tim, finding that she still sobbed, should endeavour to
console her.   As Miss La Creevy sat on a large old-
fashioned window-seat where there was ample room for
two, it was also natural that Tim should sit down beside
her; and as to Tim's being unusually spruce and particular
in his attire, that day, why it was a high festival and
a great occasion, and that was the most natural thing of
all.

Tim sat down beside Miss La Creevy, and, crossing one
leg over the other so that his foot – he had very comely
feet, and happened to be wearing the neatest shoes and
black silk stockings possible – should come easily within
the range of her eye, said in a soothing way:

"Don't cry!"

"I must," rejoined Miss La Creevy.

"No don't," said Tim.   "Please don't; pray don't."

"I am so happy!" sobbed the little woman.

"Then laugh," said Tim.   "Do laugh."

What in the world Tim was doing with his arm, it is
impossible to conjecture; but he knocked his elbow against
that part of the window which was quite on the other side
of Miss La Creevy; and it is clear that it could have no
business there.

"Do laugh," said Tim, "or I'll cry."

"Why should you cry?" asked Miss La Creevy, smiling.

"Because I'm happy too," said Tim.   "We are both
happy, and I should like to do as you do."

Surely, there never was a man who fidgeted as Tim
must have done then; for he knocked the window again –
almost in the same place – and Miss La Creevy said she
was sure he'd break it.

"I knew," said Tim, "that you would be pleased with
this scene."

"It was very thoughtful and kind to remember me,"
returned Miss La Creevy.   "Nothing could have
delighted me, half so much."

Why on earth should Miss La Creevy and Tim Linkinwater have said all this in a whisper? It was no secret. And why should Tim Linkinwater have looked so hard at Miss La Creevy, and why should Miss La Creevy have looked so hard at the ground?

"It's a pleasant thing," said Tim, "to people like us, who have passed all our lives in the world, alone, to see young folks that we are fond of, brought together with so many years of happiness before them."

"Ah!" cried the little woman with all her heart. "That it is!"

"Although," pursued Tim, "although it makes one feel quite solitary and cast away. Now, don't it?"

Miss La Creevy said she didn't know. And why should she say she didn't know? Because she must have known whether it did or not.

"It's almost enough to make us get married after all, isn't it?" said Tim.

"Oh nonsense!" replied Miss La Creevy, laughing. "We are too old."

"Not a bit," said Tim, "we are too old to be single. Why shouldn't we both be married, instead of sitting through the long winter evenings by our solitary firesides? Why shouldn't we make one fireside of it, and marry each other?"

"Oh Mr. Linkinwater, you're joking!"

"No, no, I'm not. I'm not indeed," said Tim. "I will, if you will. Do, my dear!"

"It would make people laugh so."

"Let 'em laugh," cried Tim, stoutly, "we have good tempers I know, and we'll laugh too. Why, what hearty laughs we have had since we've known each other!"

"So we have," cried Miss La Creevy – giving way a little, as Tim thought.

"It has been the happiest time in all my life; at least, away from the counting-house and Cheeryble Brothers," said Tim. "Do, my dear! Now say you will."

"No, no, we mustn't think of it," returned Miss La Creevy. "What would the Brothers say?"

"Why, God bless your soul!" cried Tim, innocently, "you don't suppose I should think of such a thing without their knowing it! Why, they left us here on purpose."

"I can never look 'em in the face again!" exclaimed Miss La Creevy, faintly.

"Come!" said Tim. "Let's be a comfortable couple. We shall live in the old house here, where I have been for four-and-forty year; we shall go to the old church, where I've been, every Sunday morning, all through that time; we shall have all my old friends about us – Dick, the archway, the pump, the flower-pots, and Mr. Frank's children, and Mr. Nickleby's children that we shall seem like grandfather and grandmother to. Let's be a comfortable couple, and take care of each other! And if we should get deaf, or lame, or blind, or bed-ridden, how glad we shall be that we have somebody we are fond of, always to talk to and sit with! Let's be a comfortable couple. Now, do, my dear!"

Five minutes after this honest and straightforward speech, little Miss La Creevy and Tim were talking as pleasantly as if they had been married for a score of years, and had never once quarrelled all the time; and five minutes after that, when Miss La Creevy had bustled out to see if her eyes were red and to put her hair to rights, Tim moved with a stately step towards the drawing-room, exclaiming as he went, "There an't such another woman in all London! I *know* there an't!"

Charles Dickens, *Nicholas Nickleby* (1838)

AN UNDERSTANDING IS REACHED

IT WAS VERY ODD to these two persons, who knew each other passing well, that the mere circumstance of their meeting in a new place and in a new way should make them so awkward and constrained. In the fields, or at her house, there had never been any embarrassment; but now that Oak had become the entertainer their lives seemed to be moved back again to the days when they were strangers.

'You'll think it strange that I have come, but –'

'O no; not at all.'

'But I thought – Gabriel, I have been uneasy in the belief that I have offended you, and that you are going away on that account. It grieved me very much, and I couldn't help coming.'

'Offended me! As if you could do that, Bathsheba!'

'Haven't I?' she asked, gladly. 'But, what are you going away for else?'

'I am not going to emigrate, you know; I wasn't aware that you would wish me not to when I told 'ee, or I shouldn't have thought of doing it,' he said, simply. 'I have arranged for Little Weatherbury Farm, and shall have it in my own hands at Lady-day. You know I've had a share in it for some time. Still, that wouldn't prevent my attending to your business as before, hadn't it been that things have been said about us.'

'What?' said Bathsheba in surprise. 'Things said about you and me. What are they?'

'I cannot tell you.'

'It would be wiser if you were to, I think. You have played the part of mentor to me many times, and I don't see why you should fear to do it now.'

'It is nothing that you have done, this time. The top and tail o't is this – that I'm sniffing about here, and waiting for poor Boldwood's farm, with a thought of getting you some day.'

'Getting me! What does that mean?'

'Marrying of 'ee, in plain British. You asked me to tell, so you mustn't blame me.'

Bathsheba did not look quite so alarmed as if a cannon had been discharged by her ear, which was what Oak had expected. 'Marrying me! I didn't know it was that you meant,' she said, quietly. 'Such a thing as that is too absurd – too soon – to think of, by far!'

'Yes; of course, it is too absurd. I don't desire any such thing; I should think that was plain enough by this time. Surely, surely you be the last person in the world I think of marrying. It is too absurd, as you say.'

' "Too – s-s-soon" were the words I used.'

'I must beg your pardon for correcting you, but you said, "too absurd", and so do I.'

'I beg your pardon too!' she returned, with tears in her eyes. ' "Too soon" was what I said. But it doesn't matter a bit – not at all – but I only meant, "too soon". Indeed, I didn't, Mr Oak, and you must believe me!'

Gabriel looked her long in the face, but the firelight being faint there was not much to be seen. 'Bathsheba,' he said, tenderly and in surprise, and coming closer: 'If I only knew one thing – whether you would allow me to love you and win you, and marry you after all – if I only knew that!'

'But you never will know,' she murmured.

'Why?'

'Because you never ask.'

'Oh – Oh!' said Gabriel, with a low laugh of joyousness. 'My own dear –'

'You ought not to have sent me that harsh letter this morning,' she interrupted. 'It shows you didn't care a bit about me, and were ready to desert me like all the rest of them! It was very cruel of you, considering I was the first sweetheart that you ever had, and you were the first I ever had; and I shall not forget it!'

'Now, Bathsheba, was ever anybody so provoking?' he

90

said, laughing. 'You know it was purely that I, as an unmarried man, carrying on a business for you as a very taking young woman, had a proper hard part to play – more particular that people knew I had a sort of feeling for 'ee; and I fancied, from the way we were mentioned together, that it might injure your good name. Nobody knows the heat and fret I have been caused by it.'

'And was that all?'

'All.'

'O, how glad I am I came!' she exclaimed, thankfully, as she rose from her seat. 'I have thought so much more of you since I fancied you did not want even to see me again. But I must be going now, or I shall be missed. Why, Gabriel,' she said, with a slight laugh, as they went to the door, 'it seems exactly as if I had come courting you – how dreadful!'

'And quite right, too,' said Oak. 'I've danced at your skittish heels, my beautiful Bathsheba, for many a long mile, and many a long day; and it is hard to begrudge me this one visit . . .'

Thomas Hardy, *Far from the Madding Crowd* (1874)

MR AND MRS DOVE

Reggie, about to go abroad, goes to say goodbye to the woman he loves.

ANNE JUMPED UP. 'Come and say good-bye to my doves,' she said. 'They've been moved to the side veranda. You do like doves, don't you, Reggie?'

'Awfully,' said Reggie, so fervently that as he opened the french window for her and stood to one side, Anne ran forward and laughed at the doves instead.

To and fro, to and fro over the fine red sand on the floor of the dove house, walked the two doves. One was

91

always in front of the other. One ran forward, uttering a little cry, and the other followed, solemnly bowing and bowing. 'You see,' explained Anne, 'the one in front, she's Mrs. Dove. She looks at Mr. Dove and gives that little laugh and runs forward, and he follows her, bowing and bowing. And that makes her laugh again. Away she runs, and after her,' cried Anne, and she sat back on her heels, 'comes poor Mr. Dove, bowing and bowing . . . and that's their whole life. They never do anything else, you know.' She got up and took some yellow grains out of a bag on the roof of the dove house. 'When you think of them, out in Rhodesia, Reggie, you can be sure that is what they will be doing. . . .'

Reggie gave no sign of having seen the doves or of having heard a word. For the moment he was conscious only of the immense effort it took to tear his secret out of himself and offer it to Anne. 'Anne, do you think you could ever care for me?' It was done. It was over. And in the little pause that followed Reginald saw the garden open to the light, the blue quivering sky, the flutter of leaves on the veranda poles, and Anne turning over the grains of maize on her palm with one finger. Then slowly she shut her hand, and the new world faded as she murmured slowly, 'No, never in that way.' But he had scarcely time to feel anything before she walked quickly away, and he followed her down the steps, along the garden path, under the pink rose arches, across the lawn. There, with the gay herbaceous border behind her, Anne faced Reginald. 'It isn't that I'm not awfully fond of you,' she said. 'I am. But' – her eyes widened – 'not in the way' – a quiver passed over her face – 'one ought to be fond of –' Her lips parted, and she couldn't stop herself. She began laughing. 'There, you see, you see,' she cried, 'it's your check t-tie. Even at this moment, when one would think one really would be solemn, your tie reminds me fearfully of the bow-tie that cats wear in pictures! Oh, please forgive me for being so horrid, please!'

Reggie caught hold of her little warm hand. 'There's no question of forgiving you,' he said quickly. 'How could there be? And I do believe I know why I make you laugh. It's because you're so far above me in every way that I am somehow ridiculous. I see that, Anne. But if I were to –'

'No, no.' Anne squeezed his hand hard. 'It's not that. That's all wrong. I'm not far above you at all. You're much better than I am. You're marvellously unselfish and ... and kind and simple. I'm none of those things. You don't know me. I'm the most awful character,' said Anne. 'Please don't interrupt. And besides, that's not the point. The point is' – she shook her head – 'I couldn't possibly marry a man I laughed at. Surely you see that. The man I marry –' breathed Anne softly. She broke off. She drew her hand away, and looking at Reggie she smiled strangely, dreamily. 'The man I marry –'

And it seemed to Reggie that a tall, handsome, brilliant stranger stepped in front of him and took his place – the kind of man that Anne and he had seen often at the theatre, walking on to the stage from nowhere, without a word catching the heroine in his arms, and after one long, tremendous look, carrying her off to anywhere. . . .

Reggie bowed to his vision. 'Yes, I see,' he said huskily.

'Do you?' said Anne. 'Oh, I do hope you do. Because I feel so horrid about it. It's so hard to explain. You know I've never –' She stopped. Reggie looked at her. She was smiling. 'Isn't it funny?' she said. 'I can say anything to you. I always have been able to from the very beginning.'

He tried to smile, to say 'I'm glad.' She went on. 'I've never known anyone I like as much as I like you. I've never felt so happy with anyone. But I'm sure it's not what people and what books mean when they talk about love. Do you understand? Oh, if you only knew how horrid I feel. But we'd be like ... like Mr. and Mrs. Dove.'

That did it. That seemed to Reginald final, and so terribly true that he could hardly bear it. 'Don't drive it home,' he said, and he turned away from Anne and looked across the lawn. There was the gardener's cottage, with the dark ilex tree beside it. A wet, blue thumb of transparent smoke hung above the chimney. It didn't look real. How his throat ached! Could he speak? He had a shot. 'I must be getting along home,' he croaked, and he began walking across the lawn. But Anne ran after him. 'No, don't. You can't go yet,' she said imploringly. 'You can't possibly go away feeling like that.' And she stared up at him frowning, biting her lip.

'Oh, that's all right,' said Reggie, giving himself a shake. 'I'll ... I'll –' And he waved his hand as much as to say 'get over it'.

'But this is awful,' said Anne. She clasped her hands and stood in front of him. 'Surely you do see how fatal it would be for us to marry, don't you?'

'Oh, quite, quite,' said Reggie, looking at her with haggard eyes.

'How wrong, how wicked, feeling as I do. I mean, it's all very well for Mr. and Mrs. Dove. But imagine that in real life – imagine it!'

'Oh, absolutely,' said Reggie, and he started to walk on. But again Anne stopped him. She tugged at his sleeve, and to his astonishment, this time, instead of laughing, she looked like a little girl who was going to cry.

'Then why, if you understand, are you so un-unhappy?' she wailed. 'Why do you mind so fearfully? Why do you look so aw-awful?'

Reggie gulped, and again he waved something away. 'I can't help it,' he said, 'I've had a blow. If I cut off now, I'll be able to –'

'How can you talk of cutting off now?' said Anne scornfully. She stamped her foot at Reggie; she was crimson. 'How can you be so cruel? I can't let you go until I know for certain that you are just as happy as you were before you asked me to marry you. Surely you must see that, it's so simple.'

But it did not seem at all simple to Reginald. It seemed impossibly difficult.

'Even if I can't marry you, how can I know that you're all that way away, with only that awful mother to write to, and that you're miserable, and that it's all my fault?'

'It's not your fault. Don't think that. It's just fate.' Reggie took her hand off his sleeve and kissed it. 'Don't pity me, dear little Anne,' he said gently. And this time he nearly ran, under the pink arches, along the garden path.

'*Roo-coo-coo-coo! Roo-coo-coo-coo!*' sounded from the veranda. 'Reggie, Reggie,' from the garden.

He stopped, he turned. But when she saw his timid, puzzled look, she gave a little laugh.

'Come back, Mr. Dove,' said Anne. And Reginald came slowly across the lawn.

Katherine Mansfield, *The Garden Party* (1922)

LOVE SONG: I AND THOU

> *Nothing is plumb, level or square:*
> *   the studs are bowed, the joists*
> *are shaky by nature, no piece fits*
> *   any other piece without a gap*
> *or pinch, and bent nails*
> *   dance all over the surfacing*
> *like maggots. By Christ*
> *   I am no carpenter. I built*
> *the roof for myself, the walls*
> *   for myself, the floors*
> *for myself, and got*
> *   hung up in it myself. I*
> *danced with a purple thumb*
> *   at this house-warming, drunk*
> *with my prime whiskey: rage.*

Oh I spat rage's nails
into the frame-up of my work:
   it held. It settled plumb,
level, solid, square and true
   for that great moment. Then
it screamed and went on through,
   skewing as wrong the other way.
God damned it. This is hell,
   but I planned it, I sawed it,
I nailed it, and I
   will live in it until it kills me.
I can nail my left palm
   to the left-hand cross-piece but
I can't do everything myself.
   I need a hand to nail the right,
a help, a love, a you, a wife.

Alan Dugan (1969)

HAROLD NICOLSON PROPOSES TO VITA SACKVILLE-WEST

HAROLD CAME BACK from Madrid at the end of that summer [1911]. He had been very ill out there, and I remember him as rather a pathetic figure wrapped up in an Ulster on a warm summer day, who was able to walk slowly round the garden with me. All that time while I was 'out' is extremely dim to me, very largely I think, owing to the fact that I was living a kind of false life that left no impression upon me. Even my liaison with Rosamund was, in a sense, superficial. I mean that it was almost exclusively physical, as, to be frank, she always bored me as a companion. I was very fond of her, however; she had a sweet nature. But she was quite stupid.

Harold wasn't. He was as gay and clever as ever, and I loved his brain and his youth, and was flattered at his

96

liking for me. He came to Knole a good deal that autumn and winter, and people began to tell me he was in love with me, which I didn't believe was true, but wished that I could believe it. I wasn't in love with him then – there was Rosamund – but I did like him better than anyone, as a companion and playfellow, and for his brain and his delicious disposition. I hoped that he would propose to me before he went away to Constantinople, but felt diffident and sceptical about it . . .

. . . It had been settled by then that Dada and Harold and I were to go to the country after luncheon as arranged. I was glad, but rather apprehensive, because by then I was sure that Harold meant to propose to me and I knew I should say yes. He had never kissed me, and I wondered whether he would.

He had never even made love to me – not by a single word – and I only knew he liked me because he always tried to be with me, and wrote to me whenever he had to go away. Besides, people had put it into my head. I had always thought they were wrong, but they weren't, and that night at the [Hatfield] ball he asked me to marry him, and I said I would. He was very shy, and pulled all the buttons one by one off his gloves; and I was frightened, and tried to prevent him from coming to the point.

He didn't kiss me, but we sat rather bewildered over supper afterwards, and talked excitedly though vaguely about the flat we would have in Rome. I had on a new dress.

From the diary of Vita Sackville-West

JACK/ERNEST IS ACCEPTED

GWENDOLEN: Pray don't talk to me about the weather, Mr. Worthing. Whenever people talk to me about the weather, I always feel quite certain that they mean something else. And that makes me so nervous.

JACK: I do mean something else.

GWENDOLEN: I thought so. In fact, I am never wrong.

JACK: And I would like to be allowed to take advantage of Lady Bracknell's temporary absence ...

GWENDOLEN: I would certainly advise you to do so. Mamma has a way of coming back suddenly into a room that I have often had to speak to her about.

JACK (*nervously*): Miss Fairfax, ever since I met you I have admired you more than any girl ... I have ever met since ... I met you.

GWENDOLEN: Yes, I am quite well aware of the fact. And I often wish that in public, at any rate, you had been more demonstrative. For me you have always had an irresistible fascination. Even before I met you I was far from indifferent to you. (JACK *looks at her in amazement*.) We live, as I hope you know, Mr. Worthing, in an age of ideals. The fact is constantly mentioned in the more expensive monthly magazines, and has now reached the provincial pulpits, I am told; and my ideal has always been to love someone of the name of Ernest. There is something in that name that inspires absolute confidence. The moment Algernon first mentioned to me that he had a friend called Ernest, I knew I was destined to love you.

JACK: You really love me, Gwendolen?

GWENDOLEN: Passionately!

JACK: Darling! You don't know how happy you've made me.

98

GWENDOLEN: My own Ernest! (*They embrace.*)

JACK: But you don't really mean to say that you couldn't love me if my name wasn't Ernest?

GWENDOLEN: But your name is Ernest.

JACK: Yes, I know it is. But supposing it was something else? Do you mean to say you couldn't love me then?

GWENDOLEN (*glibly*): Ah! that is clearly a metaphysical speculation, and like most metaphysical speculations has very little reference at all to the actual facts of real life, as we know them.

JACK: Personally, darling, to speak quite candidly, I don't much care about the name of Ernest.... I don't think the name suits me at all.

GWENDOLEN: It suits you perfectly. It is a divine name. It has a music of its own. It produces vibrations.

JACK: Well, really, Gwendolen, I must say that I think there are lots of other much nicer names. I think Jack, for instance, a charming name.

GWENDOLEN: Jack? ... No, there is very little music in the name Jack, if any at all, indeed. It does not thrill. It produces absolutely no vibrations. ... I have known several Jacks, and they all, without exception, were more than usually plain. Besides, Jack is a notorious domesticity for John! And I pity any woman who is married to a man called John. She would probably never be allowed to know the entrancing pleasure of a single moment's solitude. The only really safe name is Ernest.

JACK: Gwendolen, I must get christened at once – I mean we must get married at once. There is no time to be lost.

GWENDOLEN: Married, Mr. Worthing?

JACK (*astounded*): Well ... surely. You know that I love you, and you led me to believe, Miss Fairfax, that you were not absolutely indifferent to me.

GWENDOLEN: I adore you. But you haven't proposed to me yet. Nothing has been said at all about marriage. The subject has not even been touched on.

JACK: Well ... may I propose to you now?

GWENDOLEN: I think it would be an admirable opportunity. And to spare you any possible disappointment, Mr. Worthing, I think it only fair to tell you quite frankly beforehand that I am fully determined to accept you.

JACK: Gwendolen!

GWENDOLEN: Yes, Mr. Worthing, what have you got to say to me?

JACK: You know what I have got to say to you.

GWENDOLEN: Yes, but you don't say it.

JACK: Gwendolen, will you marry me? (*Goes on his knees.*)

GWENDOLEN: Of course I will, darling. How long you have been about it! I am afraid you have had very little experience in how to propose.

Oscar Wilde, *The Importance of Being Earnest* (1895)

VIRGINIA WOOLF REPLIES TO A PROPOSAL

Asheham [Rodmell, Sussex]

May 1st [1912]
Dearest Leonard,
    To deal with the facts first (my fingers are so cold I can hardly write) I shall be back about 7 tomorrow, so there will be time to discuss – but what does it mean? You can't take the leave, I suppose if you are going to resign certainly at the end of it. Anyhow, it shows what a career you're ruining!
    Well then, as to all the rest. It seems to me that I am

giving you a great deal of pain – some in the most casual way – and therefore I ought to be as plain with you as I can, because half the time I suspect, you're in a fog which I don't see at all. Of course I can't explain what I feel – these are some of the things that strike me. The obvious advantages of marriage stand in my way. I say to myself. Anyhow, you'll be quite happy with him; and he will give you companionship, children, and a busy life – then I say By God, I will not look upon marriage as a profession. The only people who know of it, all think it suitable; and that makes me scrutinise my own motives all the more. Then, of course, I feel angry sometimes at the strength of your desire. Possibly, your being a Jew comes in also at this point. You seem so foreign. And then I am fearfully unstable. I pass from hot to cold in an instant, without any reason; except that I believe sheer physical effort and exhaustion influence me. All I can say is that in spite of these feelings which go chasing each other all day long when I am with you, there is some feeling which is permanent, and growing. You want to know of course whether it will ever make me marry you. How can I say? I think it will, because there seems no reason why it shouldn't – But I don't know what the future will bring. I'm half afraid of myself. I sometimes feel that no one ever has or ever can share something – Its the thing that makes you call me like a hill, or a rock. Again, I want everything – love, children, adventure, intimacy, work. (Can you make any sense out of this ramble? I am putting down one thing after another). So I go from being half in love with you, and wanting you to be with me always, and know everything about me, to the extreme of wildness and aloofness. I sometimes think that if I married you, I could have everything – and then – is it the sexual side of it that comes between us? As I told you brutally the other day, I feel no physical attraction in you. There are moments – when you kissed me the other day was one – when I feel no more than a rock. And yet your caring for

101

me as you do almost overwhelms me. It is so real, and so strange. Why should you? What am I really except a pleasant attractive creature? But its just because you care so much that I feel I've got to care before I marry you. I feel I must give you everything; and that if I can't, well, marriage would only be second-best for you as well as for me. If you can still go on, as before, letting me find my own way, as that is what would please me best; and then we must both take the risks. But you have made me very happy too. We both of us want a marriage that is a tremendous living thing, always alive, always hot, not dead and easy in parts as most marriages are. We ask a great deal of life, don't we? Perhaps we shall get it; then, how splendid!

One doesn't get much said in a letter does one? I haven't touched upon the enormous variety of things that have been happening here – but they can wait.

D'you like this photograph? – rather too noble, I think. Here's another.

Yrs.
VS

Virginia Stephen to Leonard Woolf (1912)

ANEURIN BEVAN PROPOSES

ON ANOTHER OCCASION Nye said we were going to have dinner proper at the Café, so I put on my best dark-green velvet dress. When we went into the posh dining-room, waiters were hovering around the table for two that Nye had reserved for us; he had left nothing to chance, carefully ordering both food and wine before we arrived. I did not say anything, but maybe a raised eyebrow conveyed what I was thinking: this was quite outside the range of what we could normally afford. Quick as lightning, Nye answered my unspoken question with the retort: 'You can always live like a millionaire for five minutes.' This was what made Nye irresistible. He could make you laugh even when you wanted to cry.

Later he came to the main business of the evening. He said we must get married. It would do him no good in his Welsh non-conformist constituency if it became known, to use the language of those days, that he was 'living in sin'. And while he could no doubt survive, it would be fatal for me if gossip got around in North Lanark, where I was ILP candidate and expected to fight the next Election. I could feel no certainty about the future, but there was no point in handicapping ourselves by defying the conventions. We had more serious work to do, and, of course, I would never be a stumbling-block in his way.

Jennie Lee, *My Life with Nye* (1980)

from MOLLY BLOOM'S SOLILOQUY

THE SUN SHINES FOR YOU he said the day we were lying among the rhododendrons on Howth head in the grey tweed suit and his straw hat the day I got him to propose to me yes first I gave him the bit of seedcake out of my mouth and it was leapyear like now yes 16 years ago my God after that long kiss I near lost my breath yes he said I was a flower of the mountain yes so we are flowers all a womans body yes that was one true thing he said in his life and the sun shines for you today yes that was why I liked him because I saw he understood or felt what a woman is and I knew I could always get round him and I gave him all the pleasure I could leading him on till he asked me to say yes and I wouldnt answer first only looked out over the sea and the sky I was thinking of so many things he didnt know of Mulvey and Mr Stanhope and Hester and father and old captain Groves and the sailors playing all birds fly and I say stoop

and washing up dishes they called it on the pier and the
sentry in front of the governors house with the thing
round his white helmet poor devil half roasted and the
Spanish girls laughing in their shawls and their tall combs
and the auctions in the morning the Greeks and the jews
and the Arabs and the devil knows who else from all the
ends of Europe and Duke street and the fowl market all
clucking outside Larby Sharons and the poor donkeys
slipping half asleep and the vague fellows in the cloaks
asleep in the shade on the steps and the big wheels of the
carts of the bulls and the old castle thousands of years old
yes and those handsome Moors all in white and turbans
like kings asking you to sit down in their little bit of a
shop and Ronda with the old windows of the posadas.
glancing eyes a lattice hid for her lover to kiss the iron
and the wineshops half open at night and the castanets
and the night we missed the boat at Algeciras the watch-
man going about serene with his lamp and O that awful
deepdown torrent O and the sea the sea crimson sometimes like fire and the glorious sunsets and the figtrees in
the alameda gardens yes and all the queer little streets and
pink and blue and yellow houses and the rosegardens and
the jessamine and geraniums and cactuses and Gibraltar
as a girl where I was a Flower of the mountain yes when
I put the rose in my hair like the Andalusian girls used or
shall I wear a red yes and how he kissed me under the
Moorish wall and I thought well as well him as another
and then I asked him with my eyes to ask again yes and
then he asked me would I yes to say yes my mountain
flower and first I put my arms around him yes and drew
him down to me so he could feel my breasts all perfume
yes and his heart was going like mad and yes I said yes I
will Yes.

James Joyce, *Ulysses* (1922)

104

NUPTIALS

'With this ring I thee wed'

The decision made, couples proceed to the next step – the wedding itself. And although 'living together' is now a socially acceptable alternative to marriage, with little or no stigma attached, the bridal boutiques are still full on Saturdays, as the girls and their mothers, sisters and friends, lay hands on white lace, murmuring incantations of bouquets and bridesmaids – with the proper solemnity of priestesses at an ancient ritual.

I confess to discomfort at large white weddings – the spectacle symbolic of so much that is unequal in marriage: the bride given away by one male to another, like a chattel, yet queening it amongst her bridesmaids and the guests, just for this brief time, before accepting the realities of domesticity. Weddings are expensive: a family will spend a small fortune on this public statement, and the young couple may even honeymoon abroad, yet return to live in the spare room, the wedding presents still in boxes in the loft. Such conspicuous squandering is, to me, bizarre.

Yet it is inevitable – sanctioned by history and by myth. The ceremony of joining is followed by the feast in celebration – when traditional jokes may remind the couple that the true end of all this carefully followed ritual is the sexual act, legalised at last. At one time the couple were actually put to bed together. Now they sit side by side, in new clothes, as the car whisks them away on honeymoon – the day receding, to take its place in the album of memory.
(*Roses in the bride's bouquet . . .*)

WEDDING DAY

ALTHOUGH SINCE THE BEGINNING of this century marriage has changed out of recognition, weddings have altered hardly at all. Couples who 'never darken a church door' will insist (to the chagrin of the parson) on going through the whole process – not altogether because it has been artificially popularised, nor because the reception will satisfactorily kill with one stone all the courtesies due to the birds who have given presents. No, let us admit that we all go sentimental over a wedding. We like dressing up, especially in lace and veil; we like the fairytale ritual of exchange of vows and ring, the pretty procession, the raising of glasses with 'beaded bubbles winking at the brim', the ceremonial cutting of the cake, a morsel of which under the pillow will make our dreams come true. A hundred years ago, when everyone knew everyone else and all attended church or chapel, a country wedding was genuinely a sacrament. The 'foreigner' bride (from the nearest village!) was welcomed into the community, and wedding was also marriage, by which each individual there traced the common ancestry back to Adam.

Heather and Robin Tanner, *A Country Book of Days* (1986)

BENEDICTION AT THE WEDDING SERVICE

BLESSED ART THOU, O Lord our God, King of the universe, who hath created all things to thy glory.

Blessed art thou, O Lord our God, King of the universe, Creator of man.

Blessed art thou, O Lord our God, King of the universe, who hast made man in thine image, after thy likeness, and hast prepared unto him, out of his very self, a perpetual fabric. Blessed art thou, O Lord, Creator of man.

O make these loved companions greatly to rejoice, even as of old thou didst gladden thy creature in the garden of Eden. Blessed are thou, O Lord, who makest bridegroom and bride to rejoice.

Blessed art thou, O Lord our God, King of the universe, who hast created joy and gladness, bridegroom and bride, mirth and exultation, pleasure and delight, love, brotherhood, peace and fellowship. Soon may there be heard in the cities of Judah, and in the streets of Jerusalem, the voice of joy and gladness, the voice of the bridegroom and the voice of the bride, the jubilant voice of bridegrooms from their canopies, and of youths from their feasts of song. Blessed art thou, O Lord, who makest the bridegroom to rejoice with the bride.

The Hebrew Prayer Book

COMPOSED ON THE EVE OF THE MARRIAGE OF A FRIEND IN THE VALE OF GRASMERE, 1812

What need of clamorous bells, or ribands gay,
These humble nuptials to proclaim or grace?
Angels of love, look down upon the place;
Shed on the chosen vale a sun-bright day!
Yet no proud gladness would the Bride display
Even for such promise: — serious is her face,
Modest her mein; and she, whose thoughts keep pace
With gentleness, in that becoming way
Will thank you. Faultless does the maid appear,
No disproportion in her soul, no strife:
But, when the closer view of wedded life
Hath shown that nothing human can be clear
From frailty, for that insight may the Wife
To her indulgent Lord become more dear.

William Wordsworth

A WEDDING FEAST

THE TABLE WAS set out under the wagon-shed. On it were four sirloins, six fricassees of chicken, stewed veal, three legs of mutton, and, in the middle, a fine roast sucking-pig, flanked by four chitterlings cooked with sorrel. At the corners stood the brandy in decanters. The sweet cider in bottles forced out its thick froth round the corks, and all the glasses had been filled to the brim with wine in advance. Large yellow creams, which floated about of themselves in the dish at the least shaking of the table, presented to the eye, designed on their smooth surface, the monograms of the newly married couple in such arabesques as never were seen before. A pastry cook had been imported from Yvetot for the tarts and almond cakes. As he was but commencing business in the district, he had taken great pains; and he brought in himself, at dessert, an artistically built-up confection which raised cries of wonder. At the base, to begin with, it had a square of blue cardboard, representing a temple with porticoes, colonnades, and statuettes of stucco, all round in niches constellated with stars in gilt paper; then, on the second story, stood a castle made of Savoy cake, surrounded by slender fortifications in angelica, almonds, dried grapes, quarters of oranges; and, finally, on the higher level, which was a green meadow, where there were rocks with lakes of sweetmeats and boats made of nut-shells, you beheld a little Cupid, balancing himself on a chocolate swing, the two uprights of which were terminated by two natural rosebuds, by way of balls, at the top.

Till evening the eating continued. When any one was too tired of sitting he went for a stroll in the yards or to play a game of *bouchon* in the barn; then he would return to the table. Some, towards the end, went to sleep there and snored. But, at the coffee, everything brightened up again: one struck up a song, another performed feats of strength, they lifted weights, they ran under each other's arms, tried to raise carts on their shoulders, cracked broad jokes, kissed the ladies. In the evening, when the gathering broke up, the horses, gorged with oats to the nostrils, had difficulty in getting into the shafts; they kicked, reared, the harnesses broke, their masters swore or laughed, and all the night through, in the moonlight, along the roads of the district, there were runaway carriages going at a fast gallop, balancing into the dikes, springing over heaps of stones yards high, running into the banks, with women leaning out from the doors to seize the reins.

Those who remained at Les Bertaux passed the night drinking in the kitchen. The children had fallen asleep under the benches.

The bride had implored her father that she should be spared the customary pleasantries. A practical joker among their cousins, however (who had even brought a pair of boot soles for a wedding-present), was about to blow water with his mouth through the key-hole when *père* Rouault arrived, just in time to prevent him, and explained that the dignity of his son-in-law's position did not permit such improprieties. The cousin, nevertheless, yielded unwillingly to these arguments. In his own mind he accused *père* Rouault of being proud, and went to join in a corner four or five others among the guests who, having received by chance several times in succession at table the worse cuts of the joints, were also of opinion that they had been ill-entertained, whispering things to the detriment of their host, and in ambiguous words wishing his ruin.

Gustave Flaubert, *Madame Bovary* (1856)

A VILLAGE WEDDING

SEPT. YE 26. – Yester morn we up betime to be reddie for Mary Jones weddinge att 11 of the clocke. The sun didd shine and it were verrie warm. Carters wiffe cumming to help in good time we finish work erlie.

Then mee and Sarah upp to her bedd chamber, after me putting reddie Johns best velvet britches and blue silk stockeings with the purpel plusshe coate of my lordes with the gold lace, and his best shoes with two big golden buckles, and his best hat. Carters wiffe did praise Sarah much sayeing that she never in her born days did see such a daintie maid in all her finerie. Then I to my bedd chamber to put on my blue silk gown with the wide lace flounces of butter cullor; and shoes with the glass buckels, which were my dear ladies; and a blue straw bonnitt with the white ribbons; and did wear my red necklace which did look verrie fine.

Then me to help John into his britches, which he did get in to after much puffing and grunting; but indeed I was verrie proud when all reddie; and John, mighty proud to see me and Sarah lookeing so fine, did bid Carters wiffe to have a care not to over feed the black sowe and to be sure to strip the cows of all their milk. We off to the church in good time, John mighty proud to be in the cumpany of 2 such fine ladies, he did say, laffing at us.

Then mee not knowing if I had locked up the meat safe in the dairy, was about to turn about; but Sarah telling me she had done it herself, and put away turkey in the brown pot, I more content and into church, where were all the folk reddie who did stare at us with mouth agape as we did get to our seats; Sarah stopping with us till the wedding partie did cum. Mary did look verrie cumlie in her white gown with a fine lace kerchief; but my Sarah did out shine them all with her dark curlie hair and prettie pinke cheeks. A wedding be a verrie sollum thing, and not to be entered into lightlie; one do make sum verrie grate promisses which we must keep and not fail therein. I could not help but think how blest I was with my John at my side; albeit he be like a great baby at times with his show of temper. I did feel the dear God had bin good to me and my own life had fell in plessente places. The passon did read the service verrie well, and did give a good exortashun to end all. Then we all out and to the Ley Farm where we did find all reddie, so every body falling to did make a good meale; then John as becum the biggest farmer did say let us drink the brides helthe which every body did with much laffing at her blushes; then up gets Farmer Lewis from Blackmores to say lets drink to the 2 prettiest ladies in the place – Mistress Hughes and her maid Sarah; long life to both, at which I did stand up and say my thanks and say that Sarah was as good a maid as she was prettie, at which they did all shout agreement and fill their glasses.

Anne Hughes, *The Diary of a Farmer's Wife, 1796–97*

from EPITHALAMION

Open the temple gates unto my love,
Open them wide that she may enter in,
And all the postes adorne as doth behove,
And all the pillours deck with girlands trim,
For to recyve this Saynt with honour dew,
That commeth in to you.
With trembling steps and humble reverence,
She commeth in, before th'almighties vew,
Of her ye virgins learne obedience,
When so ye come into those holy places,
To humble your proud faces:
Bring her up to th'high altar, that she may
The sacred ceremonies there partake,

The which do endless matrimony make,
And let the roring Organs loudly play
The praises of the Lord in lively notes,
The whiles with hollow throates
The Choristers the joyous Antheme sing,
That al the woods may answere and their eccho ring.

Behold whiles she before the altar stands
Hearing the holy priest that to her speakes
And blesseth her with his two happy hands,
How the red roses flush up in her cheekes,
And the pure snow with goodly vermill stayne,
Like crimsin dyde in grayne,
That even th'Angels which continually,
About the sacred Altare doe remaine,
Forget their service and about her fly;
Ofte peeping in her face that seemes more fayre,
The more they on it stare.
But her sad eyes still fastened on the ground,
Are governed with goodly modesty,
That suffers not one looke to glaunce awry,
Which may let in a little thought unsownd.
Why blush ye love to give to me your hand,
The pledge of all our band?
Sing ye sweet Angels, Alleluya sing,
That all the woods may answere and your eccho ring.

Now al is done; bring home the bride againe,
Bring home the triumph of our victory,
Bring home with you the glory of her gaine,
With joyance bring her and with jollity.
Never had man more joyfull day then this,
Whom heaven would heape with blis.
Make feast therefore now all this live long day,
This day for ever to me holy is,
Poure out the wine without restraint or stay,
Poure not by cups, but by the belly full,
Poure out to all that wull,

112

And sprinkle all the postes and wals with wine,
That they may sweat, and drunken be withall.
Crowne ye God Bacchus with a coronall,
And Hymen also crowne with wreathes of vine,
And let the Graces daunce unto the rest;
For they can doo it best:
The whiles the maydens doe theyr carroll sing,
To which the woods shal answer and theyr eccho ring.

Edmund Spenser (1595)

MR WEMMICK'S WEDDING

'I KNOW YOUR ENGAGEMENTS,' said he, 'and I know you are out of sorts, Mr. Pip. But if you *could* oblige me, I should take it as a kindness. It ain't a long walk, and it's an early one. Say it might occupy you (including breakfast on the walk) from eight to twelve. Couldn't you stretch a point and manage it?'

He had done so much for me at various times, that this was very little to do for him. I said I could manage it – would manage it – and he was so very much pleased by my acquiescence, that I was pleased too. At his particular request, I appointed to call for him at the Castle at half-past eight on Monday morning, and so we parted for the time.

Punctual to my appointment, I rang at the Castle gate on the Monday morning, and was received by Wemmick himself: who struck me as looking tighter than usual, and having a sleeker hat on. Within, there were two glasses of rum-and-milk prepared, and two biscuits. The Aged must have been stirring with the lark, for, glancing into the perspective of his bedroom, I observed that his bed was empty.

When we had fortified ourselves with the rum-and-milk and biscuits, and were going out for the walk with that

113

training preparation on us, I was considerably surprised to see Wemmick take up a fishing-rod, and put it over his shoulder. 'Why, we are not going fishing!' said I. 'No,' returned Wemmick, 'but I like to walk with one.'

I thought this odd; however, I said nothing, and we set off. We went towards Camberwell Green, and when we were thereabouts, Wemmick said suddenly:

'Halloa! Here's a church!'

There was nothing very surprising in that; but again, I was rather surprised, when he said, as if he were animated by a brilliant idea:

'Let's go in!'

We went in, Wemmick leaving his fishing-rod in the porch, and looked all round. In the mean time, Wemmick was diving into his coat-pockets, and getting something out of paper there.

'Halloa!' said he. 'Here's a couple of pair of gloves! Let's put 'em on!'

As the gloves were white kid gloves, and as the post-office was widened to its utmost extent, I now began to have my strong suspicions. They were strengthened into certainty when I beheld the Aged enter at a side door, escorting a lady.

'Halloa!' said Wemmick. 'Here's Miss Skiffins! Let's have a wedding.'

That discreet damsel was attired as usual, except that she was now engaged in substituting for her green kid gloves, a pair of white. The Aged was likewise occupied in preparing a similar sacrifice for the altar of Hymen. The old gentleman, however, experienced so much difficulty in getting his gloves on, that Wemmick found it necessary to put him with his back against a pillar, and then to get behind the pillar himself and pull away at them, while I for my part held the old gentleman round the waist, that he might present an equal and safe resistance. By dint of this ingenious scheme, his gloves were got on to perfection.

The clerk and clergyman then appearing, we were ranged in order at those fatal rails. True to his notion of seeming to do it all without preparation, I heard Wemmick say to himself as he took something out of his waistcoat-pocket before the service began, 'Halloa! Here's a ring!'

I acted in the capacity of backer, or best-man, to the bridegroom; while a little limp pew-opener in a soft bonnet like a baby's, made a feint of being the bosom friend of Miss Skiffins. The responsibility of giving the lady away, devolved upon the Aged, which led to the clergyman's being unintentionally scandalised, and it happened thus. When he said, 'Who giveth this woman to be married to this man?' the old gentleman, not in the least knowing what point of the ceremony we had arrived at, stood most amiably beaming at the ten commandments. Upon which, the clergyman said again, 'WHO giveth this woman to be married to this man?' The old gentleman being still in a state of most estimable unconsciousness, the bridegroom cried out in his accustomed voice, 'Now, Aged P., you know; who giveth?' To which the Aged replied with great briskness, before saying that *he* gave, 'All right, John, all right, my boy!' And the clergyman came to so gloomy a pause upon it, that I had doubts for the moment whether we should get completely married that day.

It was completely done, however, and when we were going out of church, Wemmick took the cover off the font, and put his white gloves in it, and put the cover on again. Mrs. Wemmick, more heedful of the future, put her white gloves in her pocket and assumed her green. '*Now*, Mr. Pip,' said Wemmick, triumphantly shouldering the fishing-rod as we came out, 'let me ask you whether anybody would suppose this to be a wedding-party!'

Breakfast had been ordered at a pleasant little tavern, a mile or so away upon the rising ground beyond the green; and there was a bagatelle board in the room, in case we should desire to unbend our minds after the solemnity. It was pleasant to observe that Mrs. Wemmick no longer unwound Wemmick's arm when it adapted itself to her figure, but sat in a high-backed chair against the wall, like a violoncello in its case, and submitted to be embraced as that melodious instrument might have done.

We had an excellent breakfast, and when any one declined anything on table, Wemmick said, 'Provided by contract, you know; don't be afraid of it!' I drank to the new couple, drank to the Aged, drank to the Castle, saluted the bride at parting, and made myself as agreeable as I could.

Wemmick came down to the door with me, and I again shook hands with him, and wished him joy.

'Thankee!' said Wemmick, rubbing his hands, 'She's such a manager of fowls, you have no idea. You shall have some eggs and judge for yourself.'

Charles Dickens, *Great Expectations* (1861)

AN APRIL EPITHALAMIUM
For John and Anne Hughes

I meant to write a poem upon your wedding
Full of advice and hidden, deeper meaning.
Alas, my life has locked me out of language.
My sons skulk in their slum of drums and dinner;
Distracting wars break out on distant islands;
Rooms, uncurled in sunlight, cry for cleaning.

I'll hum some thoughts in rhythm while I'm cleaning.
Marriage, you know, is not a life-long wedding,
A launching of moony pairs to pearly islands
Where love, like light, illuminates pure meaning.
For just when truth's in sight, it's time for dinner.
Or lust (thank God) corrupts pure love of language.

NUPTIALS

Love is, of course, its appetites and language.
Nothing could be more human or more cleaning.
It seems a shame to have to think of dinner
And all the ephemeral trappings of a wedding
When what you pay for seems to cost its meaning.
Are canapes and cake somehow small islands,

Symbols in champagne of all the islands
We try to join together through our language?
John Donne was very sure about his meaning:
No John or Anne's an island. For the cleaning
up and linking up of feelings, a wedding's
A kind of causeway, then — like dinner.

O.K. A man (not John) could wed his dinner.
God help him to imagine lusty islands
Where sun and sea began life with a wedding,
Begetting — not with greedy need of language —
Greenness and creatures (winds to do the cleaning)
That ring-a-rosy in a dance of meaning,

Without which love might be the only meaning.
I mean, of course, that love and war and dinner
And politics and literature and cleaning
Are only words, flat atlases of islands.
While, with our mouths, we caterwaul a language,
Our eyes and bodies meet and make their wedding.

But look! I've spoiled your wedding with a meaning,
Tried to spice up with language good plain dinner.
Off to your island now! Leave me my cleaning.

Anne Stevenson (1985)

117

MARRIAGE OF JENNY DISTAFF

MY SISTER JENNY'S LOVER, the honest Tranquillus, for that shall be his name, has been impatient with me to dispatch the necessary directions for his marriage; that while I am taken up with imaginary schemes, as he calls them, he might not burn with real desire and the torture of expectation. When I had reprimanded him for the ardour wherein he expressed himself, which I thought had not enough of that veneration with which the marriage-bed is to be ascended, I told him, the day of his nuptials should be on the Saturday following, which was the eighth instant. On the seventh in the evening, poor Jenny came into my chamber, and having her heart full of the great change of life from a virgin condition to that of a wife, she long sat silent. I saw she expected me to entertain her on this important subject, which was too delicate a circumstance for herself to touch upon; whereupon I relieved her modesty in the following manner: 'Sister,' said I, 'you are now going from me; and be contented that you leave the company of a talkative old man for that of a sober young one. But take this along with you, that there is no mean in the state you are entering into, but you are to be exquisitely happy or miserable, and your fortune in this way of life will be wholly of your own making. In all the marriages I have ever seen, most of which have been unhappy ones, the great cause of evil has proceeded from slight occasions; and I take it to be the first maxim in a married condition, that you are to be above trifles. When two persons have so good an opinion of each other as to come together for life, they will not differ in matters of importance, because they think of each other with respect in regard to all things of consideration that may affect them, and are prepared for mutual assistance and relief in such occurrences; but for less occasions, they have formed no resolutions, but leave their minds unprepared . . .

But the wedding morning arrived, and our family being very numerous, there was no avoiding the inconvenience of making the ceremony and festival more public than the modern way of celebrating them makes me approve of. The bride next morning came out of her chamber, dressed with all the art and care that Mrs Toilet the tire-woman could bestow on her. She was on her wedding-day three and twenty. Her person is far from what we call a regular beauty; but a certain sweetness in her countenance, an ease in her shape and motion, with an unaffected modesty in her looks, had attractions beyond what symmetry and exactness can inspire without the addition of these endowments. When her lover entered the room, her features flushed with shame and joy; and the ingenuous manner, so full of passion and of awe, with which Tranquillus approached to salute her, gave me good omens of his future behaviour towards her. The wedding was wholly under my care. After the ceremony at church, I was resolved to entertain the company with a dinner suitable to the occasion, and pitched upon the 'Apollo,' at the Old Devil at Temple Bar, as a place sacred to mirth, tempered with discretion, where Ben Jonson and his sons used to make their liberal meetings . . .

Among the rest of the company there was got in a fellow you call a 'wag.' This ingenious person is the usual life of all feasts and merriments, by speaking absurdities, and putting everybody of breeding and modesty out of countenance. As soon as we sat down he drank to the bride's diversion that night; and then made twenty double meanings on the word 'thing.' We are the best-bred family, for one so numerous, in this kingdom; and indeed we should all of us have been as much out of countenance as the bride, but that we were relieved by an honest rough relation of ours at the lower end of the table, who is a lieutenant of marines. The soldier and sailor had good plain sense, and saw what was wrong as well as another; he had a way of looking at his plate, and speaking aloud in an inward manner; and whenever the wag mentioned the word 'thing,' or the words, 'that same,' the lieutenant in that voice cried, 'Knock him down.' The merry man wondering, angry, and looking round, was the diversion of the table. When he offered to recover, and say, 'To the bride's best thoughts,' 'Knock him down,' says the lieutenant, and so on. This silly humour diverted, and saved us from the fulsome entertainment of an ill-bred coxcomb; and the bride drank the lieutenant's health. We returned to my lodging, and Tranquillus led his wife to her apartment, without the ceremony of throwing the stocking, which generally costs two or three maidenheads, without any ceremony at all.

Richard Steele, writing as the columnist
Mr Bickerstaff in *The Tatler* (1709/11)

from A BALLAD UPON A WEDDING

I tell thee, Dick, where I have been;
Where I the rarest things have seen,
  O things without compare!
Such sights again cannot be found
In any place on English ground,
  Be it at wake or fair.

At Charing Cross, hard by the way
Where we, thou know'st, do sell our hay,
  There is a house with stairs;
And there did I see coming down
Such folks as are not in our town,
  Forty at least in pairs.

Among the rest one pest'lent fine,
His beard no bigger though than thine,
  Walked on before the rest:
Our landlord looks like nothing to him:

The King, God bless him!, 'twould undo him,
  Should he go still so dressed.

But wot you what? the youth was going
To make an end of all his wooing;
  The parson for him staid:
Yet by his leave, for all his haste,
He did not so much wish all past,
  Perchance, as did the maid.

The maid – and thereby hangs a tale;
For such a maid no Whitsun-ale
  Could ever yet produce:
No grape, that's kindly ripe, could be
So round, so plump, so soft as she,
  Nor half so full of juice.

Her finger was so small, the ring
Would not stay on, which they did bring;
  It was too wide a peck:
And to say truth, for out it must,
It looked like the great collar, just,
  About our young colt's neck.

Her feet beneath her petticoat
Like little mice stole in and out,
  As if they feared the light:
But O, she dances such a way!
No sun upon an Easter-day
  Is half so fine a sight.

He would have kissed her once or twice;
But she would not, she was so nice,
  She would not do't in sight:
And then she looked as who should say,
'I will do what I list to-day,
  And you shall do't at night'.

Just in the nick the cook knocked thrice,
And all the waiters in a trice

    His summons did obey:
Each serving-man, with dish in hand,
Marched boldly up, like our trained band,
    Presented, and away.

Now hats fly off, and youths carouse,
Healths first go round and then the house:
    The bride's came thick and thick;
And, when 'twas named another's health,
Perhaps he made it hers by stealth;
    And who could help it, Dick?

O' th' sudden up they rise and dance;
Then sit again and sigh and glance;
    Then dance again and kiss:
Thus several ways the time did pass,
Whilst every woman wished her place,
    And every man wished his.

By this time all were stolen aside
To counsel and undress the bride;
    But that he must not know:
But yet 'twas thought he guessed her mind,
And did not mean to stay behind
    Above an hour or so.

When in he came, Dick, there she lay
Like new-fallen snow melting away;
    'Twas time, I trow, to part:
Kisses were now the only stay,
Which soon she gave, as one would say,
    Goodbye with all my heart.

But, just as Heavens would have, to cross it,
In came the bridesmaids with the posset;
    The bridegroom ate in spite:
For, had he left the women to't,
It would have cost two hours to do't,
    Which were too much that night.

122

At length the candle's out; and now
All that they had not done they do;
*   What that is, who can tell?*
But I believe it was no more
Then thou and I have done before
*   With Bridget and with Nell.*

Sir John Suckling (1646)

THE MARRIAGE CELEBRATION OF WILL BRANGWEN AND ANNA

THE MARRIAGE PARTY went across the grave-yard to the wall, mounted it by the little steps, and descended. Oh a vain white peacock of a bride perching herself on the top of the wall and giving her hand to the bridegroom on the other side, to be helped down! The vanity of her white, slim, daintily-stepping feet, and her arched neck. And the regal impudence with which she seemed to dismiss them all, the others, parents and wedding guests, as she went with her young husband.

In the cottage big fires were burning, there were dozens of glasses on the table, and holly and mistletoe hanging up. The wedding party crowded in, and Tom Brangwen, becoming roisterous, poured out drinks. Everybody must drink. The bells were ringing away against the windows.

'Lift your glasses up,' shouted Tom Brangwen from the parlour, 'lift your glasses up, an' drink to the hearth an' home – hearth an' home, an' may they enjoy it.'

'Night an' day, an' may they enjoy it,' shouted Frank Brangwen, in addition.

'Hammer an' tongs, and may they enjoy it,' shouted Alfred Brangwen, the saturnine.

'Fill your glasses up, an' let's have it all over again,' shouted Tom Brangwen.

'Hearth and home, an' may ye enjoy it.'

There was a ragged shout of the company in response.

123

'Bed an' blessin', an' may ye enjoy it,' shouted Frank Brangwen.

There was a swelling chorus in answer.

'Comin' and goin', an' may ye enjoy it,' shouted the saturnine Alfred Brangwen, and the men roared by now boldly, and the woman said 'Just hark, now!'

There was a touch of scandal in the air.

Then the party rolled off in the carriages, full speed back to the Marsh, to a large meal of the high-tea order, which lasted for an hour and a half. The bride and bridegroom sat at the head of the table, very prim and shining both of them, wordless, whilst the company raged down the table.

The Brangwen men had brandy in their tea, and were becoming unmanageable. The saturnine Alfred had glittering, unseeing eyes, and a strange, fierce way of laughing that showed his teeth. His wife glowered at him and jerked her head at him like a snake. He was oblivious. Frank Brangwen, the butcher, flushed and florid and handsome, roared echoes to his two brothers. Tom Brangwen in his solid fashion was letting himself go at last.

These three brothers dominated the whole company. Tom Brangwen wanted to make a speech. For the first time in his life, he must spread himself wordily.

'Marriage,' he began, his eyes twinkling and yet quite profound, for he was deeply serious and hugely amused at the same time, 'Marriage,' he said, speaking in the slow, full-mouthed way of the Brangwens, 'is what we're made for —'

'Let him talk,' said Alfred Brangwen, slowly and inscrutably, 'let him talk.' Mrs Alfred darted indignant eyes at her husband.

'A man,' continued Tom Brangwen, 'enjoys being a man: for what purpose was he made a man, if not to enjoy it?'

'That a true word,' said Frank, floridly.

'And likewise,' continued Tom Brangwen, 'a woman

124

enjoys being a woman: at least we surmise she does –'

'Oh don't you bother –' called a farmer's wife.

'You may back your life they'd be summisin',' said Frank's wife.

'Now,' continued Tom Brangwen, 'for a man to be a man, it takes a woman –'

'It does that,' said a woman grimly.

'And for a woman to be a woman, it takes a *man* –' continued Tom Brangwen.

'All speak up, men,' chimed in a feminine voice.

'Therefore we have marriage,' continued Tom Brangwen.

'Hold, hold,' said Alfred Brangwen. 'Don't run us off our legs.'

And in dead silence the glasses were filled. The bride and bridegroom, two children, sat with intent, shining faces at the head of the table, abstracted.

'There's no marriage in heaven,' went on Tom Brangwen; 'but on earth there is marriage.'

'That's the difference between 'em,' said Alfred Brangwen, mocking.

'Alfred,' said Tom Brangwen, 'keep your remarks till afterwards, and then we'll thank you for them. – There's very little else, on earth, but marriage. You can talk about making money, or saving souls. You can save your own soul seven times over, and you may have a mint of money, but your soul goes gnawin', gnawin', gnawin', and it says there's something it must have. In heaven there is no marriage. But on earth there *is* marriage, else heaven drops out, and there's no bottom to it.'

'Just hark you now,' said Frank's wife.

'Go on, Thomas,' said Alfred sardonically.

'*If* we've got to be Angels,' went on Tom Brangwen, haranguing the company at large, 'and if there is no such thing as a man nor a woman amongst them, then it seems to me as a married couple makes one Angel.'

D. H. Lawrence, *The Rainbow* (1915)

SYDNEY SMITH MARRIES

FOR MANY YEARS HE HAD been engaged to a friend of his sister, Catherine Pybus, and the moment he felt that he could decently support a wife he took the plunge. With the full consent of Catherine's mother (her father being dead) and the violent opposition of her brother (who objected equally to Sydney's poor prospects and political opinions) they were married in the parish church of Cheam, Surrey, on 2 July 1800. Sydney, being an honest churchman, perceived that one of his marriage vows could be accomplished on the spot, and he endowed his wife with all his worldly goods by flinging his entire fortune into her lap. It consisted of 'six small silver teaspoons, which from much wear had become the ghosts of their former selves'. Fortunately his wife brought him a modest dowry, with, as immediate capital, a pearl necklace, which was quickly exchanged for £500, and they were able to buy the necessary plate, linen etc., for the house Sydney had taken in Edinburgh.

Hesketh Pearson, *The Smith of Smiths* (1934)

EPITHALAMION

Singing, today I married my white girl
beautiful in a barley field.
Green on thy finger a grass blade curled,
so with this ring I thee wed, I thee wed,
and send our love to the loveless world
of all the living and all the dead.

Now, no more than vulnerable human,
we, more than one, less than two,
are nearly ourselves in a barley field —

126

and only love is the rent that's due
though the bailiffs of time return anew
to all the living but not the dead.

Shipwrecked, the sun sinks down harbours
of a sky, unloads its liquid cargoes
of marigolds, and I and my white girl
lie still in the barley – who else wishes
to speak, what more can be said
by all the living against all the dead?

Come then all you wedding guests:
green ghost of trees, gold of barley,
you blackbird priests in the field,
you wind that shakes the pansy head
fluttering on a stalk like a butterfly;
come the living and come the dead.

Listen flowers, birds, winds, worlds,
tell all today that I married
more than a white girl in the barley –
for today I took to my human bed
flower and bird and wind and world,
and all the living and all the dead.

Dannie Abse (1952)

A DRUNKEN WEDDING

I NEED HARDLY REMARK that there were revelry and high frolics in this townland when my wedding day came. The neighbours arrived to congratulate me. The Old-Fellow had, by this time, drunk the dowry-money which he had procured and there was not a good drop in the house to offer to the neighbours. When they realised that matters were thus, gloom and ill humour took hold of them. Threatening whispers were heard from the men occasionally and the women set themselves to devouring all our potatoes and drinking all our buttermilk so as to inflict a three month's scarcity upon us. A species of terror came upon the Old-Fellow when he saw how matters stood with the company. He whispered privily in my ear – Fellow! said he, if this gang doesn't get spirits and tobacco from us, I'm afraid one of our pigs will be stolen from us this night. – All the pigs and my wife will be stolen as well sir, I replied.

Mabel was in the end of the house at this juncture with my mother on top of her. The poor girl was trying to escape back to her father's house and my mother endeavouring to make her see reason and informing her that it is compulsory to submit to Gaelic fate. There was great weeping and tumult that night in our house.

It was Martin O'Bannassa himself who rescued us. When everything was truly in a bad state he walked in carrying a small barrel of true water under his armpit. He quietly presented me with the barrel and congratulated me courteously on my marriage. When the company inside realised that the door of hospitality was finally opened they wished to be merry and good-humoured and commenced to drink, dance and make music with all their might. After some time, they made a racket which shook the walls of the house, dismaying and terrorising the pigs. The woman in the end of the house (his wife) was given a full cup of that fiery water – despite the fact that she had no stomach for it – and before long she ceased her struggling and fell into a drunken slumber in the rushes. According as the men drank their fill, they lost the inherited good manners and good habits they had. By the time midnight had come, blood was being spilled liberally and there were a few men in the company without a stitch of clothing about them. At three in the morning two men died after a bout of fighting which arose in the end of the house – poor Gaelic paupers without guile who had no experience of the lightning water in Martin's barrel ... I consider that it was a good thing that my wife lost her senses and was not aware of the conduct of that wedding feast.

Flann O'Brien, *The Poor Mouth* (1973)

ADAM BEDE'S WEDDING DAY

IN LITTLE MORE THAN A MONTH after that meeting on the hill – on a rimy morning in departing November – Adam and Dinah were married.

It was an event much thought of in the village. All Mr Burge's men had a holiday, and all Mr Poyser's; and most of those who had a holiday appeared in their best clothes at the wedding. I think there was hardly an inhabitant of Hayslope specially mentioned in this history and still resident in the parish on this November morning, who was not either in church to see Adam and Dinah married, or near the church door to greet them as they came forth. Mrs Irwine and her daughters were waiting at the churchyard gates in their carriage (for they had a carriage now) to shake hands with the bride and bridegroom, and wish them well; and in the absence of Miss Lydia Donnithorne at Bath, Mrs Best, Mr Mills, and Mr Craig had felt it incumbent on them to represent "the family" at the Chase on the occasion. The churchyard walk was quite lined with familiar faces, many of them faces that had first looked at Dinah when she preached on the Green; and no wonder they showed this eager interest on her marriage morning, for nothing like Dinah and the history which had brought her and Adam Bede together had been known at Hayslope within the memory of man.

Bessy Cranage, in her neatest cap and frock, was crying, though she did not exactly know why; for, as her cousin Wiry Ben, who stood near her, judiciously suggested,

129

Dinah was not going away, and if Bessy was in low spirits, the best thing for her to do was to follow Dinah's example, and marry an honest fellow who was ready to have her. Next to Bessy, just within the church door, there were the Poyser children, peeping round the corner of the pews to get a sight of the mysterious ceremony; Totty's face wearing an unusual air of anxiety at the idea of seeing cousin Dinah come back looking rather old, for in Totty's experience no married people were young.

I envy them all the sight they had when the marriage was fairly ended and Adam led Dinah out of church. She was not in black this morning; for her aunt Poyser would by no means allow such a risk of incurring bad luck, and had herself made a present of the wedding dress, made all of grey, though in the usual Quaker form, for on this point Dinah could not give way. So the lily face looked out with sweet gravity from under a grey Quaker bonnet, neither smiling nor blushing, but with lips trembling a little under the weight of solemn feelings. Adam, as he pressed her arm to his side, walked with his old erectness and his head thrown rather backward as if to face all the world better; but it was not because he was particularly proud this morning, as is the wont of bridegrooms, for his happiness was of a kind that had little reference to men's opinion of it. There was a tinge of sadness in his deep joy; Dinah knew it, and did not feel aggrieved.

There were three other couples, following the bride and bridegroom: first, Martin Poyser, looking as cheery as a bright fire on this rimy morning, led quiet Mary Burge, the bridesmaid; then came Seth serenely happy, with Mrs Poyser on his arm; and last of all Bartle Massey, with Lisbeth – Lisbeth in a new gown and bonnet, too busy with her pride in her son, and her delight in possessing the one daughter she had desired, to devise a single pretext for complaint.

Bartle Massey had consented to attend the wedding at Adam's earnest request, under protest against marriage in

general, and the marriage of a sensible man in particular.   Nevertheless, Mr Poyser had a joke against him
after the wedding dinner, to the effect that in the vestry
he had given the bride one more kiss than was necessary.

Behind this last couple came Mr Irwine, glad at heart
over this good morning's work of joining Adam and
Dinah.   For he had seen Adam in the worst moments of
his sorrow; and what better harvest from that painful
seed-time could there be than this?   The love that had
brought hope and comfort in the hour of despair, the love
that had found its way to the dark prison cell and to poor
Hetty's darker soul – this strong, gentle love was to be
Adam's companion and helper till death.

George Eliot, *Adam Bede* (1859)

WEDDING DAY

I am afraid.
Sound has stopped in the day
And the images reel over
And over. Why all those tears,

The wild grief on his face
Outside the taxi? The sap
Of mourning rises
In our waving guests.

You sing behind the tall cake
Like a deserted bride
Who persists, demented,
And goes through the ritual.

When I went to the gents
There was a skewered heart

And a legend of love. Let me
Sleep on your breast to the airport.

Seamus Heaney (1972)

ON JESSY WATSON'S ELOPEMENT

Run of is Jessy fair
Her eyes do sparkel, she's good hair.
But Mrs Leath you shal now be
Now and for all Eternity!

Marjory Fleming – aged 7
(1803–11)

ALYSE GREGORY MARRIES LLEWELYN POWYS

OCTOBER 1, 1924: yesterday was my wedding day. It is what Llewelyn wanted, but some cloud lies upon my spirit as if I had betrayed something in myself. It rained so hard. John and Marian and Richard Le Gallienne came to the little church where Hamilton married us. What should I fear? Only one fear I have, that he will cease to love me as he does. I must always be prepared for this, though he thinks this wounding to his illusions. But he is loved by every woman. This fear is the only thing that ever makes my heart sad, this and my anxiety for his health.

I have come back from New York and he loves me so sweetly, as if he could not let me go from his sight.

Alyse Gregory, *The Cry of a Gull: Journals 1923–1948*

ON THE MARRIAGE OF T.K. AND C.C.
THE MORNING STORMY

Such should this day be, so the sun should hide
His bashful face, and let the conquering Bride
Without a rival shine, whilst he forbears
To mingle his unequal beams with hers;
Or if sometimes he glance his squinting eye
Between the parting clouds, 'tis but to spy,
Not emulate her glories, so comes dressed
In veils, but as a masquer to the feast.
Thus heaven should lower, such stormy gusts should blow
Not to denounce ungentle Fates, but show
The cheerful Bridegroom to the clouds and wind
Hath all his tears, and all his sighs assigned.
Let tempests struggle in the air, but rest
Eternal calms within thy peaceful breast,
Thrice happy Youth; but ever sacrifice
To that fair hand that dried thy blubbered eyes,
That crowned thy head with roses, and turned all
The plagues of love into a cordial,
When first it joined her virgin snow to thine,
Which when today the Priest shall recombine,
From the mysterious holy touch such charms
Will flow, as shall unlock her wreathèd arms,
And open a free passage to that fruit
Which thou hast toiled for with a long pursuit.
But ere thou feed, that thou may'st better taste
Thy present joys, think on thy torments past.
Think on the mercy freed thee, think upon
Her virtues, graces, beauties, one by one,
So shalt thou relish all, enjoy the whole
Delights of her fair body, and pure soul.
Then boldly to the fight of love proceed,
'Tis mercy not to pity though she bleed,
We'll strew no nuts, but change that ancient form,

For till tomorrow we'll prorogue this storm,
Which shall confound with its loud whistling noise
Her pleasing shrieks, and fan thy panting joys.

Thomas Carew (1640)

A SECRET WEDDING

JUNE 18, 1956

Dearest Warren,

My fingers are so full of amazing news to type that I hardly know where to begin. First of all, you better stop what you are doing and be very quiet and sit down with a tall glass of cool lager and be ready to keep a huge and miraculous secret: your sister, as of 1:30 p.m., June 16, in London at the 250-year-old church of St. George the Martyr is now a married woman! Mrs. Sylvia Hughes, Mrs. Ted Hughes, Mrs. Edward James Hughes, Mrs. E. J. Hughes (wife of the internationally known poet and genius); take your pick. It is really true, and it is a dead secret between you and mummy and Ted and me. Because I am going to have another wedding at the Unitarian Church in Wellesley next June with you (I hope, if you're willing) as Ted's best man, and Frankie [*Sylvia's uncle*] giving me away, and a huge reception for all our friends and relations who will be informed by mother this fall that Ted and I are engaged.

This all seems so logical and inevitable to me that I can hardly begin to answer the questions which I know will be flocking to your mind: Why two weddings? Why a secret wedding? Why anyhow? Well, it so happens that I have at last found the one man in the world for me, which mother saw immediately (she and Ted get along beautifully, and he loves her and cares for her very much) and after three months of seeing each other every day, doing everything from writing to reading aloud to hiking

134

and cooking together, there was absolutely no shred of doubt in our minds. We are both poverty-stricken now, have no money, and are in no position to have people know we are married. Me at Newnham, where the Victorian virgins wouldn't see how I could concentrate on my studies with being married to such a handsome virile man, the Fulbright, etc., etc. Also, he is getting a job teaching English in Spain next year to earn money to come to America with me next June, so we'll have to be apart while I finish my degree for three long 8-week periods (I must do very well on my exams). I'll fly to be with him for the 5-week-long vacation at Christmas and Easter. So this marriage is in keeping with our situation: private, personal, legal, true, but limited in its way. Neither of us will think of giving up the fullest ceremony, which will be a kind of folk festival in Wellesley when we proclaim our decision to the world in another ceremony, very simple, but with a wonderful reception: then, too, we can really start our life of living together forever. So this seems the best way.

I have never been through such fantastic strenuous living in my life! Mother and I are here in Cambridge now for five days, Ted having gone off to his home in Yorkshire for two days to take all his stuff from the condemned London slum where he lived (and, thank God, will never return to). The three of us leave for London early Thursday, the 21st, fly to Paris (I wouldn't risk mother on a channel crossing) the 22nd where we will stay for a week, Ted and I seeing mother off, after showing her Paris for a week, on her flight. Ted has been simply heavenly: mother came Wednesday (I haven't been able to eat or sleep for excitement at her coming) and Ted took us to supper at Schmidt's, a good cheap German restaurant, that night, and we decided to get married while mother was in London. Our only sorrow was that you weren't there. When Ted and I see you in Europe this summer, we'll tell you all the fantastic details of our struggle to get a license (from the Archbishop of Canterbury, no less), searching for the parish church where Ted belonged and had, by law, to be married, spotting a priest on the street, Ted pointing, "That's him!" and following him home and finding he was the right one.

We rushed about London, buying dear Ted shoes and trousers, the gold wedding rings (I never wanted an engagement ring) with the last of our money, and mummy supplying a lovely pink knitted suit dress she brought (intuitively never having worn) and me in that and a pink hair ribbon and a pink rose from Ted, standing with the rain pouring outside in the dim little church, saying the most beautiful words in the world as our vows, with the curate as second witness and the dear Reverend, an old, bright-eyed man (who lives right opposite Charles Dickens' house!) kissing my cheek, and the tears just falling down from my eyes like rain – I was so happy with my dear, lovely Ted. Oh, you will love him, too. He wants so to meet you. So to the world, we are engaged, and you must help us keep this an utter secret. After mother goes on June 29th, we will be alone together for the first time and go to Spain for the summer to rent a little house by the sea and write and learn Spanish.

Sylvia Plath to her brother

A GERIATRIC WEDDING

Now to be wed a well-match'd couple came;
Twice had old Lodge been tied, and twice the dame;
Tottering they came and toying, (odious scene!)
And fond and simple, as they'd always been.
Children from wedlock we by laws restrain;
Why not prevent them, when they're such again?
Why not forbid the doting souls, to prove
Th'indecent fondling of preposterous love?

In spite of prudence, uncontroll'd by shame,
The amorous senior woos the toothless dame,
Relating idly, at the closing eve,
The youthful follies he disdains to leave;
Till youthful follies wake a transient fire,
When arm in arm they totter and retire.
   So a fond pair of solemn birds, all day,
Blink in their seat and doze the hours away;
Then by the moon awaken'd, forth they move,
And fright the songsters with their cheerless love.
   So two sear trees, dry, stunted, and unsound,
Each other catch, when dropping to the ground;
Entwine their wither'd arms 'gainst wind and weather,
And shake their leafless heads and drop together.

George Crabbe, *The Parish Register – Marriages*
(1807)

ANEURIN BEVAN MARRIES JENNIE LEE

ALL HIS LIFE NYE enjoyed complaining that I cost him two guineas: that was the fee for a special licence. Our intention was to get the marriage ceremony quietly over when no one was looking, but we had reckoned without our friends. John and Marion Balderston, who had belonged to Frank's world, not only continued to look after me but adopted Nye as well. John was doing very well at the time, as he had added to his laurels as a distinguished international journalist by becoming a successful playwright. They had a house in Trevor Square and without our knowledge had invited thirty guests to their home on the evening of our marriage. They were determined to have a celebration, and they got one in full measure. The word had got around among friends and acquaintances, so instead of thirty twice as many turned up. Ample food and drinks were produced for all. Don't ask me how it was done. I don't know. Maybe by a shuttle service to a nearby restaurant where John and Marion were well known.

Only Marion Balderston and Nye's closest friend, Archie Lush, had been invited to accompany us to the registry office. When we arrived there, the uninvited guest was Nye's older brother; he was dressed to kill, looking as a proper wedding guest ought to look, but he was in an awkward mood. Five of us instead of four went off to a private room in the Ivy restaurant, where the proprietor, our friend Abel, had prepared lunch for us. Billy Bevan refused Abel's best champagne and best wines and insisted on a special brew of beer the Ivy did not stock, causing so much fuss and bother that we wanted to strangle him. After lunch Marion went home to Trevor Square. Archie, Nye and I returned to Guilford Street, and we left brother Billy to go to the devil.

We had accepted an invitation to have an evening meal with John and Marion, and I had an idea that one or two of our friends had also been invited. But the mob that greeted us when we arrived took us completely by surprise – I mean took Nye and me completely by surprise. Archie had been in Marion's confidence. The biggest surprise of the evening was to see brother Bill handing around cocktails on a silver salver and oozing Welsh charm; Marion had taken him home with her and had completely tamed him.

Jennie Lee, *My Life with Nye* (1980)

FANCY DAY BECOMES A WIFE

F ANCY CAUSED HER LOOKS to wear as much matronly expression as was obtainable out of six hours' experience as a wife, in order that the contrast between her own state of life and that of the unmarried young women present might be duly impressed upon the company: occasionally stealing glances of admiration at her left hand, but this quite privately; for her ostensible bearing concerning the matter was intended to show that, though she undoubtedly occupied the most wondrous position in the eyes of the world that had ever been attained, she was almost unconscious of the circumstance, and that the somewhat prominent position in which that wonderfully-emblazoned left hand was continually found to be placed when handing cups and saucers, knives, forks, and glasses, was quite the result of accident.   As to wishing to excite envy in the bosoms of her maiden companions by the exhibition of the shining ring, every one was to know it was quite foreign to the dignity of such an experienced married woman.   Dick's imagination in the meantime was far less capable of drawing so much wontedness from his new condition.   He had been for two or three hours trying to feel himself merely a newly-married man, but had been able to get no further in the attempt than to realise that he was Dick Dewy, the tranter's son, at a party given by Lord Wessex's head man-in-charge, on the outlying Yalbury estate, dancing and chatting with Fancy Day.

Five country dances, including 'Haste to the Wedding,' two reels, and three fragments of hornpipes, brought them to the time for supper which, on account of the dampness of the grass from the immaturity of the summer season, was spread indoors.   At the conclusion of the meal Dick went out to put the horse in; and Fancy, with the elder half of the four bridesmaids, retired upstairs to dress for the journey to Dick's new cottage near Mellstock.

'How long will you be putting on your bonnet, Fancy?'   Dick inquired at the foot of the staircase. Being now a man of business and married he was strong on the importance of time, and doubled the emphasis of his words in conversing, and added vigour to his nods.

'Only a minute.'

'How long is that?'

'Well, dear, five.'

'Ah, sonnies!' said the tranter, as Dick retired, ''tis a talent of the female race that low numbers should stand for high, more especially in matters of waiting, matters of age, and matters of money.'

'True, true, upon my body,' said Geoffrey.

'Ye spak with feeling, Geoffrey, seemingly.'

'Anybody that d'know my experience might guess that.'

'What's she doing now, Geoffrey?'

'Claning out all the upstairs drawers and cupboards, and dusting the second-best chainey – a thing that's only done once a year. "If there's work to be done I must do it," says she, "wedding or no."'

''Tis my belief she's a very good woman at bottom.'

'She's terrible deep, then.'

Mrs. Penny turned round. 'Well, 'tis humps and hollers with the best of us; but still and for all that, Dick and Fancy stand as fair a chance of having a bit of sunsheen as any married pair in the land.'

'Ay, there's no gainsaying it.'

Mrs. Dewy came up, talking to one person and looking at another. 'Happy, yes,' she said. ''Tis always so when a couple is so exactly in tune with one another as Dick and she.'

'When they be'n't too poor to have time to sing,' said grandfather James.

'I tell ye, neighbours, when the pinch comes,' said the tranter: 'when the oldest daughter's boots be only a size less than her mother's, and the rest o' the flock close behind her. A sharp time for a man that, my sonnies; a very sharp time! Chanticleer's comb is a-cut then, 'a believe.'

'That's about the form o't', said Mr. Penny.

Thomas Hardy, *Under the Greenwood Tree* (1872)

THE WHITSUN WEDDINGS

That Whitsun, I was late getting away:
  Not till about
One-twenty on the sunlit Saturday
Did my three-quarters-empty train pull out,
All windows down, all cushions hot, all sense
Of being in a hurry gone. We ran
Behind the backs of houses, crossed a street
Of blinding windscreens, smelt the fish-dock; thence
The river's level drifting breadth began,
Where sky and Lincolnshire and water meet.

All afternoon, through the tall heat that slept
  For miles inland,
A slow and stopping curve southwards we kept.
Wide farms went by, short-shadowed cattle, and
Canals with floatings of industrial froth;
A hothouse flashed uniquely: hedges dipped
And rose: and now and then a smell of grass
Displaced the reek of buttoned carriage-cloth
Until the next town, new and nondescript,
Approached with acres of dismantled cars.

At first, I didn't notice what a noise
  The weddings made
Each station that we stopped at: sun destroys
The interest of what's happening in the shade,
And down the long cool platforms whoops and skirls
I took for porters larking with the mails,
And went on reading. Once we started, though,
We passed them, grinning and pomaded, girls
In parodies of fashion, heels and veils,
All posed irresolutely, watching us go,

As if out on the end of an event
  Waving goodbye
To something that survived it. Struck, I leant

More promptly out next time, more curiously,
And saw it all again in different terms:
The fathers with broad belts under their suits
And seamy foreheads; mothers loud and fat;
An uncle shouting smut; and then the perms,
The nylon gloves and jewellery-substitutes,
The lemons, mauves, and olive-ochres that

Marked off the girls unreally from the rest.
  Yes, from cafés
And banquet-halls up yards, and bunting-dressed
Coach-party annexes, the wedding-days
Were coming to an end. All down the line
Fresh couples climbed aboard: the rest stood round;
The last confetti and advice were thrown,
And, as we moved, each face seemed to define
Just what it saw departing: children frowned
At something dull; fathers had never known

Success so huge and wholly farcical;
  The women shared
The secret like a happy funeral;
While girls, gripping their handbags tighter, stared
At a religious wounding. Free at last,
And loaded with the sum of all they saw,
We hurried towards London, shuffling gouts of
  steam.
Now fields were building-plots, and poplars cast
Long shadows over major roads, and for
Some fifty minutes, that in time would seem

Just long enough to settle hats and say
  I nearly died,
A dozen marriages got under way.
They watched the landscape, sitting side by side
– An Odeon went past, a cooling tower,

And someone running up to bowl – and none
Thought of the others they would never meet

Or how their lives would all contain this hour.
I thought of London spread out in the sun,
Its postal districts packed like squares of wheat:

There we were aimed. And as we raced across
*   Bright knots of rail*
Past standing Pullmans, walls of blackened moss
Came close, and it was nearly done, this frail
Travelling coincidence; and what it held
Stood ready to be loosed with all the power
That being changed can give. We slowed again,
And as the tightened brakes took hold, there swelled
A sense of falling, like an arrow-shower
Sent out of sight, somewhere becoming rain.

Philip Larkin (1964)

A QUIET WEDDING FOR HENRY AND MARGARET

SHORTLY BEFORE THE MOVE, our hero and heroine were married. They have weathered the storm, and may reasonably expect peace. To have no illusions and yet to love – what stronger surety can a woman find? She had seen her husband's past as well as his heart. She knew her own heart with a thoroughness that commonplace people believe impossible. The heart of Mrs Wilcox was alone hidden, and perhaps it is superstitious to speculate on the feelings of the dead. They were married quietly – really quietly, for as the day approached she refused to go through another Oniton. Her brother gave her away, her aunt, who was out of health, presided over a few colourless refreshments. The Wilcoxes were represented by Charles, who witnessed the marriage settlement, and by Mr Cahill. Paul did send a cablegram. In a few minutes, and without the aid of music, the clergyman made them man and wife, and soon the glass shade had

143

fallen that cuts off married couples from the world. She, a monogamist, regretted the cessation of some of life's innocent odours; he, whose instincts were polygamous, felt morally braced by the change, and less liable to the temptations that had assailed him in the past.

E. M. Forster, *Howard's End* (1910)

THE WIFE OF BATH'S TALE

A handsome knight has promised to marry an old crone who has helped him out of a fix. When it comes to the point he refuses, and both have to put their cases before the court.

> *Both heard, the Judge pronounc'd against the Knight;*
> *So was he Marry'd in his own despight;*
> *And all Day after hid him as an Owl,*
> *Not able to sustain a Sight so foul.*
> *Perhaps the Reader thinks I do him wrong*
> *To pass the Marriage-Feast, and Nuptial Song:*
> *Mirth there was none, the Man was a-la-mort:*
> *And little Courage had to make his Court.*
> *To Bed they went, the Bridegroom and the Bride:*
> *Was never such an ill-pair'd Couple ty'd.*
> *Restless he toss'd and tumbled to and fro,*
> *And rowl'd, and wriggled further off; for Woe.*
> *The good old Wife lay smiling by his Side,*
> *And caught him in her quiv'ring Arms, and cry'd,*
> *When you my ravish'd Predecessor saw,*
> *You were not then become this Man of Straw;*
> *Had you been such, you might have scap'd the Law.*
> *Is this the Custom of King Arthur's Court?*
> *Are all Round-Table Knights of such a sort?*
> *Remember I am she who sav'd your Life,*
> *Your loving, lawful, and complying Wife:*
> *Not thus you swore in your unhappy Hour,*

Nor I for this return employ'd my Pow'r.
In time of Need I was your faithful Friend;
Nor did I since, nor ever will offend.
Believe me my lov'd Lord, 'tis much unkind;
What Fury has possess'd your alter'd Mind?
Thus on my Wedding-night – Without Pretence –
Come turn this way, or tell me my Offence.
If not your Wife, let Reasons Rule persuade,
Name but my Fault, amends shall soon be made.
    Amends! Nay that's impossible, said he,
What change of Age, or Ugliness can be!
Or, could Medea's Magick mend thy Face,
Thou art descended from so mean a Race,
That never Knight was match'd with such Disgrace.
What wonder, Madam, if I move my Side,
When if I turn, I turn to such a Bride?
If I am Old, and Ugly, well for you,
No leud Adult'rer will my Love pursue.
Nor Jealousy the Bane of marry'd Life,
Shall haunt you, for a wither'd homely Wife:
For Age, and Ugliness, as all agree,
Are the best Guards of Female Chastity
    Yet since I see your Mind is Worldly bent,
I'll do my best to further your Content.
And therefore of two Gifts in my dispose,
Think e'er you speak, I grant you leave to choose:
Wou'd you I should be still Deform'd, and Old,
Nauseous to Touch, and Loathsome to Behold;
On this Condition, to remain for Life
A careful, tender and obedient Wife,
In all I can contribute to your Ease,
And not in Deed or Word, or Thought displease?
Or would you rather have me Young and Fair,
And take the Chance that happens to your share?
Temptations are in Beauty, and in Youth,
And how can you depend upon my Truth?
Now weigh the Danger, with the doubtful Bliss,

And thank your self, if ought should fall amiss.
   Sore sigh'd the Knight, who this long Sermon heard,
At length considering all, his Heart he chear'd:
And thus reply'd, My Lady, and my Wife,
To your wise Conduct I resign my Life:
Choose you for me, for well you understand.
The future Good and Ill, on either Hand:
But if an humble Husband may request,
Provide and order all Things for the best;
Your's be the Care to profit, and to please:
And let your Subject-Servant take his Ease.
   Then thus in Peace, quoth she, concludes the Strife,
since I am turn'd the Husband, you the Wife:
The Matrimonial Victory is mine,
Which having fairly gain'd, I will resign;
Forgive, if I have said, or done amiss,
And seal the Bargain with a Friendly Kiss:
I promis'd you but one Content to share,
But now I will become both Good, and Fair.
No Nuptial Quarrel shall disturb your Ease,
The Business of my Life shall be to please:
And for my Beauty that, as Time shall try;
But draw the Curtain first, and cast your Eye.
   He look'd, and saw a Creature heav'nly Fair,
In bloom of Youth, and of a charming Air.
With Joy he turn'd, and seiz'd her Iv'ry Arm;
And like Pygmalion *found the Statue warm.*
Small Arguments there needed to prevail,
A Storm of Kisses pour'd as thick as Hail.
   Thus long in mutual Bliss they lay embrac'd,
And their first Love continu'd to the last:
One Sun-shine was their Life; no Cloud between;
Nor ever was a kinder Couple seen.
   And so may all our Lives like their's be led;
Heav'n send the Maids young Husbands, fresh in Bed:
May Widows Wed as often as they can,
And ever for the better change their Man.

And some devouring Plague pursue their Lives,
Who will not well be govern'd by their Wives.

Geoffrey Chaucer, *The Canterbury Tales* (1387)

THE FIRST WEDDING NIGHT

This said unanimous, and other Rites
Observing none, but adoration pure
Which God likes best, into thir inmost bower
Handed they went; and eas'd the putting off
These troublesom disguises which wee wear,
Strait side by side were laid, nor turnd I weene
Adam from his fair Spouse, nor Eve the Rites
Mysterious of connubial Love refus'd:
Whatever Hypocrites austerely talk
Of puritie and place and innocence,
Defaming as impure what God declares
Pure, and commands to som, leaves free to all.
Our Maker bids increase, who bids abstain
But our Destroyer, foe to God and Man?
Haile wedded Love, mysterious Law, true sourse
Of human ofspring, sole proprietie,
In Paradise of all things common else.
By thee adulterous lust was driv'n from men
Among the bestial herds to raunge, by thee
Founded in Reason, Loyal, Just, and Pure,
Relations dear, and all the Charities
Of Father, Son, and Brother first were known.
Farr be it, that I should write thee sin or blame,
Or think thee unbefitting holiest place,
Perpetual Fountain of Domestic sweets,

John Milton, *Paradise Lost* (1667)

'I AM GOING TO LOSE MY MAIDENHEAD'

On his wedding day in the 1690s the Reverend William Nevar writes
to a former pupil.

Sir,

I date this Letter from the happiest day of my life, a
Levitical Conjuror transformed me this morning from an
Insipid, Unrelishing Batchelour into a Loving Passionate
Husband, but in the midst of all the raptures of approaching Joys, some of my thoughts must fly to Felbrigg, and
tho I am called away 17 times in a minute to new exquisite
dainties, yet I cannot resist the inticing temptation of
conversing with you, and acquainting you, with tears in
my Eyes, that I am going to lose my Maidenhead, but
you'll think perhaps of the old Saying, that some for Joy
do cry, and some for Sorrow sing. Colonel Finch, who
honours us with his merry company, tells me of dismall
dangers I am to run before the next Sun shines upon me,
but the Spouse of my bosom being of a meek, forgiving
temper, I hope she will be mercifull, and not suffer a
young beginner to dye in the Experiment. I commend
myself to your best prayers in this dreadfull Juncture, and
wishing you speedily such a happy night, as I have now
in prospect

I remain
Your most humble and
most obedient Servant

W. Nevar

Dear Billy I am yours without reserve, and so says my
bride too.

IT WAS ALL OVER ...

SO IT WAS ALL OVER, the advance and retreat, the
doubts and hesitations. Everything finished, for better

or for worse. There we were, sheltering from the heavy rain under a large mango tree, myself, and my wife Antoinette and a little half-caste servant who was called Amélie. Under a neighbouring tree I could see our luggage covered with sacking, the two porters and a boy holding fresh horses, hired to carry us up 2,000 feet to the waiting honeymoon house.

The girl Amélie said this morning, 'I hope you will be very happy, sir, in your sweet honeymoon house.' She was laughing at me I could see. A lovely little creature but sly, spiteful, malignant perhaps, like much else in this place.

'It's only a shower,' Antoinette said anxiously. 'It will soon stop.'

I looked at the sad leaning cocoanut palms, the fishing boats drawn up on the shingly beach, the uneven row of whitewashed huts, and asked the name of the village.

'Massacre.'

'And who was massacred here? Slaves?'

'Oh no.' She sounded shocked. 'Not slaves. Something must have happened a long time ago. Nobody remembers now.'

The rain fell more heavily, huge drops sounded like hail on the leaves of the tree, and the sea crept stealthily forwards and backwards.

So this is Massacre. Not the end of the world, only the last stage of our interminable journey from Jamaica, the start of our sweet honeymoon. And it will all look very different in the sun.

It had been arranged that we would leave Spanish Town immediately after the ceremony and spend some weeks in one of the Windward Islands, at a small estate which had belonged to Antoinette's mother. I agreed. As I had agreed to everything else.

The windows of the huts were shut, the doors opened into silence and dimness. Then three little boys came to stare at us. The smallest wore nothing but a religious medal round his neck and the brim of a large fisherman's hat. When I smiled at him, he began to cry. A woman called from one of the huts and he ran away, still howling.

The other two followed slowly, looking back several times.

As if this was a signal a second woman appeared at her door, then a third.

'It's Caro,' Antoinette said. 'I'm sure it's Caro. Caroline,' she called, waving, and the woman waved back. A gaudy old creature in a brightly flowered dress, a striped head handkerchief and gold ear-rings.

'You'll get soaked, Antoinette,' I said.

'No, the rain is stopping.' She held up the skirt of her riding habit and ran across the street. I watched on critically. She wore a tricorne hat which became her, at least it shadowed her eyes which are too large and can be disconcerting. She never blinks at all it seems to me. Large, sad, dark alien eyes. Creole of pure English descent she may be, but they are not English or European either. And when did I begin to notice all this about my wife Antoinette? After we left Spanish Town I suppose. Or did I notice it before and refuse to admit what I saw? Not that I had much time to notice anything. I was married a month after I arrived in Jamaica and for nearly three weeks of that time I was in bed with fever.

The two women stood in the doorway of the hut gesticulating, talking not English but the debased French patois they use in this island. The rain began to drip down the back of my neck adding to my feeling of discomfort and melancholy.

Jean Rhys, *Wide Sargasso Sea* (1966)

THE GOOD-NIGHT
OR BLESSING

Blessings, in abundance come,
To the Bride, and to her Groome;
May the Bed, and this short night,
Know the fullness of delight!
Pleasures many, here attend ye
And ere long, a Boy, love send ye
Curld and comely, and so trimme,
Maides (in time) may ravish him.
Thus a dew of Graces fall
On ye both; Goodnight to all.

Robert Herrick (1591–1674)

DOMESTICITY

'... for the mutual society, help and comfort'

See the teenagers walking hand in hand, looking through other people's bay windows and planning their homes. The Home – this is what marriage means. If you cannot afford one, if you have to live with one set of parents, you feel rightly cheated. For marriage means a man and a woman living happily under one roof, with a child in the cot, growing, then another baby ... growing, growing ... Does it not?

This is the stuff of insurance advertisements. Indeed, domesticity may conform to this blissful picture, at least for a while. The early days of marriage may be heady, as the honeymoon continues, so that even soiled socks achieve the status of loved objects, washed with grace.

But by whom? The truth is that for many women, even today, marriage means domesticity, which in turn means a gradual wondering if life must take the form of a pile of ironing and a dirty floor – the deceitful stuff of product advertisements. A husband may 'help' – and many do. But 'help' – as a favour, without accepting an honest half of the responsibility. When babies come (as they probably will) the situation grows worse, or better – depending on how the couple are coping. The husband too may wonder, as the baby screams and his wife cries, whether this is what life is *meant* to be like. One thing is sure: it will never be quite as they thought it would be, when they gazed through others' windows. If they are fortunate, it may be richer.

(*A rose, bruised, in an ordinary, chipped vase ...*)

ADVICE FOR THE HONEYMOON

M AKE YOUR HONEYMOON a honey annum, honey life time. You can find plenty of ways to enjoy the year in concert. Study and admire Nature together, her laws and facts, beauties and wonders; attend churches, pic-nics, parties, concerts, lectures &c, for nothing cements the affection as effectively as intermingling love with the moral and intellectual faculties; because their transmission is paramount. Reading together these lectures especially, and addressing these truths kindly and intelligently, will melt into one amalgam two uncongenially married, much more two much more young lovers; for intellect naturally works with love. So together enjoy lovers' walks, talks and rides; press flowers as mementoes of these and those pleasant seasons; commune with each other while twilight tinges hills and vales with her golden hues till the queen of night throws her silvery rays over your enchanted pathway, or heaven's star-spangled dome deepens your mutual love...

Professor Fowler, *Private Lectures on Perfect Men, Women and Children in Happy Families, including Gender, Love, Matings, Married Life and Reproduction Etc.* (1883)

THE BRANGWENS' HONEYMOON

W ILL BRANGWEN had some weeks of holiday after his marriage, so the two took their honeymoon in full hands, alone in their cottage together.

And to him, as the days went by, it was as if the heavens had fallen, and he were sitting with her among the ruins, in a new world, everybody else buried, themselves two blissful survivors, with everything to squander as they would. At first, he could not get rid of a culpable sense of licence on his part. Wasn't there some duty outside, calling him and he did not come?

It was all very well at night, when the doors were locked and the darkness drawn round the two of them. Then they *were* the only inhabitants of the visible earth, the rest were under the flood. And being alone in the world, they were a law unto themselves, they could enjoy and squander and waste like conscienceless gods.

But in the morning, as the carts clanked by, and children shouted down the lane; as the hucksters came calling their wares, and the church clock struck eleven, and he and she had not got up yet, even to breakfast, he could not help feeling guilty, as if he were committing a breach of the law – ashamed that he was not up and doing.

'Doing what?' she asked. 'What is there to do? You will only lounge about.'

Still, even lounging about was respectable. One was at least in connexion with the world, then. Whereas now, lying so still and peacefully, while the daylight came obscurely through the drawn blind, one was severed from the world, one shut oneself off in tacit denial of the world. And he was troubled.

But it was so sweet and satisfying lying there talking desultorily with her. It was sweeter than sunshine, and not so evanescent. It was even irritating the way the church-clock kept on chiming: there seemed no space between the hours, just a moment, golden and still, whilst she traced his features with her finger-tips, utterly careless and happy, and he loved her to do it.

But he was strange and unused. So suddenly, everything that had been before was shed away and gone. One day, he was a bachelor, living with the world. The next day, he was with her, as remote from the world as if the two of them were buried like a seed in darkness. Suddenly, like a chestnut falling out of a burr, he was shed naked and glistening on to a soft, fecund earth, leaving behind him the hard rind of worldly knowledge and experience.

154

He heard it in the hucksters' cries, the noise of carts, the calling of children. And it was all like the hard, shed rind, discarded. Inside, in the softness and stillness of the room, was the naked kernel, that palpitated in silent activity, absorbed in reality.

Inside the room was a great steadiness, a core of living eternity. Only far outside, at the rim, went on the noise and the destruction. Here at the centre the great wheel was motionless, centred upon itself. Here was a poised, unflawed stillness that was beyond time, because it remained the same, inexhaustible, unchanging, unexhausted.

As they lay close together, complete and beyond the touch of time or change, it was as if they were at the very centre of all the slow wheeling of space and the rapid agitation of life, deep, deep inside them all, at the centre where there is utter radiance, and eternal being, and the silence absorbed in praise: the steady core of all movements, the unawakened sleep of all wakefulness. They found themselves there, and they lay still in each other's arms; for their moment they were at the heart of eternity, whilst time roared far off, forever far off, towards the rim.

Then gradually they were passed away from the supreme centre, down the circles of praise and joy and gladness, farther and farther out, towards the noise and the friction. But their hearts had burned and were tempered by the inner reality, they were unalterably glad.

Gradually they began to wake up, the noises outside became more real. They understood and answered the call outside.

D. H. Lawrence, *The Rainbow* (1915)

WEDDING-WIND

The wind blew all my wedding-day,
And my wedding-night was the night of the high wind;
And a stable door was banging, again and again,
That he must go and shut it, leaving me
Stupid in candlelight, hearing rain,
Seeing my face in the twisted candlestick,
Yet seeing nothing. When he came back
He said the horses were restless, and I was sad
That any man or beast that night should lack
The happiness I had.

                                    Now in the day
All's ravelled under the sun by the wind's blowing.
He has gone to look at the floods, and I
Carry a chipped pail to the chicken-run,
Set it down, and stare. All is the wind
Hunting through clouds and forests, thrashing
My apron and the hanging cloths on the line.
Can it be borne, this bodying-forth by wind
Of you my actions turn on, like a thread
Carrying beads? Shall I be let to sleep
Now this perpetual morning shares my bed?
Can even death dry up
These new delighted lakes, conclude
Our kneeling as cattle by all-generous waters?

                                    Philip Larkin (1955)

PLAYING WITH 'BABY'

On June 17th, 1890, Victoria Sackville-West married her first cousin,
Lionel Sackville-West. Their passionate honeymoon continued into
everyday married life. It should be pointed out that 'Baby' was
Victoria's name for her husband's penis. Their daughter was, of
course, Vita Sackville-West.

156

30 July 1890, Knole
Lionel went out to kill his first deer. I went with Amalia
to visit Miss Boscawen then we played Spillikins. I call
Lionel 'Tio'.

31 July 1890
Tio has gone out again to kill deer. Miss Boscawen came
to see us and told L. that he was looking badly. I told Tio
that this was because of e.g.! [making love].

2 August 1890
Baby very naughty this morning while I was pretending
to sleep . . .

4 August 1890
Tio went riding. Yesterday I began my embroidery for
him – a souvenir of the Château of Blois – this will be a
fire screen. I worked a lot this afternoon sitting with him
on the lawn in front of the house; all the same I was able
to play with Baby. Went to the kitchen garden and ordered
grapes to be sent to Mary and fruits to the Childrens'
Hospital.

20 August 1890
Tio is getting more passionate every day.

13 September 1890
Baby was very naughty this morning, we kept Mrs Knox
waiting for forty minutes – awful of us.

16 September 1890
Tio got up even later than usual this morning; he simply
can't leave me and often returns about 11 o'clock so that
we can have caresses that never end.

18 September 1890
Tio was perfectly mad tonight – he kissed me passionately
even in front of Amalia and Bertie, which ended in the
most delicious love making. He really is a stallion – 4
times.

28 November 1890
Delirium. Afterwards Tio said, "Was it nice, Vicky?"

22 May 1891, Knole
Every day the same thing, walking and sticking stamps
on, reading, playing the piano, making love.

27 June 1891, Knole
What a heavenly husband I have and how different our
love and union is from that of other couples.

From the Diaries of Lady Sackville

POEM ABOUT SOMETHING

When we were newly married, coy and young,
We did not fornicate, copulate, or even
'Make Love'. No – we had
Something; saying 'we had something
Last night', in the bickering dawn, to
Recapitulate love. Then (as not now) we
'Had something' on the new lino, in each new
Bed, you, afterwards, hopping, to spatter
In blessing the last seeds. In the
Conjugal bath we had something that
Churned the deeps and drowned the bathroom
Floor, and on Scottish hills, spotted
With grey wool tufts what we had
Only the sheep could tell. Now
What we have is confined to bed
And propriety. The lino's replaced,
The new kitchen floor unsanctified. You
No longer kiss me from my feet upwards and no
Wonder, seeing my bunion, my wrestler's thigh . . .
But

Broadminded now, what we do is fuck
Conscientiously and to keep in
Practice. We've had something,
I think.

Gerda Mayer (1980)

ADVICE TO A HUSBAND

I BEGAN MY YOUNG marriage days in and near Philadelphia. At one of those times to which I have just alluded, in the middle of the burning hot month of July, I was greatly afraid of fatal consequences to my wife for want of sleep, she not having, after the great danger was over, had any sleep for more than forty-eight hours. All great cities, in hot countries, are, I believe, full of dogs; and they, in the very hot weather, keep up, during the night, a horrible barking and fighting and howling. Upon the particular occasion to which I am adverting, they made a noise so terrible and so unremitted, that it was next to impossible that even a person in full health and free from pain should obtain a minute's sleep. I was, about nine in the evening, sitting by the bed: "I do think," said she, "that I could go to sleep now, if it were not for the dogs." Downstairs I went, and out I sallied, in my shirt and trousers, and without shoes and stockings; and, going to a heap of stones lying beside the road, set to work upon the dogs, going backwards and forward, and keeping them at two or three hundred yards' distance from the house. I walked thus, the whole night, barefooted, lest the noise of my shoes might possibly reach her ears; and I remember that the bricks of the causeway were, even in the night, so hot as to be disagreeable to my feet. My exertions produced the desired effect: a sleep of several hours was the consequence; and, at eight o'clock in the

159

morning, off went I to a day's business which was to end at six in the evening.

Women are all patriots of the soil; and when her neighbours used to ask my wife whether all English husbands were like hers, she boldly answered in the affirmative. I had business to occupy the whole of my time, Sundays and week-days, except sleeping hours; but I used to make time to assist her in the taking care of her baby, and in all sorts of things: get up, light her fire, boil her tea-kettle, carry her up warm water in cold weather, take the child while she dressed herself and got the breakfast ready, then breakfast, get her in water and wood for the day, then dress myself neatly, and sally forth to my business. The moment that was over I used to hasten back to her again; and I no more thought of spending a moment away from her, unless business compelled me, than I thought of quitting the country and going to sea. The thunder and lightning are tremendous in America, compared with what they are in England. My wife was, at one time, very much afraid of thunder and lightning; and, as is the feeling of all such women, and, indeed, all men too, she wanted company, and particularly her husband, in those times of danger. I knew well, of course, that my presence would not diminish the danger; but, be I at what I might, if within reach of home, I used to quit my business and hasten to her the moment I perceived a thunder-storm approaching. Scores of miles have I, first and last, run on this errand in the streets of Philadelphia! The Frenchmen who were my scholars used to laugh at me exceedingly on this account; and sometimes, when I was making an appointment with them, they would say, with a smile and a bow, "Sauve la tonnerre toujours, Monsieur Cobbett."

William Cobbett, *Advice to Young Men and (Incidentally) to Young Women* (1829)

A LETTER

Lying in bed this morning, just a year
   since our first days, I was trying to assess –
against my natural caution – my desire
   and how the fact outdid it, my happiness:
and finding the awkwardness of keeping clear
     numberless flamingo thoughts and memories,
        my dear and dearest husband, in this kind
        of rambling letter, I'll disburse my mind.

Technical problems have always given me trouble:
   a child stiff at the fiddle, my ear had praise
and my intention only; so, as was natural,
   coming to verse, I hid my lack of ease
by writing only as I thought myself able,
     escaped the crash of the bold by salt originalities.
        This is one reason for writing far from one's heart;
        a better is, that one fears it may hurt.

By an inadequate style one fears to cheapen
   glory, and that it may be blurred if seen
through the eye's used centre, not the new margin.
   It is the hardest thing with love to burn
and write it down, for what was the real passion
     left to its own words will seem trivial and thin.
        We can in making love look face to face:
        in poetry, crooked, and with no embrace.

Tolstoy's hero found in his newborn child
   only another aching, vulnerable part;
and it is true our first joy hundredfold
   increased our dangers, pricking in every street
in accidents and wars: yet this is healed
     not by reason, but the endurance of delight
        since our marriage, which, once thoroughly known,
        is known for good, though in time it were gone.

You, hopeful baby with the erring toes,
  grew, it seems to me, to a natural pleasure
in the elegant strict machine, from the abstruse
  science of printing to the rich red and azure
it plays on hoardings, rusty industrial noise,
  all these could add to your inherited treasure:
    a poise which many wish for, writing the machine
    poems of laboured praise, but few attain.

And loitered up your childhood to my arms.
  I would hold you there for ever, and know
certainly now, that though the vacuum glooms,
  quotidian dullness, in these beams don't die,
they're wrong who say that happiness never comes
  on earth, that has spread here its crystal sea.
    And since you, loiterer, did compose this wonder,
    be with me still, and may God hold his thunder.

Anne Ridler (1939)

'I CAN'T GET A MOMENT'S PEACE'

NICHOLAS SUDDENLY MOVED and cleared his throat. And at that moment little Andrew shouted from outside the door: 'Papa! Mamma's standing here!' Countess Mary turned pale with fright and made signs to the boy. He grew silent, and quiet ensued for a moment, terrible to Countess Mary. She knew how Nicholas disliked being waked. Then through the door she heard Nicholas clearing his throat again and stirring, and his voice said crossly:

'I can't get a moment's peace. Mary, is that you? Why did you bring him here?'

'I only came in to look, and did not notice ... forgive me ...'

Nicholas coughed and said no more. Countess Mary moved away from the door and took the boy back to the

162

nursery. Five minutes later little black-eyed three-year-old Natásha, her father's pet, having learnt from her brother that papa was asleep and mamma was in the sitting-room, ran to her father unobserved by her mother. The dark-eyed little girl boldly opened the creaking door, went up to the sofa with energetic steps of her sturdy little legs, and having examined the position of her father, who was asleep with his back to her, rose on tip-toe and kissed the hand which lay under his head. Nicholas turned with a tender smile on his face.

'Natásha, Natásha!' came Countess Mary's frightened whisper from the door. 'Papa wants to sleep.'

'No, mamma, he doesn't want to sleep,' said little Natásha with conviction. 'He's laughing.'

Nicholas lowered his legs, rose, and took his daughter in his arms.

'Come in, Mary,' he said to his wife.

She went in and sat down by her husband.

'I did not notice him following me,' she said timidly. 'I just looked in.'

Holding his little girl with one arm, Nicholas glanced at his wife and, seeing her guilty expression, put his other arm round her and kissed her hair.

'May I kiss mamma?' he asked Natásha.

Natásha smiled bashfully.

'Again!' she commanded, pointing with a peremptory gesture to the spot where Nicholas had placed the kiss.

'I don't know why you think I am cross,' said Nicholas, replying to the question he knew was in his wife's mind.

'You have no idea how unhappy, how lonely, I feel when you are like that. It always seems to me ...'

'Mary, don't talk nonsense. You ought to be ashamed of yourself!' he said gaily.

'It seems to me that you can't love me, that I am so plain ... always ... and now ... in this cond....'

'Oh, how absurd you are! It is not beauty that endears, it's love that makes us see beauty. It is only Malvínas and women of that kind who are loved for their beauty. But do I love my wife? I don't love her, but ... I don't know how to put it. Without you, or when something comes between us like this, I seem lost and can't do anything. Now do I love my finger? I don't love it, but just try to cut it off!'

'I'm not like that myself, but I understand. So you're not angry with me?'

'Awfully angry!' he said, smiling and getting up. And smoothing his hair he began to pace the room.

Leo Tolstoy, *War and Peace* (1863/9)

SIR THOMAS MORE TO HIS WIFE

This is the only letter from Sir Thomas More to his wife that survives. It shows his charitable nature: he is far more concerned about his poor neighbours than his own losses. It also shows the confidence of a good marriage: he knows she will cope and be cheerful, as he exhorts. And the last sentence displays a quiet satisfaction in their companionship, and ability to devise a solution to any problem that might beset them.

Woodstock, 3 September 1529

MISTRESS ALICE, in my most hearty wise I recommend me to you. And whereas I am informed by my son [-in-law] Heron of the loss of our barns and our neighbours' also with all the corn that was therein, albeit (saving God's pleasure) it were great pity of so much good corn lost – yet, sith it hath liked him to send us such a chance, we must and are bounden not only to be content but also to be glad of his visitation. He sent us all that we have lost and, since he hath by such a chance taken it away again, his pleasure be fulfilled. Let us never grudge thereat, but take in good worth and heartily thank him as well for adversity as for prosperity. And per-adventure we have more cause to thank him for our loss than for our winning, for his wisdom better seeth what is good for us than we do ourselves.

Therefore, I pray you, be of good cheer and take all the household with you to church, and there thank God both for that he hath given us and for that he hath taken from us and for that he hath left us. Which, if it please him, he can increase when he will and if it please him to leave us yet less, at his pleasure be it.

I pray you to make some good ensearch what my poor neighbours have lost and bid them take no thought therefore. For and [if] I should not leave myself a spoon, there shall no poor neighbour of mine bear no loss by any chance happened in my house. I pray you be with my children and your household merry in God, and devise somewhat with your friends what way were best to take for provision to be made for corn for our household, and for seed this year coming, if ye think it good that we keep the ground still in our hands. Yet I think it were not best suddenly thus to leave it all up and to put away our folk of our farm, till we have somewhat advised us thereon. Howbeit, if we have more now than ye shall need and which can get them other masters, ye may then discharge us of them. But I would not that any man were suddenly sent away, he wot [knew] ne'er whither.

At my coming hither I perceived none other but that I should tarry still with the King's grace. But now I shall, I think, because of this chance get leave this next week to come home and see you. And then shall we further devise together upon all things what order shall be best to take.

LOVE IN A LIFE

I

Room after room,
I hunt the house through
We inhabit together.
Heart, fear nothing, for, heart, thou shalt find her,
Next time, herself! — not the trouble behind her
Left in the curtain, the couch's perfume!
As she brushed it, the cornice-wreath blossomed anew:
Yon looking-glass gleamed at the wave of her feather.

II

Yet the day wears,
And door succeeds door;
I try the fresh fortune —
Range the wide house from the wing to the centre.
Still the same chance! she goes out as I enter.
Spend my whole day in the quest — who cares?
But 'tis twilight, you see, — with such suites to explore,
Such closets to search, such alcoves to importune!

Robert Browning, *Men and Women* (1855)

PART OF PLENTY

When she carries food to the table and stoops down
— Doing this out of love — and lays soup with its good
Tickling smell, or fry winking from the fire
And I look up, perhaps from a book I am reading
Or other work: there is an importance of beauty
Which can't be accounted for by there and then,
And attacks me, but not separately from the welcome
Of the food, or the grace of her arms.

DOMESTICITY

When she puts a sheaf of tulips in a jug
And pours in water and presses to one side
The upright stems and leaves that you hear creak,
Or loosens them, or holds them up to show me,
So that I see the tangle of their necks and cups
With the curls of her hair, and the body they are held
Against, and the stalk of the small waist rising
And flowering in the shape of breasts;

Whether in the bringing of the flowers or the food
She offers plenty, and is part of plenty,
And whether I see her stooping, or leaning with the flowers,
What she does is ages old, and she is not simply,
No, but lovely in that way.

Bernard Spencer (1949)

FARM WIFE

Hers is the clean apron, good for fire
Or lamp to embroider, as we talk slowly
In the long kitchen, while the white dough
Turns to pastry in the great oven,
Sweetly and surely as hay making
In a June meadow; hers are the hands,
Humble with milking, but still now
In her wide lap as though they heard
A quiet music, hers being the voice
That coaxes time back to the shadows
In the room's corners. O, hers is all
This strong body, the safe island
Where men may come, sons and lovers,
Daring the cold seas of her eyes.

R. S. Thomas (1958)

DORA'S HOUSEKEEPING

ONE OF OUR FIRST FEATS in the housekeeping way was a little dinner to Traddles. I met him in town, and asked him to walk out with me that afternoon. He readily consenting, I wrote to Dora, saying I would bring him home. It was pleasant weather, and on the road we made my domestic happiness the theme of conversation. Traddles was very full of it; and said, that, picturing himself with such a home, and Sophy waiting and preparing for him, he could think of nothing wanting to complete his bliss.

I could not have wished for a prettier little wife at the opposite end of the table, but I certainly could have wished, when we sate down, for a little more room. I did not know how it was, but though there were only two of us, we were at once always cramped for room, and yet had always room enough to lose everything in. I suspect it may have been because nothing had a place of its own, except Jip's pagoda, which invariably blocked up the main thoroughfare. On the present occasion, Traddles was so hemmed in by the pagoda and the guitar-case, and Dora's flower-painting, and my writing-table, that I had serious doubts of the possibility of his using his knife and fork; but he protested, with his own good-humour, "Oceans of room, Copperfield! I assure you, Oceans!"

There was another thing I could have wished; namely, that Jip had never been encouraged to walk about the table-cloth during dinner. I began to think there was something disorderly in his being there at all, even if he had not been in the habit of putting his foot in the salt or the melted-butter. On this occasion he seemed to think he was introduced expressly to keep Traddles at bay; and he barked at my old friend, and made short runs at his plate, with such undaunted pertinacity, that he may be said to have engrossed the conversation.

168

However, as I knew how tender-hearted my dear Dora was, and how sensitive she would be to any slight upon her favourite, I hinted no objection. For similar reasons I made no illusion to the skirmishing plates upon the floor; or to the disreputable appearance of the castors, which were all at sixes and sevens, and looked drunk; or to the further blockade of Traddles by wandering vegetable dishes and jugs. I could not help wondering in my own mind, as I contemplated the boiled leg of mutton before me, previous to carving it, how it came to pass that our joints of meat were of such extraordinary shapes – and whether our butcher contracted for all the deformed sheep that came into the world; but I kept my reflections to myself.

"My love," said I to Dora, "what have you got in that dish?"

I could not imagine why Dora had been making tempting little faces at me, as if she wanted to kiss me.

"Oysters, dear," said Dora, timidly.

"Was that *your* thought?" said I delighted.

"Ye-Yes, Doady," said Dora.

"There never was a happier one!" I exclaimed, laying down the carving-knife and fork. "There is nothing Traddles likes so much!"

"Ye-yes, Doady," said Dora, "and so I bought a beautiful little barrel of them, and the man said they were very good. But I – I am afraid there's something the matter with them. They don't seem right." Here Dora shook her head, and diamonds twinkled in her eyes.

"They are only opened in both shells," said I. "Take the top one off, my love."

"But it won't come off," said Dora, trying very hard, and looking very much distressed.

"Do you know, Copperfield," said Traddles, cheerfully examining the dish, "I think it is in consequence – they are capital oysters, but I *think* it is in consequence – of their never having been opened."

169

They never had been opened; and we had no oyster-knives – and couldn't have used them if we had; so we looked at the oysters and ate the mutton. At least we ate as much of it as was done, and made up with capers. If I had permitted him, I am satisfied that Traddles would have made a perfect savage of himself, and eaten a plateful of raw meat, to express enjoyment of the repast; but I would hear of no such immolation on the altar of friendship; and we had a course of bacon instead; there happening, by good fortune, to be cold bacon in the larder.

Charles Dickens, *David Copperfield* (1849/50)

URSULA IS BORN TO THE BRANGWENS

THEY WERE FRIENDS AGAIN, new, subdued friends. But there was a wanness between them. They slept together once more, very quietly, and distinct, not one together as before. And she was intimate with him as at first. But he was very quiet, and not intimate. He was glad in his soul, but for the time being he was not alive.

He could sleep with her, and let her be. He could be alone now. He had just learned what it was to be able to be alone. It was right and peaceful. She had given him a new, deeper freedom. The world might be a welter of uncertainty, but he was himself now. He had come into his own existence. He was born for a second time, born at last unto himself, out of the vast body of humanity. Now at last he had a separate identity, he existed alone, even if he were not quite alone. Before he had only existed in so far as he had relations with another being. Now he had an absolute self – as well as a relative self.

But it was a very dumb, helpless self, a crawling nursling. He went about very quiet, and in a way, submissive. He had an unalterable self at last, free, separate, independent.

170

She was relieved, she was free of him. She had given him to himself. She wept sometimes with tiredness and helplessness. But he was a husband. And she seemed, in the child that was coming, to forget. It seemed to make her warm and drowsy. She lapsed into a long muse, indistinct, warm, vague, unwilling to be taken out of her vagueness. And she rested on him also.

Sometimes she came to him with a strange light in her eyes, poignant, pathetic, as if she were asking for something. He looked and he could not understand. She was so beautiful, so visionary, the rays seemed to go out of his breast to her, like a shining. He was there for her, all for her. And she would hold his breast, and kiss it, and kiss it, kneeling beside him, she who was waiting for the hour of her delivery. And he would lie looking down at his breast, till it seemed that his breast was not himself, that he had left it lying there. Yet it was himself also, and beautiful and bright with her kisses. He was glad with a strange radiant pain. Whilst she kneeled beside him, and kissed his breast with a slow, rapt, half-devotional movement.

He knew she wanted something, his heart yearned to give it her. His heart yearned over her. And as she lifted her face, that was radiant and rosy as a little cloud, his heart still yearned over her, and now from the distance, adored her. She had a flower-like presence which he adored as he stood far off, a stranger.

The weeks passed on, the time drew near, they were very gentle, and delicately happy. The insistent, passionate, dark soul, the powerful unsatisfaction in him seemed stilled and tamed, the lion lay down with the lamb in him.

She loved him very much indeed, and he waited near her. She was a precious, remote thing to him at this time, as she waited for her child. Her soul was glad with an ecstasy because of the coming infant. She wanted a boy: oh very much she wanted a boy.

But she seemed so young and so frail. She was indeed

only a girl. As she stood by the fire washing herself – she was proud to wash herself at this time – and he looked at her, his heart was full of extreme tenderness for her. Such fine, fine limbs, her slim, round arms like chasing lights, and her legs so simple and childish, yet so very proud. Oh, she stood on proud legs, with a lovely reckless balance of her full belly, and the adorable little roundnesses, and the breasts becoming important. Above it all, her face was like a rosy cloud shining.

How proud she was, what a lovely proud thing her young body! And she loved him to put his hands on her ripe fullness, so that he should thrill also with the stir and the quickening there. He was afraid and silent, but she flung her arms round his neck with proud, impudent joy.

The pains came on, and Oh – how she cried! She would have him stay with her. And after her long cries she would look at him, with tears in her eyes and a sobbing laugh on her face, saying:

"I don't mind it really."

It was bad enough. But to her it was never deathly. Even the fierce, tearing pain was exhilarating. She screamed and suffered, but was all the time curiously alive and vital. She felt so powerfully alive and in the hands of such a masterly force of life, that her bottom-most feeling was one of exhilaration. She knew she was winning, winning, she was always winning, with each onset of pain she was nearer to victory.

Probably he suffered more than she did. He was not shocked or horrified. But he was screwed very tight in the vice of suffering.

It was a girl. The second of silence on her face when they said so showed him she was disappointed. And a great blazing passion of resentment and protest sprang up in his heart. In that moment he claimed the child.

But when the milk came, and the infant sucked her breast, she seemed to be leaping with extravagant bliss.

"It sucks me, it sucks me, it likes me – oh, it loves it!"

she cried, holding the child to her breast with her two hands covering it, passionately.

And in a few moments, as she became used to her bliss, she looked at the youth with glowing, unseeing eyes, and said:

'Anna Victrix,'

He went away, trembling, and slept. To her, the pains were the wound-smart of a victor, she was the prouder.

When she was well again she was very happy. She called the baby Ursula. Both Anna and her husband felt they must have a name that gave them private satisfaction. The baby was tawny skinned, it had a curious downy skin, and wisps of bronze hair, and the yellow grey eyes that wavered, and then became golden-brown like the father's. So they called her Ursula because of the picture of the saint.

It was a rather delicate baby at first, but soon it became stronger, and was restless as a young eel. Anna was worn out with the day-long wrestling with its young vigour.

As a little animal, she loved and adored it and was happy. She loved her husband, she kissed his eyes and nose and mouth, and made much of him, she said his limbs were beautiful, she was fascinated by the physical form of him.

And she was indeed Anna Victrix. He could not combat her any more. He was out in the wilderness, alone with her.

D. H. Lawrence, *The Rainbow* (1915)

From THE DIARY OF VIRGINIA WOOLF

Leonard Woolf has been absent, giving a lecture in Birkenhead, Cheshire. They have been married for five years.

Friday 2 November 1917
. . . But I was glad to come home, & feel my real life coming back again – I mean life here with L. Solitary is not quite the right word; one's personality seems to echo out across space, when he's not there to enclose all one's vibrations. This is not very intelligibly written; but the feeling itself is a strange one – as if marriage were a completing of the instrument, & the sound of one alone penetrates as if it were a violin robbed of its orchestra or piano. A dull wet night, so I shall sleep. The raid happened of course, with us away.

Saturday 3, Sunday 4, Monday 5 November
The raid didn't actually happen but with our nerves in the state they are (I should say Lottie's & Nelly's nerves) the dipping down of the electric lights was taken as a sign of warning: finally the lights went out, & standing on the kitchen stairs I was deluged with certain knowledge that the extinction of light is in future our warning. I looked out of the hall door, however, heard the usual patter & voices of suburbans coming home; & then, to bear out my assurance, the lights suddenly came on again. We went to bed & to sleep. I woke 5 minutes before 7, & lay listening, but heard nothing, & was about, at 8 o'clock to flatten out all my expectations when I heard L. at the door & there he was! With the softness of a mouse he had let himself in & breakfasted. We talked for as long as we could; things kept oozing out; sudden silences & spurts; divine contentment at being once more harmonious. L. travelled all night. The most pungent of his tales is to me the story of the arguing & enquiring & experimenting. Mrs Ekhard who thrust herself into all sorts of subjects, with L., while he cut down her trees. The palms of his hands are still black from the soot of Manchester bark. We walked by the river, & to bed rather early. L. having denied that he was at all tired, tumbled asleep & slept till he was called.

174

ALFRED THE GREAT

Honour and magnify this man of men
Who keeps a wife and seven children on £2 10
Paid weekly in an envelope
And yet he never has abandoned hope.

Stevie Smith (1937)

FIVE DOMESTIC INTERIORS

1

The lady of the house is on her benders;
She's scrubbed and mopped until her knees are sore.
She rests a second as her husband enters,
Then says, 'Look out! Don't walk on my clean floor.'
He looks up at the slick flies on the ceiling
And shakes his head, and goes back through the door.

2

She holds her chuckling baby to her bosom
And says, 'My honey-pie, my sugar bun,
Does Mummy love her scrumptious little darling?
You're lovely, yes, you are, my precious one!'
But when the little perisher starts bawling
She says, 'For God's sake listen to your son.'

3

Sandbagged by sleep at last the kids lie still.
The kitchen clock is nodding in warm air.
They spread the Sunday paper on the table
And each draws up a comfortable chair.
He turns the pages to the crossword puzzle,
Nonplussed they see a single large black square.

175

4

The radio is playing dated music
With lilac tune and metronomic beat.
She smiles and says, 'Remember that one, darling?
The way we used to foxtrot was a treat.'
But they resist the momentary temptation
To resurrect slim dancers on glib feet.

5

In bed his tall enthusiastic member
Receives warm welcome, and a moist one too.
She whispers, 'Do you love me? More than ever?'
And, panting, he replies, 'Of course I do.'
Then as she sighs and settles close for slumber
He thinks with mild surprise that it is true.

Vernon Scannell (1973)

THE ACADEMIC WIFE

'DO YOU HAVE TO SMOKE ALL the time, Caro?' Alan said. 'I should've thought it would be inconvenient – not to mention lung cancer.'

And expense, I thought guiltily, while reminding Alan that he used to smoke once. I still didn't like him to criticise me. Naively I had imagined that he thought me perfect and it had been a shock when he began to find fault with me, even though it was only over unimportant details.

We had first met at a university which, to my mother's grief, was neither Oxford nor Cambridge, and had fallen in love when I was slightly on the rebound from a Byronic-looking cad with political ambitions. Alan's dusty fair eyelashes, grey eyes and slight but fascinating provincial accent had attracted me. He had seemed to be the kind of person who would cherish and look after me and up to a point he was and still is.

176

I had been christened Caroline, which in my teens I had changed to Caro because of poor Lady Caroline Lamb, who said she was like the wreck of a little boat for she never came up to the sublime and beautiful. At sixteen it had seemed touching and amusing to think of oneself in this way, but as I grew older I could see that it was less admirable. After the misery of the Byronic affair, which had been the inevitable result of this early foolishness. I had tried to forget the Caro side of me, though the name still stuck.

Fiction, journalism and the conversation of other university wives, some of whom had part-time jobs, tended to make me see myself as a frustrated graduate wife, though I had married straight from university and had never had anything that might be considered as a proper job, nor was there any particular career that I wanted to follow. I was, however, conscious of lacking any special maternal feeling and this seemed an even greater inadequacy. I loved Kate and worried about her very often, but Inge was so much better with her than I was. Still, I felt proud that I had produced a child, though disappointed that I did not feel more 'fulfilled'.

'Is your hair going to be dry in time?' Alan asked.

'Of course! You don't think I'd go to the Maynards' with wet hair, do you?'

'I never quite know.'

'I've put out a clean shirt for you,' I said. 'Will you be wearing your grey suit?'

'Yes, I suppose so,' he said without interest, so different from Coco. 'I'd like a cup of tea.'

'Inge will make you one when she's finished with Kate.' Alan's liking for cups of tea at all hours had been an endearing trait which now irritated me. Of course he had developed a taste for more sophisticated and suitable drinks, but the love of tea remained.

'Inge doesn't know how to make tea properly. I'll do it myself.'

I did not offer to do it – Alan was as domesticated as I
was.

*

I looked in on Kate before we went out. One sometimes
reads in Edwardian memoirs of a child retaining a romantic memory of its mother dressed to go out to a party,
coming in to say good night. I wondered how Kate would
remember me in my trouser suit which gave little scope
for conventional glamour. Perhaps, years hence, a certain
scent would bring back the occasion, for the bottle had
upset and I was stupefied by the expensive aura.

'Is that the scent I gave you last Christmas?' Alan asked
and seemed pleased when I confirmed that it was.

'Unfortunately I spilt it, so it may overpower everybody.'

Alan smiled, as if that would add to his prestige in some
way.

Barbara Pym, An Academic Question (1986)

PAVANE FOR THE LOST CHILDREN

When you rest in my arms and your heart
quietens against mine
I think of a midnight kitchen,
the kettle muttering on the lowest gas,
and the baby forgetting to feed,
lips plumped like a little mollusc
that is almost losing its grip.
They could not relinquish survival,
those lips; I knew what they dreamed of
would keep arousing them
to fits of greedy, absent-minded tugging.
So I sat on, enthralled,
and my breasts wept ceaselessly
like the fated wedding-jars.

178

This too is our grown-up devotion
when fatigue is most pressing:
to pretend we will never put each other down
and drift singly away on
sleep's disappointing persuasions;
such lowly forms of life, so deeply marine,
we cannot move apart, or know what time is,
but are turned like bivalves on the lifting
 wave
that has promised us to the sand.

Carol Rumens (1985)

A BIRTHDAY POEM FOR MADELEINE

It was at first merely the inconvenience
– Children, we thought, would interrupt our love,
Our lovemaking, thwart our careers,
Interfere with plans for foreign travel,
Leave us less money for drink and cigarettes,
And generally be a bloody nuisance.

Then, almost without our noticing it,
There the three enchanters were, and we
Were more in love than ever, and we told
Childless friends to follow our example.

But now – three tall daughters growing taller
Every day – who am I to boast I bear
Such tall and triple responsibility?
I should be frightened, I should run away
To sea, or to some childless woman's arms,
Or to writing poems in a lonely room.

Then I see your smile upon the pillow,
And, forgetting inconvenience, responsibility,

I answer as I can to your sweet asking,
And only hope these girls deserve their mother.

T. Harri Jones (1977)

JOHN DONNE WRITES A LETTER AT HOME

SIR

I write not to you out of my poor Library, where to cast mine eye upon good Authors kindles or refreshes sometimes meditations not unfit to communicate to near friends; nor from the high way, where I am contracted, and inverted into my self; which are my two ordinary forges of Letters to you. But I write from the fire side in my Parler, and in the noise of three gamesome children; and by the side of her, whom because I have transplanted into a wretched fortune, I must labour to disguise that from her by all such honest devices, as giving her my company, and discourse, therefore I steal from her, all the time which I give this Letter, and it is therefore that I take so short a list, and gallop so fast over it . . .

John Donne (c. 1609)

FOR YOU

You have time for everything,
tireless and good, severe and comforting,
sorrow and song, day and night
always by my side,
asleep, in dreams,
in crowds, alone.
You have time for everything,
to stand and stroke my hair,
to go through piles of books,
essays and compositions, notes . . .

180

time for marking, time for reading,
time for working in the lab,
time for each child of all the hundreds
of autobiographies
of which you write a page.

Among the essays on the shelves,
piled high with books and notes,
our little girl listens to you
dreamy eyed as you tell the story of Snow White
and the seven kind dwarfs.

You have time for everything,
there where you sit among your formulas,
planning your lessons for the coming week,
tireless and good, the very heart of life.

Ion Horea (1969), translated by
Roy McGregor-Hastie

OUR DOMESTIC GRACES

The Chancellor of Gifts is an élitist.
You can't pretend he'll step out of the night
With a gilt invitation-card or flowers.
The brilliant words we wrote down in a dream
Aren't there beside our bedside after all.

Yet something calls from the great expanse
Of air we have made our latest home in.
Studio voices wake us near eight
With stories of God and how 'He moves among us
Constantly like light'. What are his tracks like?

Mystery starts no further away
Than these mossy footprints crossing the lawn
To where the raspberries are ripe again
And the panes of the greenhouse brim with tears.
Today even our lost city appears

181

From its shroud: a white dust-sheet slowly lifts
And here are all our glinting heirlooms –
The gasworks, like a coronet, queens it
Over the houses, and bridges grace
The river with their lacy hems and V s.

To have it all so clear – the congregating
Chimneypots, the lines of traffic passing
Over the heath like words being typed on a page.
Christ's fishermen must have felt like this,
Crying out, amazed, at their spangled catch.

Light falls about these rooms, silvering the face
Of what we are most used to, and ourselves,
Who on such days might think we had been
Elected at last – guest musicians
At the garden party of the gods.

Blake Morrison (1984)

A HUSBAND'S MOODS

The 'David' in this passage is the poet Edward Thomas (1878–
1917). He married Helen in 1899 when he was 21, and their married
life was a struggle, financially and emotionally. Thomas was forced
to support his young family by freelance writing and reviewing,
and called himself a 'doomed hack'. His natural tendency to
depression was exacerbated by the irregularity of work.

HOW ANXIOUSLY I waited for David's home-
coming on these days, and how with the first glance
at his face I knew what the day had been. If it had been a
bad one there was no need of words, and none were
uttered. I could do nothing, for if I said one word which
would betray that I knew what he had endured and was
enduring, his anger and despair and weariness would
break out in angry bitter words which would freeze my
heart and afterwards freeze his for having uttered them.

182

So as he ate the evening meal in silence, I talked quietly about the doings of the day, of the baby, of the walk we had been; and soon in our pretty room he would lie back in his big Oxford chair by the fire, smoking his pipe, while I sat on a stool near and sewed; and gradually the weariness would go out of his face, and the hard thin line of his mouth would relax to its lovely curve, and he would speak of an essay that had been suggested to him by something he had seen in London, or of a notable volume of poems that N. had promised he should review for the *Daily Chronicle*. Then I would slip from my stool to the floor between his knees, and he would put out his hand and rest it on my neck, and I would know that the cloud had passed.

But sometimes when his spirit had been more than usually affected by the too great strain that his circumstances put upon it, the cloud did not pass, and my chatter ran dry in the arid silence. After a ghastly hour or two with the supper still uneaten on the kitchen table he would say: "Go to bed, I'm not coming," and I would know that he would sit up all night, and in the morning would be deeper in despair than ever – or he would go out and walk till morning, and perhaps from the silence of night and from the natural sounds of early dawn, and from the peace of solitude and the beauty of intangible things he would find healing and calm. I did not sleep on these nights but took my baby into bed with me, and in suckling him and holding him close, hope and comfort came to me again.

Some days David would be at home all day writing and reading, happy and eager with the impulse for creative work which gave him greater satisfaction than anything else. If the weather was fine he would break off his work in the afternoon and putting Philip in his pram we would set out for Wimbledon or Richmond Park, somewhere where we could sit on grass and look at trees and clouds and hear birds. There the baby would play himself to sleep, while David read a book for review, or aloud to me, and we would return in the evening laden with flowers and branches of leaves or berries for our room. Some of the days at home were idle and hopeless – no commissioned work to do, and no impulse for original work – and on these days the squalid surroundings obtruded upon our spirits, and the harsh voices of the other tenants and the crying of children sounded inhuman like the sounds of hell. One of these days I remember very well. I had not got into the routine of housework and looking after the baby, and I asked David to peel the potatoes for the midday meal. This he angrily refused to do. But at dinner he praised my cooking, and I, still hurt by his unkindness, could not restrain a few tears at the welcome change of mood. Seeing my distress he jumped up from his chair, ran down the stairs into the street, and returned in two minutes with a bottle of cheap wine. Never was so homely a meal turned into such a joyous banquet. Even the baby sitting in his high chair joined in, for David dipping his finger in the wine let Philip suck it, and though he looked more surprised than pleased at the taste, he grinned at the joke when he saw us laughing.

Helen Thomas, *World Without End* (1931)

ILL-TEMPER IN WINTER WEATHER

*J*AN. YE 3. – JOHN'S MOTHER did laff verrie much at me, finding out I did write our doings in a little book, and did also give me this one to write more of our doings as they do come to pass. The weather be most cold, and the frost did freeze the new milk in the pannes this morn, thus spoiling it for the butter making; much to my distress, for I like not to see so much waste. John cumming in do say that the black sow have killed all her little pigges, and he so wroth thereby he do forget to drink his hot toddie, and did tell Sarah to come out to the yards, and we to stop our caddel in the kitchen. At this me verrie cross, but he being off I did saye nought, but did get on to the cooking.

... Later cums Passon Cross to talk to John, and it being near supper time, me and Sarah to the spinning of yarne and Johns mother to the nitting of hose, gainst the time they be needed. Then, Passon gone, we to bed.

I fear that he will take Sarah from us later. I did see his talk was but a faddel to get to see her, and I like it not, for she be a good wench and verrie useful to me.

Jan. ye 4. – This morn we did wake up to see every place covered with snow, it falling right heartilie in the night, and work on the land be at the stand still; nought bein done but to feed the stock. So today we plagued mightilie with John in the house, bringin this and that to do and mend, till my clean kitchen be verrie sluty with the snow he do bring in; and me so wroth there at, I do say to get out to the back-house with his messy jobbes, and so he goes off there-to, saying never was a man so plagued with a parcel of women, they being the verrie divvel round a man. At which we laffing, he do stamp out, banging the door mightilie.

Later me to the making of an apple pudding genst his coming in agen, and Sarah did take him out a good jorum of hot punch, whereby he better tempered on return. I do so mislike snow, it be so verrie messie, and do make a great lot of work to keep the floors clean.

Anne Hughes, *The Diary of a Farmer's Wife, 1796–97*

LES SYLPHIDES

Life in a day: he took his girl to the ballet;
Being shortsighted himself could hardly see it –
    The white skirts in the grey
    Glade and the swell of the music
    Lifting the white sails.

Calyx upon calyx, canterbury bells in the breeze
The flowers on the left mirror to the flowers on the right
    And the naked arms above
    The powdered faces moving
    Like seaweed in a pool.

Now, he thought, we are floating – ageless, oarless –
Now there is no separation, from now on
    You will be wearing white
    Satin and a red sash
    Under the waltzing trees.

But the music stopped, the dancers took their curtain,
The river had come to a lock – a shuffle of programmes –
    And we cannot continue down
    Stream unless we are ready
    To enter the lock and drop.

So they were married – to be the more together –
And found they were never again so much together,
    Divided by the morning tea,
    By the evening paper,
    By children and tradesman's bills.

Waking at times in the night she found assurance
In his regular breathing but wondered whether
    It was really worth it and where
    The river had flowed away
    And where were the white flowers.

Louis MacNeice (1939)

'THE WHOLEMEAL BREAD OF LIFE'

ALFRED AND I are happy, as happy as married people can be. We are in love, we are intellectually and physically suited in every possible way, we rejoice in each other's company. We have no money troubles and three delightful children. And yet when I consider my life, day by day, hour by hour, it seems to be composed of a series of pinpricks. Nannies, cooks, the endless drudgery of housekeeping, the nerve-racking noise and boring repetitive conversation of small children (boring in the sense that it bores into one's very brain), their absolute incapacity to amuse themselves, their sudden and terrifying illnesses, Alfred's not infrequent bouts of moodiness, his invariable complaints at meals about the pudding, the way he will use the toothpaste and will always squeeze the tube in the middle. These are the components of marriage, the wholemeal bread of life, rough, ordinary but sustaining.

Nancy Mitford, *The Pursuit of Love* (1945)

THE CONFORMERS

Yes; we'll wed, my little fay,
And you shall write you mine,
And in a villa chastely gray
We'll house, and sleep, and dine.
But those night-screened, divine,
Stolen trysts of heretofore,
We of choice ecstasies and fine
Shall know no more.

The formal faced cohue
Will then no more upbraid
With smiting smiles and whisperings two
Who have thrown less loves in shade.

We shall no more evade
The searching light of the sun,
Our game of passion will be played,
Our dreaming done.

We shall not go in stealth
To rendezvous unknown,
But friends will ask me of your health,
And you about my own.
When we abide alone,
No leapings each to each,
But syllables in frigid tone
Of household speech.

When down to dust we glide
Men will not say askance,
As now: 'How all the country side
Rings with their mad romance!'
But as they graveward glance
Remark: 'In them we lose
A worthy pair, who helped advance
Sound parish views.'

Thomas Hardy (1909)

SILVER WEDDING

In the middle of the night he started up
At a cry from his sleeping Bride,
A bat from some ruin in a heart he'd never searched
Nay, hardly seen inside:

'Want me and take me for the woman that I am,
And not for her that died,
The lovely chit Nineteen I one time was,
And am no more,' she cried.

Ralph Hodgson (1961)

COMPLICATIONS

'.. in sickness ..'

The routine of daily life, the occasional boredom, the wondering where all the romance went, the fear of growing old … may seem complication enough. The very ordinariness of it all strains any marriage from time to time. Domestic rows can leave each partner shaken, peering into the abyss and feeling at once torn between a fear of its depths and a longing to leap in.

Yet a couple may find other, sometimes unpredictable, complications scattered in their path. Absence, for instance, may be a blessing, making the heart grow fonder as the proverb says. Yet if a couple are apart, their loving letters (not so frequent this century) can hide a terrible loneliness on the part of the one left behind, and resentment too. The partner who has to travel, usually on business but sometimes by choice, may feel guilty – and perhaps will have reason to feel guilty. No marriage which survives long absences does so with ease.

And absence, of course, provides an opportunity for easy infidelity – which is the most serious and searing complication a marriage may face. John Donne was optimistic when he wrote, 'For love all love of other sights controls'. It never did and it never will, for I do not believe there is one happily married person who has not *once* glanced with a light fancy at someone else. A glance is harmless, but it is still registered upon the air. And if it leads on to love – *romantic* love – then the couple face pain. But not parting – not if they stay, try, work and *will*.
(*The rose has thorns…*)

189

THE WIFE'S COMPLAINT

I have wrought these words together out of a wryed existence,
the heart's tally, telling off
the griefs I have undergone from girlhood upwards,
old and new, and now more than ever;
for I have never not had some new sorrow,
some fresh affliction to fight against.

The first was my lord's leaving his people here:
crossed crests. To what country I knew not,
wondered where, awoke unhappy.
I left, fared any road, friendless, an outcast,
sought any service to staunch the lack of him.
Then his kinsmen ganged, began to think
thoughts they did not speak, of splitting the wedlock;
so — estranged, alienated — we lived each
alone, a long way apart; how I longed for him!

In his harshness he had me brought here;
and in these parts there were few friendly-minded,
worth trusting.
                    Trouble in the heart now:
I saw the bitterness, the bound mind
of my matched man, mourning-browed,
mirk in his mood, murder in his thoughts.

Our lips had smiled to swear hourly
that nothing should split us — save dying —
nothing else. All that has changed:
it is now as if it never had been,
our friendship. I feel in the wind
that the man dearest to me detests me.
I was banished to this knoll knotted by woods
to live in a den dug beneath an oak.
Old is this earthen room; it eats at my heart.

I see the thorns thrive up there in thick coverts
on the banks that baulk these black hollows:

190

not a gay dwelling. Here the grief bred
by lordlack preys on me. Some lovers in this world
live dear to each other, lie warm together
at day's beginning; I go by myself
about these earth caves under the oak tree.
Here I must sit the summer day through,
here weep out the woes of exile,
the hardships heaped upon me. My heart shall never
suddenly sail into slack water,
all the longings of a lifetime answered.

May grief and bitterness blast the mind
of that young man! May his mind ache
behind his smiling face! May a flock of sorrows
choke his chest! He would change his tune
if he lived alone in a land of exile
far from his folk.
                    Where my friend is stranded
frost crusts the cracked cliff-face
grey waves grind the shingle.
The mind cannot bear in such a bleak place
very much grief.
                    He remembers too often
less grim surroundings. Sorrow follows
this too long wait for one who is estranged.

Anon. Translated from the Anglo-Saxon by Michael
Alexander (10th century)

ANONYMOUS FRONTIER GUARD

While the leaves of the bamboo rustle
On a cold and frosty night,
The seven layers of clobber I wear

Are not so warm, not so warm
As the body of my wife.

Translated from the Japanese by
Geoffrey Bownas and Anthony
Thwaite (8th century AD)

SONG OF A WOMAN WHOSE HUSBAND HAD GONE TO THE COAST TO EARN MONEY

Whenever I go out of the village
and see a stone
or a tree in the distance,
I think:
It is my husband.

Baule (Ivory Coast) (20th
century African)

THE RIVER-MERCHANT'S WIFE: A LETTER

While my hair was still cut straight across my forehead
I played about the front gate, pulling flowers.
You came by on bamboo stilts, playing horse,
You walked about my seat, playing with blue plums.
And we went on living in the village of Chokan:
Two small people, without dislike or suspicion.

At fourteen I married My Lord you.
I never laughed, being bashful.
Lowering my head, I looked at the wall.
Called to, a thousand times, I never looked back.

At fifteen I stopped scowling,
I desired my dust to be mingled with yours

Forever and forever and forever.
Why should I climb the look out?

At sixteen you departed,
You went into far Ku-to-yen, by the river of swirling eddies,
And you have been gone five months.
The monkeys make sorrowful noise overhead.

You dragged your feet when you went out.
By the gate now, the moss is grown, the different mosses,
Too deep to clear them away!
The leaves fall early this autumn, in wind.
The paired butterflies are already yellow with August
Over the grass in the West garden;
They hurt me. I grow older.
If you are coming down through the narrows of the river Kiang,
Please let me know beforehand,
And I will come out to meet you
                    As far as Cho-fu-Sa.

By Rihaku (8th century AD),
translated by Ezra Pound (1915)

HORRIBLY DESOLATE AND SAD

Harold Nicolson had achieved a position in Berlin which promised
a brilliant future in diplomacy. But his wife, Vita Sackville-West,
had remained behind, unable to bear the formality of diplomatic
life. They were both unhappy, and Harold Nicolson decided at last
to resign. This was largely because, returning to Berlin from leave
in June 1929, he found a letter from Vita which was among the
most heart-broken that she ever wrote:

25th June, 1929
Long Barn

WHAT IS SO TORTURING WHEN I leave you at
these London stations and drive off, is the know-

ledge that you are *still* there – that, for half an hour or three-quarters of an hour, I could still return and find you: come up behind you, take you by the elbow, and say 'Hadji'.

I came straight home, feeling horribly desolate and sad, driving down that familiar and dreary road. I remembered Rasht and our parting there: our parting at Victoria when you left for Persia; till our life seemed made up of partings, and I wondered how long it would continue.

Then I came round the corner on to the view – our view – and I thought how you loved it, and how simple you were, really, apart from your activity; and how I loved you for being both simple and active in one and the same person.

Then I came home, and it was no consolation at all. You see, when I am unhappy for other reasons, the cottage is a real solace to me; but when it is on account of *you* that I am unhappy (because you have gone away), it is an additional pang – it is the same place, but a sort of mockery and emptiness hangs about it – I almost wish that just *once* you could lose me and then come straight back to the cottage and find it still full of me but empty of me, then you would know what I go through after you have gone away.

Anyway, you will say, it is worse for you who go back to a horrible and alien city, whereas I stay in the place we both love so much: but really, Hadji, it is no consolation to come back to a place full of coffee-cups – there was a cardboard-box lid, full of your rose-petals, still on the terrace.

You are dearer to me than anybody ever has been or ever could be. If you died suddenly, I should kill myself as soon as I had made provision for the boys. I really mean this. I could not live if I lost you. I do not think one could conceive of a love more exclusive, more tender, or more pure than I have for you. I think it is immortal, a thing which happens seldom.

Darling, there are not many people who would write such a letter after sixteen years of marriage, yet who would be saying therein only one-fiftieth of what they were feeling as they wrote it. I sometimes try to tell you the truth, and then I find that I have no words at my command which could possibly convey it to you.

NATHANIEL HAWTHORNE TO SOPHIA HAWTHORNE

Boston, 17 April, 1839

MY DEAREST, – I feel pretty secure against intruders, for the bad weather will defend me from foreign invasion; and as to Cousin Haley, he and I had a bitter political dispute last evening, at the close of which he went to bed in high dudgeon, and probably will not speak to me these three days. Thus you perceive that strife and wrangling, as well as east-winds and rain, are the methods of a kind Providence to promote my comfort, – which would not have been so well secured in any other way. Six or seven hours of cheerful solitude! But I will not be alone. I invite your spirit to be with me, – at any hour and as many hours as you please, – but especially at the twilight hour, before I light my lamp. I bid you at that particular time, because I can see visions more vividly in the dusky glow of firelight than either by daylight or lamplight. Come, and let me renew my spell against headache and other direful effects of the east-wind. How I wish I could give you a portion of my insensibility! and yet I should be almost afraid of some radical transformation, were I to produce a change in that respect. If you cannot grow plump and rosy and tough and vigorous without being changed into another nature, then I do think, for this short life, you had better remain just what you are. Yes; but you will be the same to me, because we have met in Eternity, and there our intimacy was formed. So get well as soon as you possibly can, and I shall never doubt that you are the same Sophie who have so often leaned upon my arm and needed its superfluous strength. I never, till now, had a friend who could give me repose; all have disturbed me, and, whether for pleasure or pain, it was still disturbance. But peace overflows from your heart into mine. Then I feel that there is a Now, and that Now must be always calm and happy, and that sorrow and evil are but phantoms that seem to flit across it . . .

When this week's first letter came, I held it a long time in my hand, marvelling at the superscription. How did you contrive to write it? Several times since I have pored over it, to discover how much of yourself mingled with my share of it; and certainly there is grace flung over the fac-simile, which never was seen in my harsh, uncouth autograph, and yet none of the strength is lost. You are wonderful.

What a beautiful day! and I had a double enjoyment of it – for your sake and my own. I have been to walk, this afternoon, to Bunker's Hill and the Navy Yard, and am tired, because I had not your arm to support me.

God keep you from east-winds and every other evil.

Your own friend, N.H.

BERT TO NELL

Bert Fielder (1882–1916) wrote regularly to his wife, and on one letter added a postscript: 'Please don't cry so much when you write next, as it makes them in an awful mess.' He was killed in 1916.

2nd July 1915

MY DEAREST NELL,

I think I may be able to keep here a few weeks yet, anyhow I've got hopes of staying until the Dardanelles job is over. . . . You ask me when the war is going to be over. Well, I will just tell you, only keep it secret. *In October*. You say we don't seem to be getting on very well out here; My Word if you only knew what a job we've got before us, just try to imagine a hill called Achi Baba, just fancy yourself at the bottom of a big hill with trenches and trenches piled on top of one another, made of concrete with thousands of Turks and machine-guns, five of these trenches we took one morning one after the other, but before we got to the first trench we left a good many of our chums behind, but it's no good stopping and the faster you can run the better chance you have of getting through the rain of bullets, and our boys went mad.

I have thought just lately what a lot of savages war turns us into, we see the most horrible sights of bloodshed and simply laugh at it. It seems to be nothing but blood, blood everywhere you go and on everything you touch, and you are walking amongst dead bodies all day and all night, human life seems to be of no value at all – you are joking with a chap one minute and the next minute you go to the back of the trench to do a job for yourself and then you see a little mound of earth with a little rough wooden cross on it with the name of the man you had been joking with a short time before. My dear Scrumps, I don't know whether I'm right in telling you this, because you worry so but I would not mention it only for the reason that I don't think I shall have any more of it, but I certainly *do* thank the One Above and you for your prayers at night together with our Boy for keeping me safe throughout it all.

Always you are both in my thoughts, I think of you both in that little kitchen by yourselves and know that you are thinking of me and wondering perhaps if you will ever see me come back again, every night at nine o'clock out here which is seven o'clock in England, I think that it is the Boy's bedtime and I always can picture him kneeling in his cot saying his prayers after Mummy. But

'Cheer up', my Scrumps, this will all end soon and we shall be together again and carry on the old life once more.

My dear Scrumps, I wonder if the Boy still thinks of the gun I promised to bring him home, I got hold of two Turks' guns to bring home and after keeping them for about two weeks, I got wounded and then of course I lost them as I did everything else. I might also say that the Deal Battalion have all lost their bags again, they were coming from the ship in a barge and a Turk shell hit the barge, so they sank to the bottom of the Dardanelles. The Naval Division is pretty well cut up, especially the Marines, they can only make 3 btns out of 4 even after the last lot came out from England. I think there is some move on to withdraw the Marines and Naval Division from the Dardanelles also the other troops which were in the first part of the fighting as they are in a bad state and I expect we'll get a quiet job as garrison for some place. I expect by this time you have got General Hamilton's report of the fighting here, my dear Scrumps I think I will wind up now as I've just looked at the watch and its a quarter to eleven. I've been writing ever since nine o'clock, so Night Night and God bless you.

DAVID LIVINGSTONE WRITES TO MARY

Capetown
5 May 1852

My Dearest Mary,

How I miss you now and the dear children! My heart yearns incessantly over you. How many thoughts of the past crowd into my mind! I feel as if I would treat you all much more tenderly and lovingly than ever. You have been a great blessing to me. You attended to my comfort in many, many ways. May God bless you for all your kindnesses! I see no face now to be compared with that sunburnt one which has so often greeted me with its kind looks. Let us do our duty to our Saviour and we shall meet again. I wish that time were now. You may read the letters over again which I wrote at Mabotsa, the sweet time you know. As I told you before, I tell you again, they are true, true; there is not a bit of hypocrisy in them. I never show all my feelings; but I can say truly my dearest, that I loved you when I married you, and the longer I lived with you I loved you the better.

THE CRISIS

Let me say (in anger) that since the day we were married
we have never had a towel
where anyone could find it,
the fact.
           Notwithstanding that I am not
simple to live with, not
my own judgement, but no matter.
   There are other things:

to kiss you is not
to love you.
           Or not so simply.

Laughter releases rancour, the quality of mercy is not
   strained.

Robert Creeley (1962)

from SUMMER HOME

My children weep out the hot foreign night.
We walk the floor, my foul mouth takes it out
On you and we lie stiff till dawn
Attends the pillow, and the maize, and vine

That holds its filling burden to the light.
Yesterday rocks sang when we tapped
Stalactites in the cave's old, dripping dark –
Our love calls tiny as a tuning fork.

Seamus Heaney (1972)

BRUTUS AND PORTIA

Enter Portia

PORTIA   Brutus, my lord.

BRUTUS

Portia, what mean you? Wherefore rise you now?
It is not for your health thus to commit
Your weak condition to the raw cold morning.

PORTIA

Nor for yours neither. You've ungently, Brutus,
Stole from my bed; and yesternight at supper
You suddenly arose, and walked about
Musing and sighing, with your arms across;
And when I asked you what the matter was,
You stared upon me with ungentle looks.
I urged you further; then you scratched your head,
And too impatiently stamped with your foot.
Yet I insisted; yet you answered not,
But with an angry wafture of your hand
Gave sign for me to leave you. So I did,
Fearing to strengthen that impatience
Which seemed too much enkindled, and withal
Hoping it was but an effect of humour,
Which sometime hath his hour with every man.
It will not let you eat, nor talk, nor sleep;
And could it work so much upon your shape
As it hath much prevailed on your condition,
I should not know you Brutus. Dear my lord,
Make me acquainted with your cause of grief.

BRUTUS

I am not well in health, and that is all.

PORTIA

Brutus is wise, and were he not in health
He would embrace the means to come by it.

BRUTUS

Why, so I do. Good Portia, go to bed.

PORTIA

Is Brutus sick? And is it physical
To walk unbracèd and suck up the humours
Of the dank morning? What, is Brutus sick?
And will he steal out of his wholesome bed
To dare the vile contagion of the night,
And tempt the rheumy and unpurgèd air
To add unto his sickness? No, my Brutus,
You have some sick offence within your mind,
Which by the right and virtue of my place
I ought to know of. (*Kneeling*) And upon my knees,
I charm you by my once-commended beauty,
By all your vows of love, and that great vow
Which did incorporate and make us one,
That you unfold to me, your self, your half,
Why you are heavy, and what men tonight
Have had resort to you – for here have been
Some six or seven, who did hide their faces
Even from darkness.

BRUTUS   Kneel not, gentle Portia.

PORTIA [*rising*]

I should not need if you were gentle Brutus.
Within the bond of marriage, tell me, Brutus,
Is it excepted I should know no secrets
That appertain to you? Am I your self
But as it were in sort or limitation?
To keep with you at meals, comfort your bed,
And talk to you sometimes? Dwell I but in the suburbs
Of your good pleasure? If it be no more,
Portia is Brutus' harlot, not his wife.

BRUTUS

You are my true and honourable wife,
As dear to me as are the ruddy drops
That visit my sad heart.

PORTIA

If this were true, then should I know this secret.
I grant I am a woman, but withal
A woman that Lord Brutus took to wife.
I grant I am a woman, but withal
A woman well reputed, Cato's daughter.
Think you I am no stronger than my sex,
Being so fathered and so husbanded?
Tell me your counsels; I will not disclose 'em.
I have made strong proof of my constancy,
Giving myself a voluntary wound
Here in the thigh. Can I bear that with patience,
And not my husband's secrets?

BRUTUS   O ye gods,
Render me worthy of this noble wife!

William Shakespeare, *Julius Caesar*, Act II, scene ii

AN AFTERWARDS

She would plunge all poets in the ninth circle
And fix them, tooth in skull, tonguing for brain;
For backbiting in life she'd make their hell
A rabid egotistical daisy-chain.

Unyielding, spurred, ambitious, unblunted,
Lockjawed, mantrapped, each a fastened badger
Jockeying for position, hasped and mounted
Like Ugolino on Archbishop Roger.

And when she'd make her circuit of the ice,
Aided and abetted by Virgil's wife,
I would cry out, 'My sweet, who wears the bays
In our green land above, whose is the life

Most dedicated and exemplary?'
And she: 'I have closed my widowed ears
To the sulphurous news of poets and poetry.
Why could you not have, oftener, in our years

Unclenched, and come down laughing from your room
And walked the twilight with me and your children –
Like that one evening of elder bloom
And hay, when the wild roses were fading?'

And (as some maker gaffs me in the neck)
'You weren't the worst. You aspired to a kind,
Indifferent, faults-on-both-sides tact.
You left us first, and then those books, behind.'

Seamus Heaney (1979)

MAN AND WIFE

Waking sometimes at night, your sleeping thigh
Lying against my own, which previously
Proclaimed its married dominance. I ply
Questions of love's discrepancies, then deviously
Evade the issue: kiss you or fall asleep,
Trailing, like streamers, thoughts which fail to keep
Their subtle fascination when the dawn
Edges between the curtains, cold and challenging.

Basil Payne (1971)

PILLOW TALK

'Oh yes,' she says, 'we're married:
Very much so,' says she,
Wedging the bed-clothes under her hip,
Turning her back on me.

(Japanese, 6th century AD)

203

MAN AND WIFE

Tamed by Miltown, *we lie on Mother's bed;*
the rising sun in war paint dyes us red;
in broad daylight her gilded bed-posts shine,
abandoned, almost Dionysian.
At last the trees are green on Marlborough Street,
blossoms on our magnolia ignite
the morning with their murderous five days' white.
All night I've held your hand,
as if you had
a fourth time faced the kingdom of the mad —
its hackneyed speech, its homicidal eye —
and dragged me home alive.... Oh my Petite,
clearest of all God's creatures, still all air and
      nerve:
you were in your twenties, and I,
once hand on glass
and heart in mouth,
outdrank the Rahvs in the heat
of Greenwich Village, fainting at your feet —
too boiled and shy
and poker-faced to make a pass,
while the shrill verve
of your invective scorched the traditional South.

Now twelve years later, you turn your back.
Sleepless, you hold
your pillow to your hollows like a child,
your old-fashioned tirade —
loving, rapid, merciless —
breaks like the Atlantic Ocean on my head.

Robert Lowell (1959)

204

IN NATURE THERE IS NEITHER
RIGHT NOR LEFT NOR WRONG

Men are what they do, women are what they are.
These erect breasts, like marble coming up for air
Among the cataracts of my breathtaking hair,
Are goods in my bazaar, a door ajar
To the first paradise of whores and mothers.

Men buy their way back into me from the upright
Right-handed puzzle that men fit together
From their deeds, the pieces. Women shoot from
Or dive back into its interstices
As squirrels inhabit a geometry.

We women sell ourselves for sleep, for flesh,
to those wide-awake, successful spirits, men —
Who, lying each midnight with the sinister
Beings, their dark companions, women,
Suck childhood, beasthood, from a mother's breasts.

A fat bald rich man comes home at twilight
And lectures me about my parking tickets; gowned
*   in gold*
Lamé, I look at him and think: 'You're old,
I'm old.' Husband, I sleep with you every night
And like it; but each morning when I wake
I've dreamed of my first love, the subtle serpent.

Randall Jarrell (1965)

STOREYETTE H. M.

This is an account of the marriage of Henri Matisse and his wife by someone who knew them both well, and who disapproved of the selfish way in which the painter treated his wife. The situation it describes is familiar to many marriages.

ONE WAS MARRIED TO SOME ONE. That one was going away to have a good time. The one that was married to that one did not like it very well that the one to whom that one was married then was going off alone to have a good time and was leaving that one to stay at home then. The one that was going came in all glowing. The one that was going had everything he was needing to have the good time he was wanting to be having then. He came in all glowing. The one he was leaving at home to take care of the family living was not glowing. The one that was going was saying, the one that was glowing, the one that was going was saying then, I am content, you are not content, I am content you are not content, I am content, you are not content, you are content, I am content.

Gertrude Stein, *Portraits and Prayers* (1934)

MR. MANTALINI REQUIRES CASH

THERE WAS NOT much to amuse in the room; of which the most attractive feature was, a half-length portrait in oil of Mr. Mantalini, whom the artist had depicted scratching his head in an easy manner, and thus displaying to advantage a diamond ring, the gift of Madame Mantalini before her marriage. There was, however, the sound of voices in conversation in the next room; and as the conversation was loud and the partition thin, Kate could not help discovering that they belonged to Mr. and Mrs. Mantalini.

"If you will be odiously, demnebly outr*i*geously jealous, my soul," said Mr. Mantalini, "you will be very miserable – horrid miserable – demnition miserable." And then, there was a sound as though Mr. Mantalini were sipping his coffee.

"I *am* miserable," returned Madame Mantalini, evidently pouting.

"Then you are an ungrateful, unworthy, demd unthankful little fairy," said Mr. Mantalini.

"I am not," returned Madame, with a sob.

"Do not put itself out of humour," said Mr. Mantalini, breaking an egg. "It is a pretty, bewitching little demd countenance, and it should not be out of humour, for it spoils its loveliness, and makes it cross and gloomy like a frightful, naughty, demd hobgoblin."

"I am not to be brought round in that way, always," rejoined Madame, sulkily.

"It shall be brought round in any way it likes best, and not brought round at all if it likes that better," retorted Mr. Mantalini, with his egg-spoon in his mouth.

"It's very easy to talk," said Mrs. Mantalini.

"Not so easy when one is eating a demnition egg," replied Mr. Mantalini; "for the yolk runs down the waistcoat, and yolk of egg does not match any waistcoat but a yellow waistcoat, demmit."

"You were flirting with her during the whole night," said Madame Mantalini, apparently desirous to lead the conversation back to the point from which it had strayed.

"No, no, my life."

"You were," said Madame; "I had my eye upon you all the time."

"Bless the little winking twinking eye; was it on me all the time!" cried Mantalini, in a sort of lazy rapture. "Oh, demmit!"

"And I say once more," resumed Madame, "that you ought not to waltz with anybody but your own wife; and I will not bear it, Mantalini, if I take poison first."

"She will not take poison and have horrid pains, will she?" said Mantalini; who, by the altered sound of his voice, seemed to have moved his chair, and taken up his position nearer to his wife. "She will not take poison, because she had a demd fine husband who might have married two countesses and a dowager –"

"Two countesses," interposed Madame. "You told me one before!"

"Two!" cried Mantalini. "Two demd fine women, real countesses and splendid fortunes, demmit."

"And why didn't you?" asked Madame playfully.

"Why didn't I!" replied her husband. "Had I not seen, at a morning concert, the demdest little fascinator in all the world, and while that little fascinator is my wife, may not all the countesses and dowagers in England be –"

Mr. Mantalini did not finish the sentence, but he gave Madame Mantalini a very loud kiss, which Madame Mantalini returned; after which, there seemed to be some more kissing mixed up with the progress of the breakfast.

"And what about the cash, my existence's jewel?" said Mantalini, when these endearments ceased. "How much have we in hand?"

"Very little indeed," replied Madame.

"We must have some more," said Mantalini; "we must have some discount out of old Nickleby to carry on the war with, demmit."

"You can't want any more just now," said Madame coaxingly.

"My life and soul," returned her husband, "there is a horse for sale at Scrubb's, which it would be a sin and a crime to lose – going, my senses' joy, for nothing."

"For nothing," cried Madame, "I am glad of that."

"For actually nothing," replied Mantalini. "A hundred guineas down will buy him; mane, and crest, and legs, and tail, all of the demdest beauty. I will ride him in the park before the very chariots of the rejected countesses. The demd old dowager will faint with grief and rage; the other two will say 'He is married, he has made away with himself, it is a demd thing, it is all up!' They will hate each other demnebly, and wish you dead and buried. Ha! ha! Demmit."

Madame Mantalini's prudence, if she had any, was not proof against these triumphal pictures; after a little jingling of keys, she observed that she would see what her desk contained, and rising for that purpose, opened the folding-door, and walked into the room where Kate was seated.

Charles Dickens, *Nicholas Nickleby* (1839)

EROS TURANNOS

She fears him, and will always ask
What fated her to choose him;
She meets in his engaging mask
All reason to refuse him;
But what she meets and what she fears
Are less than are the downward years,
Drawn slowly to the foamless weirs
Of age, were she to lose him.

Between a blurred sagacity
That once had power to sound him,
And Love, that will not let him be
The Judas that she found him,
Her pride assuages her almost,
As if it were alone the cost. –
He sees that he will not be lost,
And waits and looks around him.

A sense of ocean and old trees
Envelops and allures him;
Tradition, touching all he sees,
Beguiles and reassures him;
And all her doubts of what he says
Are dimmed with what she knows of days –
Till even prejudice delays
And fades, and she secures him.

The falling leaf inaugurates
The reign of her confusion:
The pounding wave reverberates
The dirge of her illusion;
And home, where passion lived and died,
Becomes a place where she can hide,
While all the town and harbour side
Vibrate with her seclusion.

We tell you, tapping on our brows,
The story as it should be, –
As if the story of a house
Were told, or ever could be;
We'll have no kindly veil between
Her visions and those we have seen, –
As if we guessed what hers have been,
Or what they are or would be.

Meanwhile we do no harm; for they
That with a god have striven,
Not hearing much of what we say,
Take what the god has given;
Though like waves breaking it may be,
Or like a changed familiar tree,
Or like a stairway to the sea
Where down the blind are driven.

Edwin Arlington Robinson (1916)

AFTER TEN YEARS ...

DR. URBINO JUSTIFIED his own weakness with grave arguments, not even asking himself if they were in conflict with the Church. He would not admit that the difficulties with his wife had their origin in the rarefied air of the house, but blamed them on the very nature of matrimony: an absurd invention that could exist

210

only by the infinite grace of God. It was against all scientific reason for two people who hardly knew each other, with no ties at all between them, with different characters, different upbringings, and even different genders, to suddenly find themselves committed to living together, to sleeping in the same bed, to sharing two destinies that perhaps were fated to go in opposite directions. He would say: "The problem with marriage is that it ends every night after making love, and it must be rebuilt every morning before breakfast." And worst of all was theirs, arising out of two opposing classes, in a city that still dreamed of the return of the Viceroys. The only possible bond was something as improbable and fickle as love, if there was any, and in their case there was none when they married, and when they were on the verge of inventing it, fate had done nothing more than confront them with reality.

That was the condition of their lives during the period of the harp. They had left behind the delicious coincidences of her coming in while he was taking a bath, when, despite the arguments and the poisonous eggplant, and despite his demented sisters and the mother who bore them, he still had enough love to ask her to soap him. She began to do it with the crumbs of love that still remained from Europe, and both allowed themselves to be betrayed by memories, softening without wanting to, desiring each other without saying so, and at last they would die of love on the floor, spattered with fragrant suds, as they heard the maids talking about them in the laundry room: "If they don't have more children it's because they don't fuck." From time to time, when they came home from a wild fiesta, the nostalgia crouching behind the door would knock them down with one blow of its paw, and then there would be a marvelous explosion in which everything was the way it used to be and for five minutes they were once again the uninhibited lovers of their honeymoon.

But except for those rare occasions, one of them was

always more tired than the other when it was time to go to bed. She would dawdle in the bathroom, rolling her cigarettes in perfumed paper, smoking alone, relapsing into her consolatory love as she did when she was young and free in her own house, mistress of her own body. She always had a headache, or it was too hot, always, or she pretended to be asleep, or she had her period again, her period, always her period. So much so that Dr. Urbino had dared to say in class, only for the relief of unburdening himself without confession, that after ten years of marriage women had their periods as often as three times a week.

Gabriel García Márquez, *Love in the Time of Cholera* (1988)

JOHN IS JEALOUS

*M*ARCH YE 13. – I have been verrie bussie this two days, what with the cooking and looking to Emily Lewis, who be much better. I fear she was but nigh clemmed for lack of food. Cousin Ned have bin verrie useful carrying this and that.

John be verrie glum and I know not the why-fore, but he do answer me verrie short and when Cousin Ned did say a word to him, he up and out saying nought, at which Ned do wonder much why. I did ask John's mother what's ado, but she knows nought, and Sarah did say the same, but fears he be not well. Later, when we to our bed chamber I do say what be wrong, but he do bounce into bed and not answer, at which I be verrie pusselled, and know not what to think, or what can be agaite, so me verrie worried.

March ye 15. – Such a to do did we have cum yesterday. John being verrie wroth still, I do say to him what be wrong, where on he did cast at me a mighty savage look,

212

and he off without answering, and did bang the door with a mightie bump.

I did ask John's mother, but she did know nought, but says she tackel him and find out first chance. So me getting him later in the kitchen I did say, what was the matter, where-on he did make for the door, but I did get in front, thereby stoping him. Then said I, why is he so churlish with us all, even Cousin Ned, who had been verrie helpful since he cum. Then says he, it be time he be gone from us, cummen atween a man and his wiffe. At this I do nought but stare, not knowing the answer; then says John's mother whatever next will he say, and me being struck by the verrie silliness of it, do nigh burst with laffing. At which he be so wroth he do start to shake me, and me laffing so hard be not able to stop him, till his mother do give him a mighty smack on his ear, and he did let me go.

Then said she, he should be ashamed to do so to such a faithful wiffe as me, and he not half a man, but just a sotte, always ready for a scratting.

Then she says, out with it, and let us know what it be all about. Then John did say what right had Cousin Ned to taking me walking every day, when I should be at the yardes, feeding the pigges. At which his mother do say what a fool he is when all that had been done was a good turn to one in need. Then said Sarah, fetch Master Ned, and the master can soon see all I had been doing; and she off out, and later Ned cum in and do tell John what we had done to help a poor wretch in need; and said he to John, that if he did but think of others with his heart instead of always his pocket, he would be the better for it. For, said he, he had got a better wiffe than any he did know, and he should be ashamed to speak so. At this John did look verrie sheepish, and did say what could a man think when he did see a man a dandering with his wiffe. At which I so wroth at such talk, did slappe his face sharply, to his great hurt. Whereon his mother says enough of this sillie rubbish, and for John to ask me and Cousin Ned to parden him his folly, and this he did, albeit verrie sulkie.

Anne Hughes, *The Diary of a Farmer's Wife, 1796–97*

'WHO IS THIS MAN?'

Llewelyn Powys was deeply in love with the American poet Gamel Woolsey – who married the writer Gerald Brenan. His wife Alyse tolerated the affair, despite great personal suffering.

JANUARY 9, 1931. YESTERDAY we talked *all day long* about Gamel, what would happen. There has not been *one second's respite, not one single second.* His sighs fall like whip lashes across my bare skin and his unhappy face drives my spirit out into the unanswering night. But again and again I turn to comfort him, his sorrow piercing my heart, beating down upon my brain – and the still days with the sun shining might be days in which I had just come from watching my lover drown. He clings to me, but we can only feel our way forward in the darkness, holding each other's hand. Never have I been so baffled. The brain, so helpless, so uninstructed – and underneath, the emotions sweeping all forward in endless catastrophes – each little moment shattered – all those moments that I lie beside Llewelyn through the nights, each one so sad, yet he breathes near me, and his kisses upon my cheek in the morning, his arms clinging about me.

January 22: Llewelyn seemed happier when we woke this morning than he has almost since we have been here. We talked about old Mr Brown, how we had followed him over to his house to look at the stagecoach whip, and Mrs Brown had stood on a chair to get it down from the shelf, and they had shown it with such pride. And all the time,

214

sitting silently in the room with bowed head, was an old man who looked like Victor Hugo, bending over a box of faded souvenirs:

> *O puissance du temps! O légères années!*
> *Vous emportez nos coeurs, nos cris et nos regrets!*
> *Mais la pitié vous prend, et sur nos fleurs fanées*
> *Vous ne marchez jamais!*

The rooms looked so homely, and this old married couple so united, so unsuspecting of the pain of hearts disloyal to an accepted tradition. Day after day, week after week, month after month, year in and year out, they had risen, side by side, through the frosts of winter and the heats of summer sharing each other's burdens – all through the treacherous whisperings of spring and the woeful warnings of autumn, never doubting each other's fidelity – when the first notes of the birds came to them on still mornings, when the hungry crows flew by over the tops of the trees, when the cows stood patiently waiting to be milked, when the wood pile was buried under a blanket of snow. Protected by their simplicity they have walked unscathed. Yet rather would I have this unhealing wound, this rack and ache, which abates only when the heart lies dead, and to have been once truly loved by so sweet a lover, loved if only for a few short years.

January 24: Again this morning he seemed so much better and his tenderness had some of the old quality. But when we went to the post and he found no letter from her, the torture returned and now he is out walking under the stars. Oh, how still, how lonely it is here while he is out in the dark pacing down the road thinking only of her. Oh, life can be cruel, unrelenting. When, over and over, he expresses his desire that she should leave Mr Brenan and go away with him, and turns to me to sympathize with and *encourage* him as I do, does he *never, never* think what his words must mean to me? I have written again *imploring* her to change, telling her she is sacrificing the one she loves best for the one she loves least.

January 25: Who is this man with whom I have lived so long? Who has whispered in my ear vows of lasting love? Where have I not followed – and now he has led me to my annihilation *and still he does not see*. No, he never sees, *he never has seen*. It is like being dragged over stones to be thrust down a precipice and left dying alone. But he does not mean to hurt me. So sweetly he turns to me in the mornings. Like two convicts we move from day to day.

Alyse Gregory, *The Cry of a Gull: Journals 1923–1948*

OF AN HEROICAL ANSWER OF A GREAT ROMAN LADY TO HER HUSBAND

A grave wise man that had a great rich lady,
Such as perhaps in these days found there may be,
Did think she played him false and more than think,
Save that in wisdom he thereat did wink.
Howbeit one time disposed to sport and play
Thus to his wife he pleasantly did say,
'Since strangers lodge their arrows in thy quiver,
Dear dame, I pray you yet the cause deliver,
If you can tell the cause and not dissemble,
How all our children me so much resemble?'
The lady blushed but yet this answer made
'Though I have used some traffic in the trade,
And must confess, as you have touched before,
My bark was sometimes steered with foreign oar,
 Yet stowed I no man's stuff but first persuaded
 The bottom with your ballast full was laded.'

Sir John Harington (1596)

216

A HUSBAND'S INFIDELITY

Johnson. "Between a man and his wife, a husband's infidelity is nothing. They are connected by children, by fortune, by serious considerations of community. Wise married women don't trouble themselves about the infidelity in their husbands." *Boswell.* "To be sure there is a great difference between the offence of infidelity in a man and that of his wife." *Johnson.* "The difference is boundless. The man imposes no bastards upon his wife."

James Boswell, *Life of Samuel Johnson* (1791)

'THIS TERRIBLE STRUGGLE'

Harold Nicolson and Vita Sackville-West were married in October 1913. They enjoyed five years together in which, she wrote, 'I should think it was hardly possible for two people to be more completely and unquestioningly happy.' Then, in 1918, Vita began a passionate love affair with Violet Trefusis, during which they ran away together. Vita never ceased to love Harold, on whom she inflicted great misery. A few letters show the strength of their love in crisis.

Vita to Harold:

OH HADJI, I COULDN'T ever hurt someone so tender and sensitive and angelic and loving as you are – at least, I know that I have hurt you, but I couldn't do anything to hurt you dreadfully and irrevocably. What a hold you have on my heart; nobody else would ever have such a hold. I love you more than myself, more than life, more than the things I love. I give you everything – like a sacrifice. I love you so much that I don't even resent it.

[*8 June 1919*]

Harold to Vita:

I KNOW THAT WE WILL win through this terrible struggle one day – both of us – but I don't want you to come out of it changed and broken, like France out of the war. Darling, when you are in London, you write so cynically, but the babies and the cottage seem to touch the ice to tears, and you write in a way that wrings my heart but doesn't break it. You say it is only for my sake that you are making this sacrifice, and it frightens me that you should say that. Why do you imagine that there is nothing between eloping with Violet and cooking my dinner? Oh what am I to do to win you back to calm and sanity? My love for you is certain; but yours for me sometimes seems so frail that it could snap.

[*9 June 1919*]

Vita to Harold:

OH MY HADJI, of course I love you. I love you unalterably. You don't know how I respond to any letter of yours. *Je m'humilie devant toi.* I have no words for my contempt for myself. Oh Hadji, you will never know. No one on this earth has the power to touch me as you have. One word from you moves me instantly, more than the tears or lamentations of anyone else. You don't know your power over me; you don't know it.

[*13 June 1919*]

[At one of the worst moments, when Harold Nicolson was unsure whether he would ever see his wife again, he wrote to her, 'I do feel that we are really closer than two people have ever been, and that whatever happens we shall come together in the end.' At the same moment Vita was writing to him:]

218

HADJI, HADJI, I feel lonely and frightened. There is so much in my heart, but I don't want to write it, for *à quoi bon*? Only if I were you, and you were me, I would battle so hard to keep you – partly, I dare say, because I would not have the courage and the reserve to do like you and say nothing. Oh Hadji, the reason why I sometimes get you to say things, to say that you would miss me, is that I long for weapons with which to fortify myself; and when you do say things, I treasure them up, and in moments of temptation I say them over to myself, and I think 'Then he *does* mind, he *would* mind, you *are* essential to him. It *is* worth while making yourself unhappy to keep him happy', and so on. But when you say things like you don't miss me in Paris, and that scandal matters, I think, 'Well, if it is only on account of scandal and convenience and above all *because I am his wife* and permanent and legitimate – if it isn't more personal than that, is it worth while my breaking my heart to give him, not positive happiness, but mere negative contentment?'

So I fish and fish, and sometimes I catch a lovely little silver trout, but never the great salmon that lashes and fights and *convinces* me that it is fighting for its life. You just say, 'Darling Vita', and leave me to invent my own conviction out of your silence.

But I *have* struggled. I tore myself away and came to Paris in June last year. And it was only, only, out of love for you; nothing else would have weighed for me the weight of a hair, so you can see how strong a temptation it must have been to sweep everything aside, and you must see also how strongly my love for you must be. My darling, I shall love you till I die; you know I shall.

[1 February 1920]

219

Harold to Vita:

WHEN DID I SAY that I didn't miss you in Paris? Darling, I miss you all the time. I suppose I said I didn't miss you in Paris as much as in England. If I said that, I meant that it was rather as if I was a soldier and said I didn't miss you in the trenches. It would be quite true – but it wouldn't mean that I didn't *want* you. I want you all the time, wherever I may be – and if I were not to see you again, I cannot contemplate what my attitude would be. It would be despair like one can't imagine – a sort of winter night (Sunday) at Aberdeen, and me in the streets alone with only a temperance hotel to sleep in.

Then about my general attitude. You see, what appeal can I make except that of love? I can't appeal to your pity and it would be doing that if I let you see what I feared and suffered. It would be ridiculous to appeal to your sense of duty – that's all rubbish. So what is there left except to appeal to love – my love for you, and yours for me? How can that appeal be anything but inarticulate? If you left me, I should never love anyone else. I see that quite clearly. I should be so lonely, so terribly lonely; it would be worse than that, for even my memories would be painful.

And you are all wrong to think that I look on you as my *légitime*. You are not a person with whom one can associate law, order, duty – or any of the conventional ties of life. I never think of you that way – not even from the babies' point of view. I just look on you as the person whom I love best in the world, and without whom life would lose all its light and meaning.

[*4 February 1920*]

from MODERN LOVE

1

By this he knew she wept with waking eyes:
That, at his hand's light quiver by her head,
The strange low sobs that shook their common bed,
Were called into her with a sharp surprise,
And strangled mute, like little gaping snakes,
Dreadfully venomous to him. She lay
Stone-still, and the long darkness flowed away
With muffled pulses. Then, as midnight makes
Her giant heart of Memory and Tears
Drink the pale drug of silence, and so beat
Sleep's heavy measure, they from head to feet
Were moveless, looking through their dead black years,
By vain regret scrawled over the blank wall.
Like sculptured effigies they might be seen
Upon their marriage-tomb, the sword between;
Each wishing for the sword that severs all.

16

In our old shipwrecked days there was an hour,
When in the firelight steadily aglow,
Joined slackly, we beheld the red chasm grow
Among the clicking coals. Our library-bower
That eve was left to us: and hushed we sat
As lovers to whom Time is whispering.
From sudden-opened doors we heard them sing:
The nodding elders mixed good wine with chat.
Well knew we that Life's greatest treasure lay
With us, and of it was our talk. 'Ah, yes!
Love dies!' I said: I never thought it less.
She yearned to me that sentence to unsay.
Then when the fire domed blackening, I found
Her cheek was salt against my kiss, and swift
Up the sharp scale of sobs her breast did lift:—
Now am I haunted by that taste! that sound!

17

At dinner, she is hostess, I am host.
Went the feast ever cheerfuller? She keeps
The Topic over intellectual deeps
In buoyancy afloat. They see no ghost.
With sparkling surface-eyes we play the ball:
It is in truth a most contagious game:
HIDING THE SKELETON, shall be its name.
Such play as this, the devils might appal!
But here's the greater wonder: in that we
Enamoured of an acting nought can tire,
Each other, like true hypocrites, admire;
Warm-lighted looks, Love's ephemeroie,
Shoot gaily o'er the dishes and the wine.
We waken envy of our happy lot.
Fast, sweet, and golden, shows the marriage-knot.
Dear guests, you now have seen Love's corpse-light shine.

George Meredith (1862)

ONE FLESH

Lying apart now, each in a separate bed,
He with a book, keeping the light on late,
She like a girl dreaming of childhood,
All men elsewhere – it is as if they wait
Some new event: the book he holds unread,
Her eyes fixed on the shadows overhead.

Tossed up like flotsam from a former passion,
How cool they lie. They hardly ever touch,
Or if they do it is like a confession
Of having little feeling – or too much.
Chastity faces them, a destination
For which their whole lives were a preparation.

COMPLICATIONS

Strangely apart, yet strangely close together,
Silence between them like a thread to hold
And not wind in. And time itself's a feather
Touching them gently. Do they know they're old,
These two who are my father and my mother
Whose fire from which I came, has now grown cold?

Elizabeth Jennings (1979)

ACCOMMODATIONS

'. . . and in health'

Scandal in the newspapers: men cover their faces with guilty arms, wives stare tight-lipped, their faces haggard with the grief of shattered pride – and then the astonishing, but magical sentence, 'She is standing by him'.

The girls fingering over-priced wedding dresses in bridal boutiques might titter in disbelief, the boys in the bar might snort, 'If my missus carried on like that she'd be out on her ear' – all demonstrating a sad ignorance. Some might say they would not wish for the experience that might lead to wisdom. Yet why? The slow and painful recognition of imperfection in a partner, and the *accommodation* of that recognition, will leave a marriage shaken but strengthened.

Perhaps recognition comes after an affair, following disgrace in business, or simple low-level crime; maybe one partner cannot cope; sometimes it might be illness and attendant ill-humour . . . all these can be accommodated. Elastic sides of the marriage bond give and stretch in response to the demands placed upon it – almost, but never quite, snapping. The cynic might say that partners 'accommodate' each other because they are afraid of isolation. I prefer to imagine that the 'injured' partner sees weakness and need in the other's face – then peers in the mirror to see the same, turning back to forgive.

'I'll stand by you' – that phrase is more moving (though possibly as untrue – for none of us can know the rage hidden by that brave sentiment of conventional loyalty) than much of what is promised in the marriage service.

(*The thorns, grasped firmly, cease to hurt* . . .)

224

SOME MAXIMS

Love is not weakness. It is strong. Only the sacrament of marriage can contain it.

Boris Pasternak, *Dr Zhivago* (1958)

A lady of forty-seven who has been married 27 years and has six children knows what love really is and once described it for me like this: 'Love is what you've been through with someone'.

James Thurber (1894–1961), quoted in *Life* magazine

It is a lovely thing to have a husband and a wife developing together and having the feeling of falling in love again. That is what marriage really means. Helping one another to reach the full status of being persons, responsible and autonomous beings who do not run away from life.

Paul Tournier, *The Meaning of Persons* (1957)

To keep your marriage brimming,
With love in the loving cup,
Whenever you're wrong admit it;
Whenever you're right, shut up.

Ogden Nash (1902–71), *Marriage Lines*

'LOVE WILL NOT BE CONSTRAINED BY MASTERY'

In old Armorica, now Brittany,
There was a knight that loved and strove, did he
To serve a lady in the highest wise;
And many a labour, many a great emprise
He wrought for her, or ever she was won.
For she was of the fairest under sun,
And therewithal come of so high kindred
That scarcely could this noble knight, for dread,
Tell her his woe, his pain, and his distress.
But at the last she, for his worthiness,
And specially for his meek obedience,
Had so much pity that, in consequence,
She secretly was come to his accord
To take him for her husband and her lord,
Of such lordship as men have over wives;
And that they might be happier in their lives,
Of his free will he swore to her, as knight,
That never in his life, by day or night,
Would he assume a right of mastery
Against her will, nor show her jealousy,
But would obey and do her will in all
As any lover of his lady shall;
Save that the name and show of sovereignty,
Those would he have, lest he shame his degree.
*   She thanked him, and with a great humbleness*
She said: "Since, sir, of your own nobleness
You proffer me to have so loose a rein
Would God there never come between us twain,
For any guilt of mine, a war or strife.
Sir, I will be your humble, faithful wife,
Take this as truth till heart break in my breast."
Thus were they both in quiet and in rest.

For one thing, sirs, I safely dare to say,
That friends each one the other must obey
If they'd be friends and long keep company.
Love will not be constrained by mastery;
When mastery comes, the god of love anon
Beats his fair wings, and farewell! He is gone!
Love is a thing as any spirit free;
Women by nature love their liberty,
And not to be constrained like any thrall,
And so do men, if say the truth I shall.
Observe who is most patient in his love,
He is advantaged others all above.
Patience is virtue high, and that's certain;
For it does vanquish, as these clerks make plain.
Things that oppression never could attain.
One must not chide for trifles nor complain.
Learn to endure, or else, so may I go,
You'll have to learn it, whether you will or no.
For in this world, it's certain, no one is
Who never does or says sometimes amiss.
Sickness, or woe, or what the stars have sent,
Anger, or wine, or change of temperament
Causes one oft to do amiss or speak.
For every wrong one may not vengeance wreak;
Conditions must determine temperance
In all who understand good governance.
And therefore did this wise and worthy knight,
To live in quiet, patience to her plight,
And unto him full truly did she swear
That never should he find great fault in her.
Here may men see an humble wise accord;
Thus did she take her servant and her lord,
Servant in love and lord in their marriage;
So was he both in lordship and bondage;
In bondage? Nay, but in lordship above,
Since he had both his lady and his love;
His lady truly, and his wife also,

To which the law of love accords, we know.
And when he was in this prosperity,
Home with his wife he went to his country,
Not far from Penmarch, where his dwelling was.
And there he lived in bliss and all solace.
*   Who could relate, save those that wedded be,*
The joy, the ease, and the prosperity
That are between a husband and a wife?

Geoffrey Chaucer, 'The Franklin's
Tale', *The Canterbury Tales* (1387)

MARGERY KEMPE'S HUSBAND

The Book of Margery Kempe is the earliest surviving autobiographical
writing in the English language, and tells of the religious life of a
medieval anchoress – or recluse. Margery Kempe was born in about
1373, and the early part of her *Book* describes her struggle to achieve
chastity within marriage. In fact, she bore fourteen children, and
her husband, John Kempe, appears to have been remarkably long-
suffering. Her first madness and spiritual crisis followed the birth
of her first child; thereafter, the following extracts give insight into
their marriage.

A ND AFTER THIS TIME she never had any desire
to have sexual intercourse with her husband, for
paying the debt of matrimony was so abominable to her
that she would rather, she thought, have eaten and drunk
the ooze and muck in the gutter than consent to intercourse, except out of obedience.

And so she said to her husband, 'I may not deny you
my body, but all the love and affection of my heart is
withdrawn from all earthly creatures and set on God
alone.' But he would have his will with her, and she

obeyed with much weeping and sorrowing because she could not live in chastity. And often this creature advised her husband to live chaste and said that they had often (she well knew) displeased God by their inordinate love, and the great delight that each of them had in using the other's body, and now it would be a good thing if by mutual consent they punished and chastised themselves by abstaining from the lust of their bodies. Her husband said it was good to do so, but he might not yet – he would do so when God willed. And so he used her as he had done before, he would not desist. And all the time she prayed to God that she might live chaste, and three or four years afterwards, when it pleased our Lord, her husband made a vow of chastity, as shall be written afterwards, by Jesus's leave.

*

It happened one Friday, Midsummer Eve, in very hot weather – as this creature was coming from York carrying a bottle of beer in her hand, and her husband a cake tucked inside his clothes against his chest – that her husband asked his wife this question: 'Margery, if there came a man with a sword who would strike off my head unless I made love with you as I used to do before, tell me on your conscience – for you say you will not lie – whether you would allow my head to be cut off, or else allow me to make love with you again, as I did at one time?'

'Alas, sir,' she said, 'why are you raising this matter, when we have been chaste for these past eight weeks?'

'Because I want to know the truth of your heart.'

And then she said with great sorrow, 'Truly I would rather see you being killed, than that we should turn back to our uncleanness.'

And he replied, 'You are no good wife.'

And then she asked her husband what was the reason that he had not made love to her for the last eight weeks, since she lay with him every night in his bed. And he said that he was made so afraid when he would have touched her, that he dared do no more.

'Now, good sir, mend your ways and ask God's mercy, for I told you nearly three years ago that you[r desire for sex] would suddenly be slain – and this is now the third year, and I hope yet that I shall have my wish. Good sir, I pray you to grant what I shall ask, and I shall pray for you to be saved through the mercy of our Lord Jesus Christ, and you shall have more reward in heaven than if you wore a hair-shirt or wore a coat of mail as a penance. I pray you, allow me to make a vow of chastity at whichever bishop's hand that God wills.'

'No,' he said, 'I won't allow you to do that, because now I can make love to you without mortal sin, and then I wouldn't be able to.'

Then she replied, 'If it be the will of the Holy Ghost to fulfil what I have said, I pray God that you may consent to this; and if it be not the will of the Holy Ghost, I pray God that you never consent.'

Then they went on towards Bridlington and the weather was extremely hot, this creature all the time having great sorrow and great fear for her chastity. And as they came by a cross her husband sat down under the cross, calling his wife to him and saying these words to her: 'Margery, grant me my desire, and I shall grant you your desire. My first desire is that we shall still lie together in one bed as we have done before; the second, that you shall pay my debts before you go to Jerusalem; and the third, that you shall eat and drink with me on Fridays as you used to do.'

'No, sir,' she said. 'I will never agree to break my Friday fast as long as I live.'

'Well,' he said, 'then I'm going to have sex with you again.'

She begged him to allow her to say her prayers, and he kindly allowed it. Then she knelt down beside a cross in the field and prayed in this way, with a great abundance of tears: 'Lord God, you know all things. You know what sorrow I have had to be chaste for you in my body all these three years, and now I might have my will and I dare not, for love of you. For if I were to break that custom of fasting from meat and drink on Fridays which you commanded me, I should now have my desire. But, blessed Lord, you know I will not go against your will, and great is my sorrow now unless I find comfort in you. Now, blessed Jesus, make your will known to my unworthy self, so that I may afterwards follow and fulfil it with all my might.'

And then our Lord Jesus Christ with great sweetness spoke to this creature, commanding her to go again to her husband and pray him to grant her what she desired: 'And he shall have what he desires. For, my beloved daughter, this was the reason why I ordered you to fast, so that you should the sooner obtain your desire, and now it is granted to you. I no longer wish you to fast, and therefore I command you in the name of Jesus to eat and drink as your husband does.'

Then this creature thanked our Lord Jesus Christ for his grace and his goodness, and afterwards got up and went to her husband, saying to him, 'Sir, if you please, you shall grant me my desire, and you shall have your desire. Grant me that you will not come into my bed, and I grant you that I will pay your debts before I go to Jerusalem. And make my body free to God, so that you never make any claim on me requesting any conjugal debt after this day as long as you live – and I shall eat and drink on Fridays at your bidding.'

Then her husband replied to her, 'May your body be as freely available to God as it has been to me.'

This creature thanked God greatly, rejoicing that she had her desire, praying her husband that they should say three paternosters in worship of the Trinity for the great grace that had been granted them. And so they did, kneeling under a cross, and afterwards they ate and drank

231

together in great gladness of spirit. This was on a Friday, on Midsummer's Eve.

THE BOOK OF MARGERY KEMPE (15th century),
translated by B. A. Windeatt

NATÁSHA AND PIERRE

NATÁSHA HAD MARRIED in the early spring of 1813, and in 1820 already had three daughters, besides a son for whom she had longed and whom she was now nursing. She had grown stouter and broader, so that it was difficult to recognize the slim lively Natásha of former days in this robust motherly woman. Her features were more defined and had a calm, soft and serene expression. In her face there was none of the ever-glowing animation that had formerly burned there and constituted its charm. Now her face and body were often all that one saw, and her soul was not visible at all. All that struck the eye was a strong, handsome and fertile woman. The old fire very rarely kindled in her face now. That happened only when, as was the case that day, her husband returned home, or a sick child was convalescent, or when she and Countess Mary spoke of Prince Andrew (she never mentioned him to her husband, who she imagined was jealous of Prince Andrew's memory), or on the rare occasions when something happened to induce her to sing, a practice she had quite abandoned since her marriage. At the rare moments when the old fire kindled in her handsome fully-developed body she was even more attractive than in former days.

Since their marriage Natásha and her husband had lived in Moscow, in Petersburg, on their estate near Moscow, or with their mother, that is to say, in Nicholas's house. The young Countess Bezúkhova was not often seen in society, and those who met her there were not

232

pleased with her and found her neither attractive nor amiable. Not that Natásha liked solitude – she did not know whether she liked it or not, she even thought that she did not – but with her pregnancies, her confinements, the nursing of her children, and sharing every moment of her husband's life, she had demands on her time which could only be satisfied by renouncing society. All who had known Natásha before her marriage wondered at the change in her as at something extraordinary. Only the old countess, with her maternal instinct, had realized that all Natásha's outbursts had been due to her need of children and a husband – as she herself had once exclaimed at Otrádnoe not so much in fun as in earnest – and her mother was now surprised by the surprise expressed by those who had never understood Natásha, and kept saying that she had always known that Natásha would make an exemplary wife and mother.

'Only she lets her love of her husband and children overflow all bounds,' said the countess, 'so that it even becomes absurd.'

Natásha did not follow the golden rule advocated by clever folk, especially the French, which says that a girl should not let herself go when she marries, should not neglect her accomplishments, should be even more careful of her appearance than when she was unmarried, and should fascinate her husband as much as she did before he became her husband. Natásha, on the contrary, had at once abandoned all her witchery, of which her singing had been an unusually powerful part. She gave it up just because it was so powerfully seductive. She took no pains with her manners, or with delicacy of speech, or with her toilet, or to show herself to her husband in her most becoming attitudes, or to avoid inconveniencing him by being too exacting. She acted in contradiction to all those rules. She felt that the allurements instinct had formerly taught her to use would now be merely ridiculous in the eyes of her husband, to whom she had from the first moment given herself up entirely – that is, with her whole soul, leaving no corner of it hidden from him.   She felt that her unity with her husband was not maintained by the poetic feelings that had attracted him to her, but by something else – indefinite but firm as the bond between her own body and soul.

To fluff out her curls, put on fashionable dresses, and sing romantic songs to fascinate her husband, would have seemed as strange as to adorn herself to attract herself.   To adorn herself for others might perhaps have been agreeable – she did not know – but she had no time at all for it.   The chief reason for devoting no time either to singing, to dress, or to choosing her words, was that she really had no time to spare for these things.

It is known that man has the faculty of becoming completely absorbed in a subject however trivial it may be.   And it is known that there is no subject so trivial that it will not grow to infinite proportions if one's entire attention is devoted to it.

The subject which wholly engrossed Natásha's attention was her family, that is, her husband whom she had to keep so that he should belong entirely to her and to the home – and the children whom she had to bear, bring into the world, nurse, and bring up.

And the deeper she penetrated, not with her mind only but with her whole soul, her whole being, into the subject that absorbed her, the larger did that subject grow and the weaker and more inadequate her own powers appeared, so that she concentrated them all on that one thing and yet was unable to accomplish all that she considered necessary.

There were then, as there are now, conversations and discussions about women's rights, the relations of husband and wife, and their freedom and rights, though these themes were not yet termed *questions* as they are now; but these topics were not merely uninteresting to Natásha, she positively did not understand them.

Those questions, then as now, existed only for those

who see nothing in marriage but the pleasure married people get from one another, that is, only the beginnings of marriage and not its whole significance, which lies in the family.

Discussions and questions of that kind, which are like the question of how to get the greatest gratification from one's dinner, did not then, and do not now, exist for those for whom the purpose of a dinner is the nourishment it affords, and the purpose of marriage is the family.

If the purpose of dinner is to nourish the body, a man who eats two dinners at once may perhaps get more enjoyment, but will not attain his purpose for his stomach will not digest the two dinners.

If the purpose of marriage is the family, the person who wishes to have many wives or husbands may perhaps obtain much pleasure, but in that case will not have a family.

If the purpose of food is nourishment, and the purpose of marriage is the family, the whole question resolves itself into not eating more than one can digest, and not having more wives or husbands than are needed for the family – that is, one wife or one husband. Natásha needed a husband. A husband was given her, and he gave her a family. And she not only saw no need of any other or better husband, but as all the powers of her soul were intent on serving that husband and family she could not imagine, and saw no interest in imagining, how it would be if things were different.

Natásha did not care for society in general, but prized the more the society of her relatives – Countess Mary and her brother, her mother, and Sónya. She valued the company of those to whom she could come striding dishevelled from the nursery in her dressing-gown, and with joyful face show a yellow instead of a green stain on baby's napkin, and from whom she could hear reassuring words to the effect that baby was much better.

To such an extent had Natásha let herself go, that the

way she dressed and did her hair, her ill-chosen words, and her jealousy – she was jealous of Sónya, of the governess, and of every woman, pretty or plain – were habitual subjects of jest to those about her. The general opinion was that Pierre was under his wife's thumb, which was really true. From the very first days of their married life Natásha had announced her demands. Pierre was greatly surprised by his wife's view, to him a perfectly novel one, that every moment of his life belonged to her and to the family. His wife's demands astonished him, but they also flattered him, and he submitted to them.

Pierre's subjection consisted in the fact that he not only dared not flirt with, but dared not even speak smilingly to, any other woman; did not dare to dine at the Club as a pastime, did not dare to spend money on a whim, and did not dare absent himself for any length of time, except on business – in which his wife included his intellectual pursuits, which she did not in the least understand but to which she attributed great importance. To make up for this, Pierre had the right of completely regulating his life at home as he chose, as well as that of the whole family. At home Natásha placed herself in the position of a slave to her husband, and the whole household went on tip-toe when he was occupied – that is, was reading or writing in his study. Pierre had but to show a partiality for anything, to get just what he liked done always. He had only to express a wish and Natásha would jump up and run to fulfil it.

The entire household was governed according to Pierre's supposed orders, that is, by his wishes which Natásha tried to guess. Their way of life and place of residence, their acquaintances and ties, Natásha's occupations, the children's upbringing, were all selected not merely with regard to Pierre's expressed wishes, but to what Natásha supposed his wishes to be from the thoughts he expressed in conversation. And she deduced the essentials of his wishes quite correctly, and having once arrived at them clung to them tenaciously. When Pierre himself wanted to change his mind she would fight him with his own weapons.

Thus in a time of trouble ever memorable to him, after the birth of their first child who was delicate, when they had to change the wet-nurse three times and Natásha fell ill from despair, Pierre one day told her of Rousseau's view, with which he quite agreed, that to have a wet-nurse is unnatural and harmful. When her next baby was born, despite the opposition of her mother, the doctors, and even of her husband himself – who were all vigorously opposed to her nursing her baby herself, a thing then unheard of and considered injurious – she insisted on having her own way, and after that nursed all her babies herself.

It very often happened that in a moment of irritation husband and wife would have a dispute, but long afterwards Pierre, to his surprise and delight, would find in his wife's ideas and actions the very thought against which she had argued, but divested of everything superfluous that in the excitement of the dispute he had added when expressing his opinion.

After seven years of marriage Pierre had the joyous and firm consciousness that he was not a bad man, and he felt this because he saw himself reflected in his wife. He felt the good and bad within himself inextricably mingled and overlapping. But only what was really good in him was reflected in his wife, all that was not quite good was rejected. And this was not the result of logical reasoning but was a direct and mysterious reflection.

Leo Tolstoy, *War and Peace* (1863/9)

MRS MICAWBER IS LOYAL

"I NEVER WILL DESERT Mr. Micawber. Mr. Micawber may have concealed his difficulties from me in the first instance, but his sanguine temper may have led him to expect that he would overcome them. The pearl necklace and bracelets which I inherited from mamma, have been disposed of for less than half their value; and the set of coral, which was the wedding gift of my papa, has been actually thrown away for nothing. But I never will desert Mr. Micawber. No!" cried Mrs. Micawber, more affected than before, "I never will do it! It's of no use asking me!"

I felt quite uncomfortable – as if Mrs. Micawber supposed I had asked her to do anything of the sort – and sat looking at her in alarm.

"Mr. Micawber has his faults. I do not deny that he is improvident. I do not deny that he has kept me in the dark as to his resources and his liabilities, both," she went on, looking at the wall; "but I never will desert Mr. Micawber!"

Mrs. Micawber having now raised her voice into a perfect scream, I was so frightened that I ran off to the club-room, and disturbed Mr. Micawber in the act of presiding at a long table, and leading the chorus of –

> *Gee up, Dobbin,*
> *Gee ho, Dobbin,*
> *Gee up, Dobbin,*
> *Gee up, and gee ho-o-o!*

– with the tidings that Mrs. Micawber was in an alarming state, upon which he immediately burst into tears, and came away with me with his waistcoat full of the heads and tails of shrimps, of which he had been partaking.

"Emma, my angel!" cried Mr. Micawber, running into the room; "what is the matter?"

"I never will desert you, Micawber!" she exclaimed.

"My life!" said Mr. Micawber, taking her in his arms. "I am perfectly aware of it."

"He is the parent of my children! He is the father of my twins! He is the husband of my affections," cried Mrs. Micawber, struggling; "and I ne-ver-will-desert Mr. Micawber!"

Mr. Micawber was so deeply affected by this proof of her devotion (as to me, I was dissolved in tears) that he hung over her in a passionate manner, imploring her to look up and to be calm. But the more he asked Mrs. Micawber to look up, the more she fixed her eyes on nothing; and the more he asked her to compose herself, the more she wouldn't. Consequently Mr. Micawber was soon so overcome, that he mingled his tears with hers and mine; until he begged me to do him the favour of taking a chair on the staircase, while he got her into bed.

Charles Dickens, *David Copperfield* (1849)

AN ARRANGED MARRIAGE

In 1440 the Paston family arranged for John Paston to be married to Margaret Mautby, an heiress. This match was clearly designed to further the family fortunes. The marriage took place in the summer or early autumn of 1440, whilst John was still a student at Peterhouse in Cambridge. Margaret's first surviving letter to him is fairly businesslike:

'RIGHT REVEREND AND WORSHIPFUL HUSBAND, I commend myself to you with all my simple heart. This is to let you know that 1100 Flemish landed at Waxham, of whom 800 were captured, killed or drowned. If they had not been, you would have been at home this Whitsuntide, and I expect that you will be at home before very long.

'I thank you for your letter, for I had none from you since I last spoke with you about the business of John Marriott. The inquest did not take place today, for my lord of Norfolk was in town for Wetherby's case; and for that reason he would not let it take place. As far as I know, neither Finch nor Kilby are scheming to do him any good.

'I write no more to you this time, but the Holy Trinity have you in their keeping.

'Written at Norwich on Trinity Sunday.'

Your Margaret Paston

[Soon, the tone changes. Margaret is pregnant.]

14 [?] December, 1441

'Right reverend and worshipful husband, I commend myself to you, desiring heartily to hear of your welfare, thanking you for the token that you sent me by Edmund Perys. Please let me tell you that my mother sent to my father in London for some grey woollen gown cloth, to make me a gown, and he told my mother and me when he came home that he had instructed you to buy it after you left London. If it is not yet bought, please be so kind as to buy it and send it home as soon as you can, for I have no gown to wear this winter except my black and green one with tapes, and that is so cumbersome that I am tired of wearing it.

'As to the girdle that my father promised me, I spoke to him about it a little while before he last went to London, and he said to me that it was your fault, because you would not think about having it made: but I expect that it is not so – he said it just as an excuse. I ask you, if you

240

dare take it upon you, to be so good as to have it made in time for your return home, for I never needed it more than I do now, for I have grown so fat that no belt or girdle that I have will go round me.

'Elisabeth Peverel has lain sick for fifteen or sixteen weeks with sciatica, but she sent my mother word by Kate that she would come here when God sent time, even if she had to be wheeled in a barrow.

'John Damme was here, and my mother revealed my secret to him and he said by his troth that he was not so pleased by anything he had heard for the last twelve months as he was by that news. I can no longer live by cunning; my secret is revealed to everyone who sees me. I sent you word of all the other things that you desired me to send word of in a letter I wrote on Our Lady's day last [8 December].

'The Holy Trinity have you in their keeping. Written at Oxnead in very great haste on the Thursday before St Thomas' day.

'Please wear the ring with the image of St Margaret that I sent you as a keepsake until you come home. You have left me such a keepsake as makes me think of you both day and night when I want to sleep.'

Yours, M.P.

[Later still, we have a love-letter, touching and intimate in tone:]

28 September, 1443

Right worshipful husband, I commend myself to you, desiring with all my heart to hear how you are and thanking God for your recovery from the great illness you have had; and I thank you for the letter you sent me, for I swear that my mother-in-law and I were not easy in our hearts from the time that we knew of your sickness until

241

we knew for certain of your recovery. My mother-in-law has promised another image of wax weighing as much as you for our lady of Walsingham, and she sent four nobles (26s 8d) to the four orders of friars in Norwich to pray for you. I have promised to go on a pilgrimage to Walsingham and St Leonard's Priory (in Norwich) for you. By my troth, I have never had such a weary time as I had from the time that I knew of your sickness to the time I knew of your recovery, and even now I am not very much at ease, nor shall I be until I know that you are completely better.

'Your father and mine was at Beccles a week ago today on the prior of Bromholm's business, and he stayed at Geldeston that night; he was there until nine o'clock the next day. And I sent a message asking for a gown from there, and my mother said that I could not have one until I went there again; and so they could not get one. My stepfather Garneys sent word that he would be here next week, and my aunt too, and would have some sport with their hawks; and they want to take me home with them. And, so God help me, I shall make an excuse for not going there, if I can, because I expect that I shall get news from you here more easily than I would have there.

'I shall send my mother a token that she gave me, for I suppose the time has come to send it to her if I am to keep the promise that I have made – I think that I have told you what it was. I beg you with all my heart to be kind and send me a letter as quickly as you can, if writing is not difficult for you, and that you will send me word how your sore is. If I could have had my way, I would have seen you before now. I wish you were at home, if you would have been more comfortable here, and your sore might have been as well looked after here as it is where you are now; I would rather have you here than be given a new gown, even though it was a scarlet one. Please, if your sore is healed and you can bear to ride, when my father comes to London, ask him for leave and come home when the horses are sent home again, for I think you will be looked after as tenderly here as you are in London.

'I cannot find time to write half a quarter as much as I would tell you if I could speak to you. I shall send you another letter as soon as I can. I shall be grateful if you can remember my girdle, and if you can write to me now, because I expect writing has been difficult for you. Almighty God have you in his keeping and send you health. Written at Oxnead in very great haste on St Michael's eve.

Yours, M. Paston

'My mother-in-law sends you greetings and God's blessing and hers, and asks you, as I do also, to keep to a good diet of meat and drink, for that will do more than anything to help you to recover. Your son is well, blessed be God.'

The Paston Letters

HELEN

And you, Helen, what should I give you?
So many things I would give you
Had I an infinite great store
Offered me and I stood before
To choose. I would give you youth,
All kinds of loveliness and truth,
A clear eye as good as mine,
Lands, waters, flowers, wine,
As many children as your heart
Might wish for, a far better art
Than mine can be, all you have lost
Upon the travelling waters tossed,
Or given to me. If I could choose
Freely in that great treasure-house
Anything from any shelf,

I would give you back yourself,
And power to discriminate
What you want and want it not too late,
Many fair days free from care
And heart to enjoy both foul and fair,
And myself, too, if I could find
Where it lay hidden and it proved kind.

Edward Thomas (1916)

DOROTHEA PITIES HER HUSBAND

The young and idealistic Dorothea Brooke has married the elderly, pedantic scholar, Mr Casaubon, and this unlikely union is not happy. At this point they have both been informed, separately, that Mr Casaubon's heart condition is likely to lead to sudden death.

DOROTHEA HAD BEEN AWARE when Lydgate had ridden away, and she had stepped into the garden, with the impulse to go at once to her husband. But she hesitated, fearing to offend him by obtruding herself; for her ardour, continually repulsed, served, with her intense memory, to heighten her dread, as thwarted energy subsides into a shudder; and she wandered slowly round the nearer clumps of trees until she saw him advancing. Then she went towards him, and might have represented a heaven-sent angel coming with a promise that the short hours remaining should yet be filled with that faithful love which clings the closer to a comprehended grief. His glance in reply to hers was so chill that she felt her timidity increased; yet she turned and passed her hand through his arm.

Mr Casaubon kept his hands behind him and allowed her pliant arm to cling with difficulty against his rigid arm.

244

There was something horrible to Dorothea in the sensation which this unresponsive hardness inflicted on her. That is a strong word, but not too strong: it is in these acts called trivialities that the seeds of joy are for ever wasted, until men and women look round with haggard faces at the devastation their own waste has made, and say, the earth bears no harvest of sweetness – calling their denial knowledge. You may ask why, in the name of manliness, Mr Casaubon should have behaved in that way. Consider that his was a mind which shrank from pity: have you ever watched in such a mind the effect of a suspicion that what is pressing it as a grief may be really a source of contentment, either actual or future, to the being who already offends by pitying? Besides, he knew little of Dorothea's sensations, and had not reflected that on such an occasion as the present they were comparable in strength to his own sensibilities about Carp's criticisms.

Dorothea did not withdraw her arm, but she could not venture to speak. Mr Casaubon did not say, "I wish to be alone," but he directed his steps in silence towards the house, and as they entered by the glass door on this eastern side, Dorothea withdrew her arm and lingered on the matting, that she might leave her husband quite free. He entered the library and shut himself in, alone with his sorrow.

She went up to her boudoir. The open bow-window let in the serene glory of the afternoon lying in the avenue, where the lime-trees cast long shadows. But Dorothea knew nothing of the scene. She threw herself on a chair, not heeding that she was in the dazzling sun-rays: if there were discomfort in that, how could she tell that it was not part of her inward misery?

She was in the reaction of a rebellious anger stronger than any she had felt since her marriage. Instead of tears there came words: –

"What have I done – what am I – that he should treat me so? He never knows what is in my mind – he never cares. What is the use of anything I do? He wishes he had never married me."

She began to hear herself, and was checked into stillness. Like one who has lost his way and is weary, she sat and saw as in one glance all the paths of her young hope which she should never find again. And just as clearly in the miserable light she saw her own and her husband's solitude – how they walked apart so that she was obliged to survey him. If he had drawn her towards him, she would never have surveyed him – never have said, "Is he worth living for?" but would have felt him simply a part of her own life. Now she said bitterly, "It is his fault, not mine." In the jar of her whole being, Pity was overthrown. Was it her fault that she had believed in him – had believed in his worthiness? – And what, exactly, was he? – She was able enough to estimate him – she who waited on his glances with trembling, and shut her best soul in prison, paying it only hidden visits, that she might be petty enough to please him. In such a crisis as this, some women begin to hate.

The sun was low when Dorothea was thinking that she would not go down again, but would send a message to her husband saying that she was not well and preferred remaining up-stairs. She had never deliberately allowed her resentment to govern her in this way before, but she believed now that she could not see him again without telling him the truth about her feeling, and she must wait till she could do it without interruption. He might wonder and be hurt at her message. It was good that he should wonder and be hurt. Her anger said, as anger is apt to say, that God was with her – that all heaven, though it were crowded with spirits watching them, must be on her side. She had determined to ring her bell, when there came a rap at the door.

Mr Casaubon had sent to say that he would have his dinner in the library. He wished to be quite alone this evening, being much occupied.

"I shall not dine, then, Tantripp."

"Oh, madam, let me bring you a little something?"

"No; I am not well. Get everything ready in my dressing-room, but pray do not disturb me again."

Dorothea sat almost motionless in her meditative struggle, while the evening slowly deepened into night. But the struggle changed continually, as that of a man who begins with a movement towards striking and ends with conquering his desire to strike. The energy that would animate a crime is not more than is wanted to inspire a resolved submission, when the noble habit of the soul reasserts itself. That thought with which Dorothea had gone out to meet her husband – her conviction that he had been asking about the possible arrest of all his work, and that the answer must have wrung his heart, could not be long without rising beside the image of him, like a shadowy monitor looking at her anger with sad remonstrance. It cost her a litany of pictured sorrows and of silent cries that she might be the mercy for those sorrows – but the resolved submission did come; and when the house was still, and she knew that it was near the time when Mr Casaubon habitually went to rest, she opened her door gently and stood outside in the darkness waiting for his coming up-stairs with a light in his hand. If he did not come soon she thought that she would go down and even risk incurring another pang. She would never again expect anything else. But she did hear the library door open, and slowly the light advanced up the staircase without noise from the footsteps on the carpet. When her husband stood opposite to her, she saw that his face was more haggard. He started slightly on seeing her, and she looked up at him beseechingly, without speaking.

"Dorothea!" he said, with a gentle surprise in his tone. "Were you waiting for me?"

"Yes, I did not like to disturb you."

"Come, my dear, come. You are young, and need not to extend your life by watching."

When the kind quiet melancholy of that speech fell on Dorothea's ears, she felt something like the thankfulness that might well up in us if we had narrowly escaped hurting a lamed creature. She put her hand into her husband's, and they went along the broad corridor together.

George Eliot, *Middlemarch* (1871)

MR AND MRS RAMSAY GO FOR A WALK

THAT WAS A GOOD BIT OF WORK on the whole – his eight children. They showed he did not damn the poor little universe entirely, for on an evening like this, he thought, looking at the land dwindling away, the little island seemed pathetically small, half swallowed up in the sea.

'Poor little place,' he murmured with a sigh.

She heard him. He said the most melancholy things, but she noticed that directly he had said them he always seemed more cheerful than usual. All this phrase-making was a game, she thought, for if she had said half what he said, she would have blown her brains out by now.

It annoyed her, this phrase-making, and she said to him, in a matter-of-fact way, that it was a perfectly lovely evening. And what was he groaning about, she asked, half laughing, half complaining, for she guessed what he was thinking – he would have written better books if he had not married.

He was not complaining, he said. She knew that he did not complain. She knew that he had nothing whatever to complain of. And he seized her hand and raised it to his lips and kissed it with an intensity that brought the tears to her eyes, and quickly he dropped it.

They turned away from the view and began to walk up the path where the silver-green spear-like plants grew, arm in arm. His arm was almost like a young man's arm, Mrs Ramsay thought, thin and hard, and she thought with delight how strong he still was, though he was over sixty, and how untamed and optimistic, and how strange it was that being convinced, as he was, of all sorts of horrors, seemed not to depress him, but to cheer him. Was it not odd, she reflected? Indeed he seemed to her sometimes made differently from other people, born blind, deaf, and dumb, to the ordinary things, but to the extraordinary things, with an eye like an eagle's. His understanding often astonished her. But did he notice the flowers? No. Did he notice the view? No. Did he even notice his own daughter's beauty, or whether there was pudding on his plate or roast beef? He would sit at table with them like a person in a dream. And his habit of talking aloud, or saying poetry aloud, was growing on him, she was afraid; for sometimes it was awkward –

Best and brightest, come away!

poor Miss Giddings, when he shouted that at her, almost jumped out of her skin. But then, Mrs Ramsay, though instantly taking his side against all the silly Giddingses in the world, then, she thought, intimating by a little pressure on his arm that he walked up hill too fast for her, and she must stop for a moment to see whether those were fresh mole-hills on the bank, then, she thought, stooping down to look, a great mind like his must be different in every way from ours. All the great men she had ever known, she thought, deciding that a rabbit must have got in, were like that, and it was good for young men (though the atmosphere of lecture-rooms was stuffy and depressing to her beyond endurance almost) simply to hear him, simply to look at him. But without shooting rabbits, how was one to keep them down? she wondered. It might be a rabbit; it might be a mole. Some creature anyhow was ruining her Evening Primroses. And looking up, she saw above the thin trees the first pulse of the full-throbbing star, and wanted to make her husband look at it; for the sight gave her such keen pleasure. But she stopped herself. He never looked at things. If he did, all he would say would be, poor little world, with one of his sighs.

At that moment, he said, 'Very fine,' to please her, and pretended to admire the flowers. But she knew quite well that he did not admire them, or even realize that they were there. It was only to please her ... Ah, but was that not Lily Briscoe strolling along with William Bankes? She focused her short-sighted eyes upon the backs of a retreating couple. Yes, indeed it was. Did that not mean that they would marry? Yes, it must! What an admirable idea! They must marry!

Virginia Woolf, *To the Lighthouse* (1927)

MR BLACKETT IS FORGIVEN

The downtrodden Mrs Blackett has finally rebelled against her conceited, domineering husband, and told him that she loathed their honeymoon and has resented his selfishness and stupidity for twenty years. Shocked and confused, he rushes out, leaving his wife to wonder if he had understood any part of what she had said:

S HE FELT RATHER ASHAMED, but she knew she felt more kindly towards him than she had done since their wedding day and could see him simply now as another faulty human creature like herself.

[Much later, Mr Blackett returns from wandering the streets:]

Exactly where he went he never rightly knew. He heard the front door bang behind him with an awful sound of finality and it seemed to him that it was Bertha who had

250

thrust him out, her rough hand which had slammed the door on him, that hand hitherto so soft and deft, and for a time he proceeded in a queer shambling trot, very different from the normal, assured gait of Mr. Herbert Blackett. And those cruel words had come from her whose speech had seldom been less gentle than her words! It was no wonder he moved with such uncertainty for he felt that the ground was shaking under his feet. Yet he could not believe all this had really happened. It must be a nightmare. He could not live without the steady foundations on which he had built his life, without his supports and props and, since he was quite certainly alive, he must surely be under some delusion. This questionably happy idea soon deserted him. Here, when he lifted his dropped head, he saw houses and streets he knew, taking on none of the fantastic shapes incident to dreams and, realizing that he was indeed awake, he straightened his back though he did not slacken his pace. He pushed past merry groups of people who were celebrating their release from fear; he heard distant sounds of revelry from the city and the shouting and the laughter added to the confusion in his mind and this very gradually cleared to the necessity of accepting a horrible reality. He could not change it, for all his adroitness, into anything but what it was. He did not try to defend himself against anything his wife had said. Whether it was true or false was not his present concern. What had brought a great lump of misery into his chest, what drove him round about the roads of Upper Radstowe, was the thought of the woman whose fancied love and admiration had been the unacknowledged background to his life. She had been hating and despising him for years, his wife, who had made a home which had seemed as near perfection as it could be and to which he must eventually return. For, he asked himself, standing still and breathing hard, as though he had temporarily evaded his pursuers and could afford a moment's rest, what else could

251

he do? And as he stood there, instinctively seeking the shadow of a drooping tree, it seemed to him, who was rarely imaginative except about himself, that the world must be thronged with people who, for a while, might wander in the protective darkness of the night but, sooner or later, must go back to houses they hated, to houses where they were not wanted, because there was no other shelter for them, and he was one of them, like some sad old dog who had been beaten for a fault he did not know he had committed, but must trundle home meekly to his kennel.

Stealthily he put his key in the lock and found he need not turn it. The door was opened for him.

'Why, Bertha, Bertha!' he stammered in meek surprise, remembering that, in all their days together, she had never been at a door to welcome him.

'I was listening for you,' she said, and when she saw the queer, homeless look he had, she was aghast at her presumption in tampering with another person's soul and she knew that if he was humiliated, so was she, but sensibly she said, 'Shall we go into the kitchen and have something hot to drink?' and hearing the new friendliness in her own voice, she gave him an amused, questioning glance, as though to ask whether he heard it too, and with, as it were, an uncertain wag of his tail, he followed her down the basement stairs for, again, what else could he do?

E. H. Young, *Chatterton Square* (1947)

MRS BULSTRODE FACES DISGRACE

Harriet Bulstrode has just heard that her husband has been involved in shady dealings, and now faces a public scandal.

S HE LOCKED HERSELF IN HER ROOM. She needed time to get used to her maimed consciousness, her poor lopped life, before she could walk steadily to the place allotted her. A new searching light had fallen on her husband's character, and she could not judge him leniently: the twenty years in which she had believed in him and venerated him by virtue of his concealments came back with particulars that made them seem an odious deceit. He had married her with that bad past life hidden behind him, and she had no faith left to protest his innocence of the worst that was imputed to him. Her honest ostentatious nature made the sharing of a merited dishonour as bitter as it could be to any mortal.

But this imperfectly-taught woman, whose phrases and habits were an odd patchwork, had a loyal spirit within her. The man whose prosperity she had shared through nearly half a life, and who had unvaryingly cherished her – now that punishment had befallen him it was not possible to her in any sense to forsake him. There is a forsaking which still sits at the same board and lies on the same couch with the forsaken soul, withering it the more by unloving proximity. She knew, when she locked her door, that she should unlock it ready to go down to her unhappy husband and espouse his sorrow, and say of his guilt, I will mourn and not reproach. But she needed time to gather up her strength; she needed to sob out her farewell to all the gladness and pride of her life. When she had resolved to go down, she prepared herself by some little acts which might seem mere folly to a hard onlooker; they were her way of expressing to all spectators visible or invisible that she had begun a new life in which she embraced humiliation. She took off all her ornaments and put on a plain black gown, and instead of wearing her much-adorned cap and large bows of hair, she brushed her hair down and put on a plain bonnet-cap, which made her look suddenly like an early Methodist.

Bulstrode, who knew that his wife had been out and had come in saying that she was not well, had spent the time in an agitation equal to hers. He had looked forward to her learning the truth from others, and had acquiesced in that probability, as something easier to him than any confession. But now that he imagined the moment of her knowledge come, he awaited the result in anguish. His daughters had been obliged to consent to leave him, and though he had allowed some food to be brought to him, he had not touched it. He felt himself perishing slowly in unpitied misery. Perhaps he should never see his wife's face with affection in it again. And if he turned to God there seemed to be no answer but the pressure of retribution.

It was eight o'clock in the evening before the door opened and his wife entered. He dared not look up at her. He sat with his eyes bent down, and as she went towards him she thought he looked smaller – he seemed so withered and shrunken. A movement of new compassion and old tenderness went through her like a great wave, and putting one hand on his which rested on the arm of the chair, and the other on his shoulder, she said, solemnly but kindly –

"Look up, Nicholas."

He raised his eyes with a little start and looked at her half amazed for a moment: her pale face, her changed, mourning dress, the trembling about her mouth, all said, "I know"; and her hands and eyes rested gently on him. He burst out crying and they cried together, she sitting at his side. They could not yet speak to each other of the shame which she was bearing with him, or of the acts which had brought it down on them. His confession was silent, and her promise of faithfulness was silent. Openminded as she was, she nevertheless shrank from the words which would have expressed their mutual consciousness, as she would have shrunk from flakes of fire. She could not say, "How much is only slander and false suspicion?" and he did not say, "I am innocent."

George Eliot, *Middlemarch* (1871)

GODFREY CASS MAKES HIS CONFESSION

"EVERYTHING COMES TO LIGHT, Nancy, sooner or later. When God Almighty wills it, our secrets are found out. I've lived with a secret on my mind, but I'll keep it from you no longer. I wouldn't have you know it by somebody else, and not by me – I wouldn't have you find it out after I'm dead. I'll tell you now. It's been 'I will' and 'I won't' with me all my life – I'll make sure of myself now."

Nancy's utmost dread had returned. The eyes of the husband and wife met with awe in them, as at a crisis which suspended affection.

"Nancy," said Godfrey, slowly, "when I married you, I hid something from you – something I ought to have told you. That woman Marner found dead in the snow – Eppie's mother – that wretched woman – was my wife: Eppie is my child."

He paused, dreading the effect of his confession. But Nancy sat quite still, only that her eyes dropped and ceased to meet his. She was pale and quiet as a meditative statue, clasping her hands on her lap.

"You'll never think the same of me again," said Godfrey, after a little while, with some tremor in his voice.

She was silent.

"I oughtn't to have left the child unowned: I oughtn't to have kept it from you. But I couldn't bear to give you up, Nancy. I was led away into marrying her – I suffered for it."

Still Nancy was silent, looking down; and he almost expected that she would presently get up and say she would go to her father's. How could she have any mercy for faults that must seem so black to her, with her simple severe notions?

But at last she lifted up her eyes to his again and

255

spoke. There was no indignation in her voice – only deep regret.

"Godfrey, if you had but told me this six years ago, we could have done some of our duty by the child. Do you think I'd have refused to take her in, if I'd known she was yours?"

At that moment Godfrey felt all the bitterness of an error that was not simply futile, but had defeated its own end. He had not measured this wife with whom he had lived so long. But she spoke again, with more agitation.

"And – O, Godfrey – if we'd had her from the first, if you'd taken to her as you ought, she'd have loved me for her mother – and you'd have been happier with me: I could better have bore my little baby dying, and our life might have been more like what we used to think it'ud be."

The tears fell, and Nancy ceased to speak.

"But you wouldn't have married me then, Nancy, if I'd told you," said Godfrey, urged, in the bitterness of his self-reproach, to prove to himself that his conduct had not been utter folly. "You may think you would now, but you wouldn't then. With your pride and your father's, you'd have hated having anything to do with me after the talk there'd have been."

"I can't say what I should have done about that, Godfrey. I should never have married anybody else. But I wasn't worth doing wrong for – nothing is in this world. Nothing is so good as it seems before-hand – not even our marrying wasn't, you see." There was a faint sad smile on Nancy's face as she said the last words.

"I'm a worse man than you thought I was, Nancy," said Godfrey, rather tremulously. "Can you forgive me ever?"

"The wrong to me is but little, Godfrey: you've made it up to me – you've been good to me for fifteen years. It's another you did the wrong to; and I doubt it can never be all made up for."

"But we can take Eppie now," said Godfrey.   "I won't mind the world knowing at last.   I'll be plain and open for the rest o' my life."

"It'll be different coming from us, now she's grown up," said Nancy, shaking her head sadly.   "But it's your duty to acknowledge her and provide for her; and I'll do my part by her, and pray to God Almighty to make her love me."

"Then we'll go together to Silas Marner's this very night, as soon as everything's quiet at the Stone-pits."

[They go and tell Eppie that she is Godfrey's illegitimate child, and offer her a home. She says that she considers Silas Marner, who brought her up, to be her father, and that she will stay with him and marry a working man. Her decision has to be accepted . . .]

Nancy and Godfrey walked home under the starlight in silence.   When they entered the oaken parlour, Godfrey threw himself into his chair, while Nancy laid down her bonnet and shawl, and stood on the hearth near her husband, unwilling to leave him even for a few minutes, and yet fearing to utter any word lest it might jar on his feelings.   At last Godfrey turned his head towards her, and their eyes met, dwelling in that meeting without any movement on either side.   That quiet mutual gaze of a trusting husband and wife is like the first moment of rest or refuge from a great weariness or a great danger – not to be interfered with by speech or action which would distract the sensations from the fresh enjoyment of repose.

But presently he put out his hand, and as Nancy placed hers within it, he drew her towards him, and said –

"That's ended!"

George Eliot, *Silas Marner* (1861)

THE FALL OF ADAM

Thus Eve *with Countnance blithe her storie told;*
But in her Cheek distemper flushing glowd.
On th' other side, Adam, *soon as he heard*
The fatal Trespass don by Eve, *amazd,*
Astonied stood and Blank, while horror chill
Ran through his veins, and all his joynt relax'd;
From his slack hand the Garland wreath'd for Eve
Down drop'd, and all the faded Roses shed:
Speechless he stood and pale, till thus at length
First to himself he inward silence broke.
O fairest of Creation, last and best
Of all Gods Works, Creature in whom excell'd
Whatever can to sight or thought be formd,
Holy, divine, good, amiable, or sweet!
How art thou lost, how on a sudden lost,
Defac't, deflourd, and now to Death devote?
Rather how hast thou yeelded to transgress
The strict forbiddance, how to violate
The sacred Fruit forbidd'n! som cursed fraud
Of Enemie hath beguil'd thee, yet unknown,
And mee with thee hath ruind, for with thee
Certain my resolution is to Die;
How can I live without thee, how forgoe
Thy sweet Converse and Love so dearly joyn'd,
To live again in these wilde Woods forlorn?
Should God create another Eve, *and I*
Another Rib afford, yet loss of thee
Would never from my heart; no no, I feel
The Link of Nature draw me: Flesh of Flesh,
Bone of my Bone thou art, and from thy State
Mine never shall be parted, bliss or woe.

John Milton, *Paradise Lost* (1667)

NIGEL NICOLSON ON HIS PARENTS' MARRIAGE

TO THIS EASY RELATIONSHIP they gave a moral base, both having analytical minds, and they evolved a 'formula' for their marriage, 'a firm, elastic formula', said Harold, 'which makes it so easy for us both to duplicate the joys of love and life, and to halve their miseries'; or, as she put it to him, 'We are sure of each other, in this odd, strange, detached, intimate, mystical relationship which we could never explain to any outside person.' The formula ran something like this: what mattered most was that each should trust the other absolutely. 'Trust', in most marriages, means fidelity. In theirs it meant that they would always tell each other of their infidelities, give warning of approaching emotional crises and, whatever happened, return to their common centre in the end. Vita once put her 'little creed' for Harold in these words: 'To love me whatever I do. To believe my motives are not mean. Not to credit tales without hearing my own version. To give up everything and everybody for me in the last resort.'

The basis of their marriage was mutual respect, enduring love and 'a common sense of values' . . .

In 1929 they debated on BBC radio their ideas about marriage, and this was their conclusion:

> Harold: You agree that a successful marriage is the greatest of human benefits?
>
> Vita: Yes.
>
> Harold: And that it must be based on love guided by intelligence?
>
> Vita: Yes.
>
> Harold: That an essential condition is a common sense of values?

Vita: Yes.
Harold: That the only things that will stave off marital nerves are modesty, good humour and, above all, occupation?
Vita: Yes.
Harold: And give and take?
Vita: And give and take.
Harold: And mutual esteem. I do not believe in the permanence of any love which is based on pity, or the protective or maternal instincts. It must be based on respect.
Vita: Yes, I agree. The caveman plus sweet-little-thing theory is long past. It was a theory insulting to the best qualities of both.

Marriage, they thought (but not for a BBC audience in 1929), was 'unnatural'. Marriage was only tolerable for people of strong character and independent minds if it were regarded as a lifetime association between intimate friends. It was a bond which should last only as long as both wanted it to. (Both, for this reason, were strongly in favour of easier divorce.) But as a happy marriage is 'the greatest of human benefits', husband and wife must strive hard for its success. Each must be subtle enough to mould their characters and behaviour to fit the other's, facet to facet, convex to concave. The husband must develop the feminine side of his nature, the wife her masculine side. He must cultivate the qualities of sympathy and intuition; she those of detachment, reason and decision. He must respond to tears; she must not miss trains.

Nigel Nicolson, *Portrait of a Marriage* (1973)

LYDGATE'S RESIGNATION

Dorothea Casaubon has just left Rosamond Lydgate, wife of the Middlemarch doctor, Tertius Lydgate. Their marriage is a union of opposites; there is no understanding between them. Lydgate says goodbye to Dorothea, whom he greatly admires, ...

WHEN HE CAME BACK to Rosamond, she had already thrown herself on the sofa, in resigned fatigue.

"Well, Rosy," he said, standing over her, and touching her hair, "what do you think of Mrs Casaubon now you have seen so much of her?"

"I think she must be better than any one," said Rosamond, "and she is very beautiful. If you go to talk to her so often, you will be more discontented with me than ever!"

Lydgate laughed at the "so often." "But has she made you any less discontented with me?"

"I think she has," said Rosamond, looking up in his face. "How heavy your eyes are, Tertius – and do push your hair back." He lifted up his large white hand to obey her, and felt thankful for this little mark of interest in him. Poor Rosamond's vagrant fancy had come back terribly scourged – meek enough to nestle under the old despised shelter. And the shelter was still there: Lydgate had accepted his narrowed lot with sad resignation. He had chosen this fragile creature, and had taken the burthen of her life upon his arms. He must walk as he could, carrying that burthen pitifully.

George Eliot, *Middlemarch* (1871)

MR BOMPAS IS PROUD OF HIS WIFE

Henry, a beautiful youth of eighteen, is passionately in love with Aurora Bompas, who is thirty-seven. She has just made it clear that she has no intention of leaving her husband, when that gentleman interrupts them. He has found the love poems Henry wrote to his wife, but Henry protests innocence ...

HE [*earnestly*] Believe me, you are I assure you, on my honor as a gentleman, that I have never had the slightest feeling for Mrs Bompas beyond the ordinary esteem and regard of a pleasant acquaintance.

HER HUSBAND [*shortly, showing ill humor for the first time*] Oh, indeed. [*He leaves his hearth and begins to approach Henry slowly, looking him up and down with growing resentment*].

HE [*hastening to improve the impression made by his mendacity*] I should never have dreamt of writing poems to her. The thing is absurd.

HER HUSBAND [*reddening ominously*] Why is it absurd?

HE [*shrugging his shoulders*] Well, it happens that I do not admire Mrs Bompas – in that way.

HER HUSBAND [*breaking out in Henry's face*] Let me tell you that Mrs Bompas has been admired by better men than you, you soapy headed little puppy, you.

HE [*much taken aback*] There is no need to insult me like this. I assure you, on my honor as a –

HER HUSBAND [*too angry to tolerate a reply, and boring Henry more and more towards the piano*] You dont admire Mrs Bompas! You would never dream of writing poems to Mrs Bompas! My wife's not good enough for you, isnt she. [*Fiercely*] Who are you, pray, that you should be so jolly superior?

HE. Mr Bompas: I can make allowances for your jealousy –

HER HUSBAND. Jealousy! do you suppose I'm jealous of

you? No, nor of ten like you. But if you think I'll stand here and let you insult my wife in her own house, youre mistaken.

HE [*very uncomfortable with his back against the piano and Teddy standing over him threateningly*] How can I convince you? Be reasonable. I tell you my relations with Mrs Bompas are relations of perfect coldness – of indifference –

HER HUSBAND [*scornfully*] Say it again: say it again. Youre proud of it, arnt you? Yah! you're not worth kicking.

HE. This is ridiculous. I assure you Mrs Bompas is quite –

HER HUSBAND. What is Mrs Bompas to you, I'd like to know. I'll tell you what Mrs Bompas is. She's the smartest woman in the smartest set in South Kensington, and the handsomest, and the cleverest, and the most fetching to experienced men who know a good thing when they see it, whatever she may be to conceited penny-a-lining puppies who think nothing good enough for them. It's admitted by the best people; and not to know it argues yourself unknown. Three of our first actor-managers have offered her a hundred a week if she'll go on the stage when they start a repertory theatre; and I think they know what theyre about as well as you. The only member of the present Cabinet that you might call a handsome man has neglected the business of the country to dance with her, though he dont belong to our set as a regular thing. One of the first professional poets in Bedford Park wrote a sonnet to her, worth all your amateur trash. At Ascot last season the eldest son of a duke excused himself from calling on me on the ground that his feelings for Mrs Bompas were not consistent with his duty to me as host; and it did him honor and me too. But [*with gathering fury*] she isnt good enough for you, it seems. You regard her with coldness, with indifference; and you have the cool cheek to tell me so to my face. For two pins I'd flatten your nose in to teach

you manners.   Introducing a fine woman to you is casting
pearls before swine [*yelling at him*] before SWINE! d'ye hear?

George Bernard Shaw, *How He Lied To Her Husband*
(1905)

SONNET NO. 19

My one requirement: that you stay with me.
I want to hear you, grumble as you may.
If you were deaf I'd need what you might say
If you were dumb I'd need what you might see.

If you were blind I'd want you in my sight
For you're the sentry posted to my side:
We're hardly half way through our lengthy ride
Remember we're surrounded yet by night.

Your 'let me lick my wounds' is no excuse now.
Your 'anywhere' (not here) is no defence
There'll be relief for you, but no release now.

You know whoever's needed can't go free
And you are needed urgently by me
I speak of me when us would make more sense.

Bertold Brecht (c. 1940), translated by John Willett

'NOT THE HERO OF HER DREAMS'

Lizzie West has at last married the widower, Vincent Deering,
whom first she loved when she was his daughter's teacher. Lizzie
has become wealthy, and Vincent has returned from America to
France to marry her, swearing that his long silence was to avoid
pain for them both. Now Lizzie has just found, in an old trunk, all
the letters she wrote to him in America, letters he swore made him
suffer – unopened. In a flash she sees her husband as weak, that

264

their happiness is built on a lie, and resolves to leave. Then she reflects: their marriage *is* genuinely happy, and what would life be like without him? Anxiously she looks from the window, awaiting his return:

A S HER HUSBAND advanced up the path she had a sudden vision of their three years together. Those years were her whole life; everything before them had been colorless and unconscious, like the blind life of the plant before it reaches the surface of the soil. The years had not been exactly what she had dreamed; but if they had taken away certain illusions they had left richer realities in their stead. She understood now that she had gradually adjusted herself to the new image of her husband as he was, as he would always be. He was not the hero of her dreams, but he was the man she loved, and who had loved her. For she saw now, in this last wide flash of pity and initiation, that, as a comely marble may be made out of worthless scraps of mortar, glass, and pebbles, so out of mean mixed substances may be fashioned a love that will bear the stress of life.

Edith Wharton, *Tales of Men and Ghosts* (1910)

CELEBRATIONS

'... let no man put asunder'

The anniversaries come and go. 'I don't like remembering them,' my partner said to me, years ago, 'because they remind me too much of the passage of time.'

Yet people send cards to congratulate the married couple, at the fifth, the tenth ... each year until the big celebrations – the silver, the ruby, the golden, the diamond. And so they should. Yet do they stop to reflect on the oddity of the business? Why *congratulate*?

Because, of course, something has been achieved. In an unhappy marriage each month might be a notch in a gunbelt, signifying slaughter. Even in most marriages each passing year is an obstacle in a race, or a task in an endurance test, as well as a ring in a tree – signifying growth.

Once imperfection is recognised, the inevitable shortfall in happiness accepted, mutual needs and weaknesses accommodated ... then something extraordinary can happen, for which the only word is rebirth. It is possible to look at your partner again one day, one month, one chilly year, when lines show more clearly on the brow – and fall in love once more. This is the kind of love which burns slowly, when passion has long consumed itself and lies cold, in ashes. It is to do with companionship, with mutuality and friendship: the realisation that you want to grow old with no one else, and that *this* person makes growing old bearable. It raises a glass in celebration.

(The rose, at summer's height, is magnificent ...)

THE ANNIVERSARIE

All Kings, and all their favourites,
   All glory of honours, beauties, wits,
The sun itself, which makes times, as they pass,
Is elder by a year now than it was
When thou and I first one another saw:
All other things to their destruction draw,
   Only our love hath no decay;
This no tomorrow hath, nor yesterday,
Running it never runs from us away,
But truly keeps his first, last, everlasting day.

   Two graves must hide thine and my corse;
   If one might, death were no divorce.
Alas, as well as other Princes, we
(Who Prince enough in one another be)
Must leave at last in death these eyes and ears,
Oft fed with true oaths, and with sweet salt tears;
   But souls where nothing dwells but love
(All other thoughts being inmates) then shall prove
This, or a love increasèd there above,
When bodies to their graves, souls from their graves remove.

   And then we shall be thoroughly blessed;
   But we no more than all the rest.
Here upon earth we're Kings, and none but we
Can be such Kings, nor of such subjects be;
Who is so safe as we? where none can do
Treason to us, except one of us two.
   True and false fears let us refrain,
Let us love nobly, and live, and add again
Years and years unto years, till we attain
To write threescore: this is the second of our reign.

John Donne (1635)

MRS MILBURN'S BIRTHDAY CELEBRATION

Clara Milburn was born in 1883 and died in 1961. In 1905 she married Jack, a draughtsman, and her diaries, kept from 1939 until 1945, are a touching but matter-of-fact chronicle of civilian life in wartime.

Saturday 24th June 1944
Midsummer Day and, yes, it's her birthday again – she who scribes this page. There was a bumper post from most of the right people, and the rest, I know, are too busy. So I enjoyed all the letters that came and spent the afternoon answering some of them. Jack and I went out in the car to the butcher and the village, where I stood in a queue for peas, potatoes, asparagus and tomatoes, for this evening we had a birthday meal. And didn't we enjoy it, complete with half of the half-bottle of Graves?

Every day and night planes attack the enemy. Launching ramps at the Pas de Calais have been heavily bombed again. Nevertheless there were flying-bombs over in the night and this morning, with the sad toll of casualties and damage. In Italy the enemy's resistance has stiffened near Perugia. Our successes in Burma are being followed up.

Mrs Milburn's Diaries, edited by Peter Donnelly (1980)

OLIVER CROMWELL TO HIS WIFE

Dunbar, 4 September, 1650

For My Beloved Wife Elizabeth Cromwell,
at the Cockpit:
My Dearest,
I have not leisure to write much, but I could chide thee that in many of thy letters thou writest to me, that I should

268

not be unmindful of thee and thy little ones. Truly, if I love thee not too well, I think I err not on the other hand much. Thou are dearer to me than any creature; let that suffice.

The Lord hath showed us an exceeding mercy: who can tell how great it is . . .

THOMAS CARLYLE TO JANE WELSH CARLYLE

Chelsea, 13 July, 1846

Dearest,

I hope the Seaforth Post-Office will exert itself, and endeavour to be punctual on this occasion for once! I send thee a poor little Card-case, a small memorial of Bastille-day, and of another day also very important to me and thee! My poor little Jeannie, no heart ever wished another more truly 'many happy returns'; or if 'happy returns' are not in our vocabulary then 'wise returns', wise and true and brave, which after all are the only 'happiness', as I conjecture, that we have any right to look for in this segment of Eternity that we are traversing together, thou and I. God bless thee, Darling; and know thou always, in spite of the chimeras and delusions that thou art dearer to me than any earthly creature. That *is* a fact, if it can be of any use to thy poor soul to know. And so accept my little Gift, and kiss it as I have done; and say, In the name of Heaven it shall yet all be well; and my poor Husband *is* the man I have always known him from of old, is and will be!

I meant to write a longer Letter; but the moments are counted for me; and I am nearly roasted to death before starting. Such a passage in that Steamer: it seems to me I will never set foot in one again. I *walked* out to Addis-combe on Saturday afternoon; carrying a clean shirt and comb in my pocket; and did very well with that luggage, and indeed very well altogether; the Lady 'sick'; Baring engaged in agricultural donothingisms; nobody else there at all: a very quiet time, and even considerable sleep and rest; but this horrid baking – for two hours on the River has spoiled all! ...

Adieu Dearest
T.

FRED VINCY AND MARY GARTH LIVE
HAPPILY EVER AFTER

EVERY LIMIT IS a beginning as well as an ending. Who can quit young lives after being long in company with them, and not desire to know what befell them in their after-years? For the fragment of a life, however typical, is not the sample of an even web: promises may not be kept, and an ardent outset may be followed by declension; latent powers may find their long-waited opportunity: a past error may urge a grand retrieval.

Marriage, which has been the bourne of so many narratives, is still a great beginning, as it was to Adam and Eve, who kept their honeymoon in Eden, but had their first little one among the thorns and thistles of the wilderness. It is still the beginning of the home epic – the gradual conquest or irremediable loss of that complete union which makes the advancing years a climax, and age the harvest of sweet memories in common.

Some set out, like Crusaders of old, with a glorious equipment of hope and enthusiasm and get broken by the way, wanting patience with each other and the world.

All who have cared for Fred Vincy and Mary Garth will like to know that these two made no such failure, but achieved a solid mutual happiness. Fred surprised his neighbours in various ways. He became rather distinguished in his side of the county as a theoretic and

270

practical farmer, and produced a work on the 'Cultivation of Green Crops and the Economy of Cattle-Feeding' which won him high congratulations at agricultural meetings. In Middlemarch admiration was more reserved: most persons there were inclined to believe that the merit of Fred's authorship was due to his wife, since they had never expected Fred Vincy to write on turnips and mangel-wurzel.

But when Mary wrote a little book for her boys, called 'Stories of Great Men, taken from Plutarch,' and had it printed and published by Gripp & Co., Middlemarch, every one in the town was willing to give the credit of this work to Fred, observing that he had been to the University, "where the ancients were studied," and might have been a clergyman if he had chosen.

In this way it was made clear that Middlemarch had never been deceived, and that there was no need to praise anybody for writing a book, since it was always done by somebody else.

Moreover, Fred remained unswervingly steady. Some years after his marriage he told Mary that his happiness was half owing to Farebrother, who gave him a strong pull-up at the right moment. I cannot say that he was never again misled by his hopefulness: the yield of crops or the profits of a cattle sale usually fell below his estimate; and he was always prone to believe that he could make money by the purchase of a horse which turned out badly – though this, Mary observed, was of course the fault of the horse, not of Fred's judgment. He kept his love of horsemanship but he rarely allowed himself a day's hunting; and when he did so, it was remarkable that he submitted to be laughed at for cowardliness at the fences, seeming to see Mary and the boys sitting on the five-barred gate, or showing their curly heads between hedge and ditch.

There were three boys: Mary was not discontented that she brought forth men-children only; and when Fred

271

wished to have a girl like her, she said, laughingly, "That would be too great a trial to your mother." ...

... Fred never became rich – his hopefulness had not led him to expect that; but he gradually saved enough to become owner of the stock and furniture at Stone Court, and the work which Mr Garth put into his hands carried him in plenty through those "bad times" which are always present with farmers. Mary, in her matronly days, became as solid in figure as her mother; but, unlike her, gave the boys little formal teaching, so that Mrs Garth was alarmed lest they should never be well grounded in grammar and geography. Nevertheless, they were found quite forward enough when they went to school; perhaps, because they had liked nothing so well as being with their mother. When Fred was riding home on winter evenings he had a pleasant vision beforehand of the bright hearth in the wainscoted parlour, and was sorry for other men who could not have Mary for their wife; especially for Mr Farebrother. "He was ten times worthier of you than I was," Fred could now say to her, magnanimously. "To be sure he was," Mary answered; "and for that reason he could do better without me. But you – I shudder to think what you would have been – a curate in debt for horse-hire and cambric pocket-handkerchiefs!"

On inquiry it might possibly be found that Fred and Mary still inhabit Stone Court – that the creeping plants still cast the foam of their blossoms over the fine stone-wall into the field where the walnut-trees stand in stately row – and that on sunny days the two lovers who were first engaged with the umbrella-ring may be seen in white-haired placidity at the open window from which Mary Garth, in the days of old Peter Featherstone, had often been ordered to look out for Mr Lydgate.

George Eliot, *Middlemarch* (1871)

IN TIME OF WAR

Harold Nicolson to Vita Sackville-West:

26th May, 1940
4 King's Bench Walk, E.C.4

WHAT A GRIM interlude in our lives! The Government may decide to evacuate Kent and Sussex of all civilians. If, as I hope, they give orders instead of advice, then those orders will either be 'Go' or 'Stay'. If the former, then you know what to do. If the latter, we are faced with a great predicament. I don't think that even if the Germans occupied Sissinghurst they would harm you, in spite of the horrified dislike which they feel for me. But to be quite sure that you are not put to any humiliation, I think you really ought to have a 'bare bodkin' handy so that you can take your quietus when necessary. I shall have one also. I am not in the least afraid of such sudden and honourable death. What I dread is being tortured and humiliated. But how can we find a bodkin which will give us our quietus quickly and which is easily portable? I shall ask my doctor friends.

My dearest, I felt so close to you yesterday. We never need to put it all in words. If I believe in anything surviving, I believe in a love like ours surviving: it is all so completely unmaterial in every way.

Vita replies:

27th May, 1940
Sissinghurst

I could not trust myself to say much to you yesterday, but I expect you know what I felt. Every time we meet now, it must be in both our minds that we may possibly never meet again; but it must also be in both our minds (as you said) that we have known what few people know: a great happiness and a great unalterable love.

CHARLES DARWIN TO HIS SONS

YOU ALL KNOW your mother, and what a good mother she has ever been to all of you. She has been my greatest blessing and I can declare that in my whole life I have never heard her utter one word which I would rather have been unsaid. She has never failed in kindest sympathy towards me, and has borne with the utmost patience my frequent complaints of ill-health and discomfort. I do not believe she has ever missed an opportunity of doing a kind action to anyone near her. I marvel at my good fortune, that she, so infinitely my superior in every single moral quality, consented to be my wife. She has been my wise adviser and cheerful comforter throughout life, which without her would have been during a very long period a miserable one from ill-health. She has earned the love and admiration of every soul near her.

Charles Darwin, *Life and Letters, Including an Autobiographical Chapter* (1887)

RAMSAY AND MARGARET MacDONALD

Ramsay MacDonald (the first Labour Prime Minister, who held office in 1924 and again in 1929–31) married Margaret Gladstone in 1896.

Margaret to Aunt Elizabeth.

23 May 1897

I should like to say something to you of the blessedness I feel in [my marriage]; but it is difficult to express it in words: only it is a growing happiness as all true love ought to be.

Ramsay to Margaret.

29 May 1897
The Progressive Review

My dearest Wiffie

I am very wretched for this morning. I forgot myself –
why? I do not know, & would give anything to undo it.
This is a special day with us too. But I have been sending
telegrams all morning & think I have been receiving
them. Ever, my dearie, your own unsatisfactory man.

X X X X

[Years later, their second son Malcolm wrote of his parents' marriage:]

A ... fact about my mother's and father's partnership
deeply impressed me in my early years. This was the
superlative affection which bound them together. Their
profound love for one another made them ideal companions in their private life, whilst their zealous joint
political work made them perfect comrades in their public
lives. For a while the relationship caused me to suppose
that human existence is invariably blessed with supreme
life-long joy ...

Malcolm MacDonald, *People and Places* (1969)

TO MY DEAR AND LOVING HUSBAND

If ever two were one, then surely we.
If ever man were lov'd by wife, then thee;
If ever wife was happy in a man,
Compare with me ye women if you can.
I prize thy love more than whole Mines of gold,
Or all the riches that the East doth hold.

My love is such that Rivers cannot quench,
Nor ought but love from thee, give recompence.
Thy love is such I can no way repay,
The heavens reward thee manifold I pray.
Then while we live, in love lets so persever,
That when we live no more, we may live ever.

Ann Bradstreet (1650)

TO HIS WIFE ON THE FOURTEENTH
ANNIVERSARY OF HER WEDDING-DAY,
WITH A RING

'Thee, Mary, with this ring I wed,'
So, fourteen years ago, I said.
Behold another ring! 'For what?'
To wed thee o'er again – why not?

With that first ring I married youth,
Grace, beauty, innocence, and truth;
Taste long admired, sense long revered,
And all my Molly then appeared.

If she, by merit since disclosed,
Prove twice the woman I supposed,
I plead that double merit now,
To justify a double vow.

Here then, to-day, – with faith as sure,
With ardour as intense and pure,
As when amidst the rites divine
I took thy troth, and plighted mine, –
To thee, sweet girl, my second ring,
A token, and a pledge, I bring;
With this I wed, till death us part,
Thy riper virtues to my heart;
Those virtues which, before untried,

276

The wife has added to the bride –
Those virtues, whose progressive claim,
Endearing wedlock's very name,
My soul enjoys, my song approves,
For conscience' sake as well as love's.

For why? – They show me every hour
Honour's high thought, affection's power,
Discretion's deed, sound judgment's sentence,
And teach me all things – but repentance.

Samuel Bishop (1731–95)

JOHN HERVEY (FIRST EARL OF BRISTOL) TO ELIZABETH HERVEY

Newmarket, 3 May, 1697

My ever-new Delight

Knowing how kind a welcome all my scribbles meet with where they are addressed, neither heart nor hand can forbear, when any opportunity offers, to tell thee (tho' but by faint images of the former) how much I long to be in the place of this my harbinger, tho' perhaps thou mayst not see it but few hours before my arrival, which by the grace of God shall not be deferred one moment beyond Wednesday night; for all time is worse than lost that's spent where thou art not, thou only relish to all other pleasures. Tis you alone that sweetens life, and makes one wish the wings of time were clipt, which not only seems but really flies away too fast, much too fast, for those that love (shall I be vain and say) like us; for that instead of breeding a satiety in either, (you see I answer for you boldly,) the common fate of vulgar friendships, does but heighten the vehemence of our desires for a more intimate (if that be possible) and lasting enjoyment of each others conversation and love. Ah! my dear, how I could expatiate on this fruitful theme, were it not day-

light already, which if thou knewest, I am sure, Pray, my
dear, goe to bed, would be your request to, my dearest
life, your faithful friend and constant lover, J. Hervey

ELIZABETH HERVEY TO JOHN HERVEY

Bury, 25 October, 1697

My dear dear love,

Ye hundred things I had to say when you left me, (&
shoud endeed have so if you weir to be with me as many
years,) must now be only to repeat how much and dearly
I love you & have wanted you these few but tedious hours
you have been absent.... Though I coud dwell for ever
on this subject, yet I am sure you would be angry with
me if I did not tel ye wants those bills you left me to pay
has put me in more then I thought for; but £20 will
effectuially do my bisnes, which sum, if it is not easy for
you to send, a note for Mr. Cook to receive it at London
will do as well; for he can let me have that or any other
sum I want; but I shall nead no more.

'I TAKE PLEASURE IN IT'

The painter, William Hogarth, to his wife, Jenny:

June 6 1749

Dear Jenny

I write to you now, not because I think you may expect
it only, but because I find a pleasure in it, which is more
than I can say of writing to any body else, and I insist on
it you don't take it as a mere complement, your last letter
pleased more than I'll say, but this I will own if the
postman should knock at the door in a weeks time after

the receipt of this I shall think there is more musick in't
than the beat of a Kettle Drum, & if the words to the
tune are made by you, (to carry on metafor) and brings
news of all your coming so soon to town I shall think the
words much better than the musick, but dont hasten out
of a scene of Pleasure to make me one (I wish I could
contribute to it) you'l see by the Enclosed that I shall be
glad to make a small contributer to it. I dont know
whether or no you knew that Garrick was going to be
married to the Violette when you went away. I supt with
him last night and had a deal of talk about her. I can't
write any more than what this side will contain, you know
I wont turn over a new leaf I am so obstinate, but then I
am no less obstinate in being your affectionate Husband

Wm Hogarth

A DEDICATION TO MY WIFE

To whom I owe the leaping delight
That quickens my senses in our wakingtime
And the rhythm that governs the repose of our sleepingtime,
The breathing in unison

Of lovers whose bodies smell of each other
Who think the same thoughts without need of speech
And babble the same speech without need of meaning.

No peevish winter wind shall chill
No sullen tropic sun shall wither
The roses in the rose-garden which is ours and ours only

But this dedication is for others to read:
These are private words addressed to you in public.

T. S. Eliot (1959)

A SMALL CELEBRATION

On the wall of the south transept in the parish church of St Cuthbert, Wells, Somerset, is a simple plaque which reads as follows:

Laus Deo

In thanks for a happy married life the 15th Century ceiling over this chapel hidden by plaster for many years was uncovered and restored 1960.

E.U.O.B.   H.A.B.

'HALF A PERSON'

MAY 4TH. [1948] I quite often look back at the pleasures and pains of youth – love, jealousy, recklessness, vanity – without forgetting their spell but no longer desiring them; while middle-aged ones like music, places, botany, conversation seem to be just as enjoyable as those wilder ones, in which there was usually some potential anguish lying in wait, like a bee in a flower. I hope there may be further surprises in store, and on the whole do not fear the advance into age ...

May 5th. Ralph to London to the dentist. I have sprained my ankle so cannot go with him, but as the years pass I *hate* being parted from him even for an hour or so; I feel only half a person by myself, with one arm, one leg and half a face.

Warmer, softer, sweeter day: the birds sing very loudly and the pollarded trees on the road to Hungerford station seem to be holding little bunches of greenery in their fists.

Frances Partridge, *Everything to Lose: Diaries 1945–1960*

JEÄNE

We now mid hope vor better cheer,
My smilèn wife o' twice vive year.
Let others frown, if thou bist near
   Wi' hope upon thy brow, Jeäne;
Vor I vu'st lov'd thee when thy light
Young sheäpe vu'st grew to woman's height;
I loved thee near, an' out o'zight,
   An' I do love thee now, Jeäne.

An' we've a-trod the sheenèn bleäde,
Ov eegrass in the summer sheäde,
An' when the leäves begun to feäde
   Wi' zummer in the weäne, Jeäne;
And we've a-wander'd drough the groun'
O' swayèn wheat a-turnèn brown,
An' we've a-stroll'd together roun'
   The brook an' drough the leäne, Jeäne.

An' nwone but I can ever tell
Ov all thy tears that have a-vell
When trials meäde thy bosom zwell,
   An' nwone but thou o' mine, Jeäne;
An' now my heart, that heaved wi' pride
Back then to have thee at my zide,
Do love thee mwore as years do slide,
   An' leäve them times behind, Jeäne.

eegrass – *arrish, aftermath, after the haymaking.*

William Barnes (1879)

'MY HUSBAND LIVES IN THAT HOUSE'

In the early 1930s, years after her marriage, Virginia Woolf was talking with an old friend, Bobo Mayer, who remembered the conversation thus:

'(she) said – and as though addressing herself rather than

me: "What do you think is probably the happiest moment in one's whole life?" While I was wondering how I should answer this sudden question, she went on, with a strange but very quiet radiance in her voice: "I think it's the moment when one is walking in one's garden, perhaps picking off a few dead flowers, and suddenly one thinks: My husband lives in that house – And he loves me." Her face shone as I had never seen it.'

George Spater and Ian Parsons, *A Marriage of True Minds*
(1977)

MRS LEO HUNTER

"MY WIFE, SIR – MRS. LEO HUNTER – is proud to number among her acquaintance all those who have rendered themselves celebrated by their works and talents.   Permit me, sir, to place in a conspicuous part of the list the name of Mr. Pickwick, and his brother-members of the club that derives its name from him."

"I shall be extremely happy to make the acquaintance of such a lady, sir," replied Mr. Pickwick.

"You *shall* make it, sir," said the grave man.   "To-morrow morning, sir, we give a public breakfast – a *fête champêtre* – to a great number of those who have rendered themselves celebrated by their works and talents.   Permit Mrs. Leo Hunter, sir, to have the gratification of seeing you at the Den."

"With great pleasure," replied Mr. Pickwick.

"Mrs. Leo Hunter has many of these breakfasts, sir," resumed the new acquaintance – " 'feasts of reason,' sir, 'and flows of soul,' as somebody who wrote a sonnet to Mrs. Leo Hunter on her breakfasts, feelingly and orig-inally observed."

"Was *he* celebrated for his works and talents?" inquired Mr. Pickwick.

"He was, sir," replied the grave man, "all Mrs. Leo

Hunter's acquaintances are; it is her ambition, sir, to have no other acquaintance."

"It is a very noble ambition," said Mr. Pickwick.

"When I inform Mrs. Leo Hunter, that that remark fell from *your* lips, sir, she will indeed be proud," said the grave man. "You have a gentleman in your train, who has produced some beautiful little poems, I think, sir."

"My friend Mr. Snodgrass has a great taste for poetry," replied Mr. Pickwick.

"So has Mrs. Leo Hunter, sir. She dotes on poetry, sir. She adores it; I may say that her whole soul and mind are wound up, and entwined with it. She has produced some delightful pieces, herself, sir. You may have met with her 'Ode to an Expiring Frog,' sir."

"I don't think I have," said Mr. Pickwick.

"You astonish me, sir," said Mr. Leo Hunter. "It created an immense sensation. It was signed with an 'L' and eight stars, and appeared originally in a lady's magazine. It commenced —

> *'Can I view thee panting, lying*
> *On thy stomach, without sighing;*
> *Can I unmoved see thee dying*
> > *On a log,*
> *Expiring frog!'"*

"Beautiful!" said Mr. Pickwick.

"Fine," said Mr. Leo Hunter; "so simple."

"Very," said Mr. Pickwick.

"The next verse is still more touching. Shall I repeat it?"

"If you please," said Mr. Pickwick.

"It runs thus," said the grave man, still more gravely,

> *" 'Say, have fiends in shape of boys,*
> *With wild halloo, and brutal noise,*
> *Hunted thee from marshy joys,*
> > *With a dog,*
> *Expiring frog!'" '*

"Finely expressed," said Mr. Pickwick.

"All point, sir," said Mr. Leo Hunter; "but you shall hear Mrs. Leo Hunter repeat it. *She* can do justice to it, sir. She will repeat it, in character, sir, to-morrow morning."

"In character!"

"As Minerva."

Charles Dickens, *The Pickwick Papers* (1837)

'OPEN AND TRUE'

MY LOVE FOR HIM never lost its passionate intensity. My letters to him were love-letters, and his home coming meant for me to be lifted into Heaven.

We cannot say why we love people. There is no reason for passionate love. But the quality in him that I most admired was his sincerity. There was never any pretence between us. All was open and true. Often he was bitter and cruel, but I could bear it because I knew all. There was nothing left for me to guess at, no lies, no falsity. All was known, all was suffered and endured; and afterwards there was no reserve in our joy. If we love deeply we must also suffer deeply; for the price for the capacity for ecstatic joy is anguish. And so it was with us to the end.

Helen Thomas, *World Without End* (1931)

TIGER-SHOOTING

'MY VIEW WOULD BE husband first, if the children are all right. You are responsible for your children and you love them, your job with them is to get them to the point where they lead their own lives. *Your* life is with your husband, not just while the children are there, but afterwards, too. That's the most important bonding, and that's the way we've always played it.

'What do I get from marriage? My whole life, travel, fascinating things. I'd be highly unlikely to have become Foreign Secretary myself, and I can't imagine arriving at the sort of job with those opportunities any other way.

'I don't think within a marriage one even needs to ask if they love you because you jolly well know they do. You need reassurances now and then, but you *know*. And, of course, in the early days it was more physically expressed and more continuously expressed, but in a way it's rather nicer later on because it's a part of your whole life: mutual love and respect.

'Geoffrey does need less sleep than me. When the children were young he was marvellous, he would amuse them, as I got up gradually. I don't think it matters needing different amounts of sleep as long as you sometimes get in the same bed together!

'I can't imagine myself married to anyone else. Geoffrey is very solid, that's the wrong word, it sounds boring and he's by no means boring. He's got a good grasp of what is right and just and what should be striven for. That's what makes him tick. The tiger-shooting syndrome is an interesting one: if you were tiger-shooting and something went wrong, would you be saved by the person you went with? I'd go tiger-shooting with Geoffrey.'

Lady Elspeth Howe, wife of Sir Geoffrey Howe (1988)

HUSBAND TO WIFE: PARTY GOING

Turn where the stairs bend
In this other house; statued in other light,
Allow the host to ease you from your coat.
Stand where the stairs bend,
A formal distance from me, then descend
With delicacy conscious but not false
And take my arm, as if I were someone else.

Tonight, in a strange room
We will be strangers: let our eyes be blind
To all our customary stances –
Remark how well I'm groomed,
I will explore your subtly-voiced nuances
Where delicacy is conscious but not false,
And take your hand, as if you were someone else.

Home forgotten, rediscover
Among chirruping of voices, chink of glass,
Those simple needs that turned us into lovers,
How solitary was the wilderness
Until we met, took leave of hosts and guests,
And with delicate consciousness of what was false
Walked off together, as if there were no one else.

Brian Jones (1966)

MR AND MRS RAMSAY IN LOVE

BUT SHE WAS BECOMING conscious of her husband looking at her. He was smiling at her, quizzically, as if he were ridiculing her gently for being asleep in broad daylight, but at the same time he was thinking, Go on reading. You don't look sad now, he thought. And he wondered what she was reading, and exaggerated her ignorance, her simplicity, for he liked to think that she was not clever, not book-learned at all. He wondered if she understood what she was reading. Probably not, he thought. She was astonishingly beautiful. Her beauty seemed to him, if that were possible, to increase.

> *Yet seem'd it winter still, and, you away,*
> *As with your shadow I with these did play,*

she finished.

'Well?' she said, echoing his smile dreamily, looking up from her book.

> *As with your shadow I with these did play,*

she murmured putting the book on the table.

What had happened she wondered, as she took up her knitting, since she had last seen him alone? She remembered dressing, and seeing the moon; Andrew holding his plate too high at dinner; being depressed by something William had said; the birds in the trees; the sofa on the landing; the children being awake; Charles Tansley waking them with his books falling – oh no, that she had invented; and Paul having a wash-leather case for his watch. Which should she tell him about?

'They're engaged,' she said, beginning to knit, 'Paul and Minta.'

'So I guessed,' he said. There was nothing very much to be said about it. Her mind was still going up and down, up and down with the poetry; he was still feeling very vigorous, very forthright, after reading about Steenie's funeral. So they sat silent. Then she became aware that she wanted him to say something.

Anything, anything, she thought, going on with her knitting. Anything will do.

'How nice it would be to marry a man with a wash-leather bag for his watch,' she said, for that was the sort of joke they had together.

He snorted. He felt about this engagement as he always felt about any engagement; the girl is much too good for that young man. Slowly it came into her head, why is it then that one wants people to marry? What was the value, the meaning of things? (Every word they said now would be true.) Do say something, she thought, wishing only to hear his voice. For the shadow, the thing folding them in was beginning, she felt, to close round her again. Say anything, she begged, looking at him, as if for help.

He was silent, swinging the compass on his watch-chain to and fro, and thinking of Scott's novels and Balzac's novels. But through the crepuscular walls of their intimacy, for they were drawing together, involuntarily, coming side by side, quite close, she could feel his mind like a raised hand shadowing her mind; and he was beginning now that her thoughts took a turn he disliked – towards this 'pessimism' as he called it – to fidget, though he said nothing, raising his hand to his forehead, twisting a lock of hair, letting it fall again.

'You won't finish that stocking tonight,' he said, pointing to her stocking. That was what she wanted – the asperity in his voice reproving her. If he says it's wrong to be pessimistic probably it is wrong, she thought; the marriage will turn out all right.

'No,' she said, flattening the stocking out upon her knee, 'I shan't finish it.'

And what then? For she felt that he was still looking at her, but that his look had changed. He wanted something – wanted the thing she always found it so difficult to give him; wanted her to tell him that she loved him. And that, no, she could not do. He found talking so much easier than she did. He could say things – she never could.

So naturally it was always he that said the things, and then for some reason he would mind this suddenly, and would reproach her. A heartless woman he called her; she never told him that she loved him. But it was not so – it was not so. It was only that she never could say what she felt. Was there no crumb on his coat? Nothing she could do for him? Getting up she stood at the window with the reddish-brown stocking in her hands, partly to turn away from him, partly because she did not mind looking now, with him watching, at the Lighthouse. For she knew that he had turned his head as she turned; he was watching her. She knew that he was thinking, You are more beautiful than ever. And she felt very beautiful. Will you not tell me just for once that you love me? He was thinking that, for he was roused, what with Minta and his book, and its being the end of the day and their having quarrelled about going to the Lighthouse. But she could not do it; she could not say it. Then, knowing that he was watching her, instead of saying anything she turned, holding her stocking, and looked at him. And as she looked at him she began to smile, for though she had not said a word, he knew, of course, that she loved him. He could not deny it. And smiling she looked out of the window and said (thinking to herself, Nothing on earth can equal this happiness) –

'Yes, you were right. It's going to be wet tomorrow.' She had not said it, but he knew it. And she looked at him smiling. For she had triumphed again.

Virginia Woolf, *To The Lighthouse* (1927)

NATÁSHA AND PIERRE

"I love you awfully!" Natásha suddenly said. "Awfully, awfully!"

"No, he would not have approved," said Pierre, after reflection. "What he would have approved of is our family life. He was always so anxious to find seemliness, happiness, and peace in everything, and I should have been proud to let him see us. There now – you talk of my absence, but you wouldn't believe what a special feeling I have for you after a separation. . . ."

"Yes, I should think . . ." Natásha began.

"No, it's not that. I never leave off loving you. And one couldn't love more, but this is something special. . . . Yes, of course –" he did not finish because their eyes meeting said the rest.

"What nonsense it is," Natásha suddenly exclaimed, "about honeymoons, and that the greatest happiness is at first! On the contrary, now is the best of all."

Leo Tolstoy, *War and Peace* (1863/9)

MY WIFE

Trusty, dusky, vivid, true,
With eyes of gold and bramble-dew,
Steel true and blade-straight,
The great artificer
Made my mate.

Honour, anger, valour, fire,
A love that life could never tire,
Death quench or evil stir;
The mighty master
Gave to her.

Teacher, tender, comrade, wife,
A fellow-farer true through life,
Heart-whole and soul-free,
The august father
Gave to me.

Robert Louis Stevenson
(1896)

THE AUTHOR TO HIS WIFE, OF A WOMAN'S ELOQUENCE

My Mall, I mark that when you mean to prove me
To buy a velvet gown, or some rich border,
Thou call'st me good sweet heart, thou swear'st to
*   love me,*
Thy locks, thy lips, thy looks, speak all in order,
Thou think'st, and right thou think'st, that these
*   do move me,*
That all these severally thy suit do further:
*   But shall I tell thee what most thy suit advances?*
*   Thy fair smooth words? no, no, thy fair smooth*
*   haunches*

Sir John Harington (1596)

LOVE'S VISION

There is no happy life
But in a wife;
The comforts are so sweet
When they do meet:
'Tis plenty, peace, a calm
Like dropping balm:
Love's weather is so fair,
Perfumèd air,
Each word such pleasure brings
Like soft-touched strings;
Love's passion moves the heart
On either part.
Such harmony together,
So pleased in either,
No discords, concords still,
Sealed with one will.
By love, God man made one,
Yet not alone:
Like stamps of king and queen
It may be seen,
Two figures but one coin;
So they do join,
Only they not embrace,
We face to face.

William Cavendish,
Duke of Newcastle
(17th century)

LETTER FROM OSCAR WILDE TO HIS WIFE

The Balmoral,
Edinburgh, Tuesday.
(postmarked 16th December, 1884)

Dear and Beloved,

Here am I, and you at the Antipodes. O excrable facts, that keep our lips from kissing, though our souls are one.

What can I tell you by letter? Alas! nothing that I would tell you. The messages of the gods to each other travel not by pen and ink and indeed your bodily presence here would not make you more real: for I feel your fingers in my hair and your cheek brushing mine.

The air is full of the music of your voice, my soul and body seem no longer mine, but mingled in some exquisite ecstasy with yours. I feel incomplete without you.

Ever and ever yours
Oscar

Here I stay till Sunday.

PERFECT WOMAN

She was a phantom of delight
When first she gleam'd upon my sight;
A lovely apparition, sent
To be a moment's ornament;
Her eyes as stars of twilight fair;
Like twilight's, too, her dusky hair;
But all things else about her drawn
From May-time and the cheerful dawn;
A dancing shape, an image gay,
To haunt, to startle, and waylay.

I saw her upon nearer view,
A Spirit, yet a Woman too!

Her household motions light and free,
And steps of virgin liberty;
A countenance in which did meet
Sweet records, promises as sweet;
A creature not too bright or good
For human nature's daily food;
For transient sorrows, simple wiles,
Praise, blame, love, kisses, tears, and smiles.

And now I see with eye serene
The very pulse of the machine;
A being breathing thoughtful breath,
A traveller between life and death;
The reason firm, the temperate will,
Endurance, foresight, strength, and skill;
A perfect Woman, nobly plann'd,
To warn, to comfort, and command;
And yet a Spirit still, and bright
With something of angelic light.

William Wordsworth (1804)

SIR WINSTON CHURCHILL TO HIS WIFE, CLEMENTINE

10 November 1909
You ought to trust me for I do not love and will never love any woman in the world but you, and my chief desire is to link myself to you week by week by bonds which shall ever become more intimate and profound.

Beloved I kiss your memory – your sweetness and beauty have cast a glory upon my life.

You will find me always
Your loving and
devoted husband W

294

from THE TUNNYNG OF ELYNOUR
RUMMYNGE

This is so short there seems no point in 'translating' it, since the
original *looks*, as well as sounds, so rumbustiously coarse.

> *Beholde, she sayde, and se*
> *How bryght I am of ble!*
> *Ich am not cast away,*
> *That can my husband say,*
> *Whan we kys and play*
> *In lust and in lykyng;*
> *He calleth me his whytyng,*
> *His mullyng and his mytyng,*
> *His nobbes and his conny,*
> *His swetyng and his honny,*
> *With Bas, my pretty bonny*
> *Thou art worth good and monny,*
> *This make I my falyre fonny,*
> *Til that he dreme and dronny;*
> *For, after all our sport,*
> *Than wyll he rout and snort;*
> *Than swetely together we ly,*
> *As two pygges in a sty.*

John Skelton (16th century)

MR AND MRS CHERRY OWEN HAVE
BREAKFAST

MR AND MRS CHERRY OWEN, in their Donkey
Street room that is bedroom, parlour, kitchen, and
scullery, sit down to last night's supper of onions boiled

295

in their overcoats and broth of spuds and baconrind and leeks and bones.

MRS C. O.:   See that smudge on the wall by the picture of Auntie Blossom? That's where you threw the sago.

                (Cherry Owen laughs with delight)
You only missed me by an inch.

CHERRY O.:   I always miss Auntie Blossom too.

MRS C. O.:   Remember last night? In you reeled, my boy, as drunk as a deacon with a big wet bucket and a fish-frail full of stout and you looked at me and you said, 'God has come home!' you said, and then over the bucket you went, sprawling and bawling, and the floor was all flagons and eels.

CHERRY O.:   Was I wounded?

MRS C.O.:   And then you took off your trousers and you said, 'Does anybody want a fight!' Oh, you old baboon.

CHERRY O.:   Give me a kiss.

MRS C. O.:   And then you sang 'Bread of Heaven', tenor and bass.

CHERRY O.:   I *always* sing 'Bread of Heaven'.

MRS C. O.:   And then you did a little dance on the table.

CHERRY O.:   I did?

MRS. C. O.:   Drop dead!

CHERRY O.:   And then what did I do?

MRS C. O.:   Then you cried like a baby and said you were a poor drunk orphan with nowhere to go but the grave.

CHERRY O.:   And what did I do next, my dear?

MRS C. O.:   Then you danced on the table all over again and said you were King Solomon Owen and I was your Mrs Sheba.

CHERRY O.:   And then?

MRS C. O.: And then I got you into bed and you snored
all night like a brewery.
(Mr and Mrs Cherry Owen laugh delightedly
together)

Dylan Thomas, *Under Milk Wood* (1954)

WHEN SEX HAS DIED OUT

IT'S NOT TILL SEX HAS DIED out between a man
and a woman that they can really love. And now I
mean affection. Now I mean to be *fond of* (as one is fond
of oneself) – to hope, to be disappointed, to live inside
the other heart. When I look back on the pain of sex, the
love like a wild fox so ready to bite, the antagonism that
sits like a twin beside love, and contrast it with affection,
so deeply unrepeatable, of two people who have lived a
life together (and of whom one must die), it's the affection
I find richer. It's that I would have again. Not all those
doubtful rainbow colours (But then she's old, one must
say).

Enid Bagnold, *Autobiography* (1969)

SO SWEET LOVE SEEMED

So sweet love seemed that April morn,
When first we kissed beside the thorn
So strangely sweet, it was not strange
We thought that love could never change.

But I can tell – let truth be told –
That love will change in growing old;
Though day by day is nought to see,
So delicate his motions be.

297

And in the end 'twill come to pass
Quite to forget what once he was
Nor even in fancy to recall
The pleasure that was all in all.

His little spring, that sweet we found,
So deep in summer floods is drowned
I wonder, bathed in joy complete,
How love so young could be so sweet.

Robert Bridges (1844–1930)

CONJUGAL CONSPIRACY

SHE CLUNG TO HER HUSBAND. And it was just at the time when he needed her most, because he suffered the disadvantage of being ten years ahead of her as he stumbled alone through the mists of old age, with the even greater disadvantage of being a man and weaker than she was. In the end they knew each other so well that by the time they had been married for thirty years they were like a single divided being, and they felt uncomfortable at the frequency with which they guessed each other's thoughts without intending to, or the ridiculous accident of one of them anticipating in public what the other was going to say. Together they had overcome the daily incomprehension, the instantaneous hatred, the reciprocal nastiness and fabulous flashes of glory in the conjugal conspiracy. It was the time when they loved each other best, without hurry or excess, when both were most conscious of and grateful for their incredible victories over adversity. Life would still present them with other mortal trials, of course, but that no longer mattered: they were on the other shore.

Gabriel García Márquez, *Love in the Time of Cholera* (1988)

O FAIN WOULD I, BEFORE I DIE

O, fain would I, before I die,
Bequeath to thee a legacy,
That thou may'st say, when I am gone,
None had my heart but thee alone!
Had I as many hearts as hairs,
As many lives as lovers' fears,
As many lives as years have hours,
They all and only should be yours!

Dearest, before you condescend
To entertain a bosom-friend,
Be sure you know your servant well
Before your liberty you sell:
For love's a fire in young and old,
'Tis sometimes hot and sometimes cold,
And now you know that, when they please,
They can be sick of love's disease.

Then wisely choose a friend that may
Last for an age, and not a day,
Who loves thee not for lip or eye,
But for thy mutual sympathy.
Let such a friend thy heart engage,
For he will comfort thee in age,
And kiss thy wrinkled, furrowed brow
With as much joy as I do now.

Anon: from *Westminster Drollery* (17th
century)

QUIET SONG IN TIME OF CHAOS

Here
Is home.
Is peace.
Is quiet.

Here
Is love
That sits by the hearth
And smiles into the fire,
As into a memory
Of happiness,
As into the eyes
Of quiet.

Here
Is faith
That can be silent.
It is not afraid of silence.
It knows happiness
Is a deep pool
Of quiet.

Here
Sadness, too,
Is quiet.
Is the earth's sadness
On autumn afternoons
When days grow short,
And the year grows old,
When frost is in the air,
And suddenly one notices
Time's hair
Has grown whiter.

Here?
Where is here?
But you understand.

In my heart
Within your heart
Is home.
Is peace.
Is quiet.

Eugene O'Neill
(1888–1953) to
Carlotta on her
birthday

COURTESY

I AM BY NATURE CONVENTIONAL and straightforward, but Yün was a stickler for forms, like the Confucian schoolmasters. Whenever I put on a dress for her or tidied up her sleeves, she would say 'So much obliged' again and again, and when I passed her a trowel or a fan, she must receive it standing up. At first I disliked this and said to her: 'Do you mean to tie me down with all this ceremony? There is a proverb which says, "One who is overcourteous is crafty."' Yün blushed all over and said: 'I am merely trying to be polite and respectful; why do you charge me with craftiness?' 'True respect is in the heart, and does not require such empty forms,' said I, but Yün said, 'There is no more intimate relationship than that between children and their parents. Do you mean to say that children should behave freely towards their parents and keep their respect only in their heart?' 'Oh! I was only joking,' I said. 'The trouble is,' said Yün, 'most marital troubles begin with joking. Don't you accuse me of disrespect later, for then I shall die of grief without being able to defend myself.' Then I held her close to my breast and caressed her and then she smiled. From then on our conversations were full of "I'm sorry's" and "I beg your pardon's." And so we remained courteous

301

to each other for twenty-three years of our married life like Liang Hung and Meng Kuang of old, and the longer we stayed together, the more passionately attached we became to each other. Whenever we met each other in the house, whether it be in a dark room or in a narrow corridor, we used to hold each other's hands and ask: "Where are you going?" and we did this on the sly as if afraid that people might see us. As a matter of fact, we tried at first to avoid being seen sitting or walking together, but after a while, we did not mind it any more. When Yün was sitting and talking with somebody and saw me come, she would rise and move sideways for me to sit down together with her. All this was done naturally almost without any consciousness, and although at first we felt uneasy about it, later on it became a matter of habit. I cannot understand why all old couples must hate each other like enemies. Some people say "if they weren't enemies, they would not be able to live together until old age." Well, I wonder!

Shen Fu, *Wedded Bliss*

A CHURCH ROMANCE

She turned in the high pew, until her sight
Swept the west gallery, and caught its row
Of music-men with viol, book, and bow
Against the sinking sad tower-window light.

She turned again; and in her pride's despite
One strenuous viol's inspirer seemed to throw
A message from his string to her below,
Which said: 'I claim thee as my own forthright!'

Thus their hearts' bond began, in due time signed.
And long years thence, when Age had scared Romance,

At some old attitude of his or glance
That gallery-scene would break upon her mind,
With him as minstrel, ardent, young, and trim,
Bowing 'New Sabbath' or 'Mount Ephraim'.

Thomas Hardy (c. 1835)

from BY THE FIRESIDE

XXI

My perfect wife, my Lèonor,
*   Oh, heart my own, oh, eyes, mine too,*
Whom else could I dare look backward for,
*   With whom beside should I dare pursue*
The path grey heads abhor?

XXII

For it leads to a crag's sheer edge with them;
*   Youth, flowery all the way, there stops –*
Not they; age threatens and they contemn,
*   Till they reach the gulf wherein youth drops,*
One inch from our life's safe hem!

XXIII

With me, youth led ... I will speak now,
*   No longer watch you as you sit*
Reading by fire-light, that great brow
*   And the spirit-small hand propping it,*
Mutely, my heart knows how –

XXIV

When, if I think but deep enough,
*   You are wont to answer, prompt as rhyme;*
And you, too, find without a rebuff
*   The response your soul seeks many a time*
Piercing its fine flesh-stuff.

303

XXV

My own, confirm me! If I tread
  This path back, is it not in pride
To think how little I dreamed it led
  To an age so blest that by its side
Youth seems the waste instead?

XXVI

My own, see where the years conduct!
  At first, 'twas something our two souls
Should mix as mists do; each is sucked
  Into each now: on, the new stream rolls,
Whatever rocks obstruct.

XXVII

Think, when our one soul understands
  The great Word which makes all things new —
When earth breaks up and Heaven expands —
  How will the change strike me and you
In the House not made with hands?

XXVIII

Oh, I must feel your brain prompt mine,
  Your heart anticipate my heart,
You must be just before, in fine,
  See and make me see, for your part,
New depths of the Divine!

XXIX

But who could have expected this,
  When we two drew together first
Just for the obvious human bliss,
  To satisfy life's daily thirst
With a thing men seldom miss?

Robert Browning (1864)

'KILL ME TOO'

Julius Fucik, a journalist, was born in Prague on 23rd February, 1903, and was among the leaders of the Communist resistance movement in Czechoslovakia. He was arrested by the Gestapo on 24th April, 1942, and executed on 8th September, 1943. Notes he made during his imprisonment were found subsequently, amongst which was this:

I T WAS DURING the period of martial law. The middle of June of last year. She was seeing me for the first time since our arrest, after six weeks of suffering spent in solitude in her cell, brooding over reports that announced my death. They called her in to soften me up.

'Talk to him,' the division chief said to her on confronting her with me. 'Urge him to be reasonable. If he won't think of himself, he might at least think of you. You have an hour to think it over. If he is still obdurate after that, you will be shot tonight. Both of you.'

She caressed me with her glance and answered simply: 'Officer, that's no threat for me, that's my last wish: If you are going to kill him, Kill me too.'

MY OLD DUTCH

I've got a pal,
A reg'lar out an' outer:
She's a dear good old gal,
I'll tell yer all about 'er;
It's many years since fust we met,
'Er 'air was then as black as jet,
It's whiter now, but she don't fret,

305

Not my old gal . . .
We've been together now for forty years,
An' it don't seem a day too much,
There ain't a lady livin' in the land,
As I'd swap for my dear old Dutch.
There ain't a lady livin' in the land,
As I'd swap for my dear old Dutch.

Albert Chevalier, popular song
(c. 1900)

JOHN ANDERSON, MY JO

John Anderson, my jo, John,
 When we were first acquent;
Your locks were like the raven,
 Your bonie brow was brent;
But now your brow is beld, John,
 Your locks are like the snaw;
But blessings on your frosty pow,
 John Anderson, my jo.

John Anderson, my jo, John,
 We clamb the hill thegither;
And mony a cantie day, John,
 We've had wi' ane anither:
Now we maun totter down, John,
 And hand in hand we'll go,
And sleep thegither at the foot,
 John Anderson, my jo.

Robert Burns (1780s)

CELEBRATIONS

'I MUST NOT TELL HOW DEAR YOU ARE TO ME'

In the middle of the Second World War, Vita Sackville-West wrote for Harold Nicolson a poem which was read by the Poet Laureate, Cecil Day-Lewis, at their joint memorial service in 1968:

I must not tell how dear you are to me.
It is unknown, a secret from myself
Who should know best. I would not if I could
Expose the meaning of such mystery.

I loved you then, when love was Spring, and May.
Eternity is here and now, I thought;
The pure and perfect moment briefly caught
As in your arms, but still a child, I lay.

Loved you when summer deepened into June
And those fair, wild, ideal dreams of youth
Were true yet dangerous and half unreal
As when Endymion kissed the mateless moon.

But now when autumn yellows all the leaves
And thirty seasons mellow our long love,
How rooted, how secure, how strong, how rich,
How full the barn that holds our garnered sheaves!

307

REVERBERATIONS

'... till death us do part'

'I can't bear to think that one of us will have to die first.'
'Nor can I.'
'Let's not think about it.'
You say that when you are first in love, first married; then as the years pass you stop saying it, because you are forced to think about it. You hear of a young woman you once met, a beautiful young mother in her thirties, who has sickened and died within nine months, leaving her husband inconsolable. An old friend dies, a man of eighty-six who met his wife when they were in their teens – and you visit his widow, bowed a little but trying to be cheerful, still talking about him in the present tense...

Then the soul trembles, as it always has, at the thought of the one goodbye that must be the last.

Few of us want to be the one to remain, though we might hesitate to confess such selfishness. Yet the questions that flicker through the mind before marriage ('How will it be for *me*?') are rephrased into 'What will I do, left alone? How will I cope?', after death brings its own divorce. Perhaps the fear of loneliness is what has kept the pair together all those years. The heart has its reasons, some of which may only start to make sense afterwards, in memory, when at last we realise (with great joy as well as grief) the truth about the life of the spirit.
(*Essence of dead rose petals in a still room.*)

JANET DEMPSTER FORGIVES HER BRUTAL HUSBAND

R OBERT WOULD GET BETTER; this illness might alter him; he would be a long time feeble, needing help, walking with a crutch, perhaps. She would wait on him with such tenderness, such all-forgiving love, that the old harshness and cruelty must melt away for ever under the heart-sunshine she would pour around him. Her bosom heaved at the thought, and delicious tears fell. Janet's was a nature in which hatred and revenge could find no place; the long bitter years drew half their bitterness from her ever-living remembrance of the too short years of love that went before; and the thought that her husband would ever put his hand to his lips again, and recall the days when they sat on the grass together, and he laid scarlet poppies on her black hair, and called her his gypsy queen, seemed to send a tide of loving oblivion over all the harsh and stony space they had traversed since. The Divine Love that had already shone upon her would be with her; she would lift up her soul continually for help; Mr Tryan, she knew, would pray for her. If she felt herself failing, she would confess it to him at once; if her feet began to slip, there was that stay for her to cling to. Oh, she could never be drawn back into that cold damp vault of sin and despair again; she had felt the morning sun, she had tasted the sweet pure air of trust and penitence and submission.

*

There was profound stillness in the house. She heard no sound but her husband's breathing and the ticking of the watch on the mantelpiece. The candle, placed high up, shed a soft light down on the one object she cared to see. There was a smell of brandy in the room; it was given to her husband from time to time; but this smell,

which at first had produced in her a faint shuddering
sensation, was now becoming indifferent to her: she did
not even perceive it; she was too unconscious of herself
to feel either temptations or accusations. She only felt
that the husband of her youth was dying; far, far out of
her reach, as if she were standing helpless on the shore,
while he was sinking in the black storm-waves; she only
yearned for one moment in which she might satisfy the
deep forgiving pity of her soul by one look of love, one
word of tenderness.

Her sensations and thoughts were so persistent that she
could not measure the hours, and it was a surprise to her
when the nurse put out the candle, and let in the faint
morning light. Mrs Raynor, anxious about Janet, was
already up, and now brought in some fresh coffee for her;
and Mr Pilgrim having awaked, had hurried on his clothes,
and was come in to see how Dempster was.

This change from candle-light to morning, this recom-
mencement of the same round of things that had happened
yesterday, was a discouragement rather than a relief to
Janet. She was more conscious of her chill weariness;
the new light thrown on her husband's face seemed to
reveal the still work that death had been doing through
the night; she felt her last lingering hope that he would
ever know her again forsake her.

But now, Mr Pilgrim, having felt the pulse, was putting
some brandy in a tea-spoon between Dempster's lips;
the brandy went down, and his breathing became
freer. Janet noticed the change, and her heart beat faster
as she leaned forward to watch him. Suddenly a slight
movement, like the passing away of a shadow was visible
in his face, and he opened his eyes full on Janet.

It was almost like meeting him again on the resurrection
morning, after the night of the grave.

'Robert, do you know me?'

He kept his eyes fixed on her, and there was a faintly
perceptible motion of the lips, as if he wanted to speak.

310

But the moment of speech was for ever gone – the moment for asking pardon of her, if he wanted to ask it. Could he read the full forgiveness that was written in her eyes? She never knew; for, as she was bending to kiss him, the thick veil of death fell between them, and her lips touched a corpse.

George Eliot, *Janet's Repentance* (1857)

from CLEARANCES

In the last minutes he said more to her
Almost than in all their life together.
'You'll be in New Row on Monday night
And I'll come up for you and you'll be glad
When I walk in the door ... Isn't that right?'
His head was bent down to her propped-up head.
She could not hear but we were overjoyed.
He called her good and girl. Then she was dead,
The searching for a pulsebeat was abandoned
And we all knew one thing by being there.
The space we stood around had been emptied
Into us to keep, it penetrated
Clearances that suddenly stood open.
High cries were felled and a pure change happened.

Seamus Heaney (1987)

THE DEATH OF RALPH PARTRIDGE

November 28th, 1960 ... Last night before dinner I missed Ralph for a while. For the thousandth time I wondered, 'Is he all right? Could he perhaps be feeling ill?' Usually after the first panic and wild wobblings on my base, my equilibrium has been restored. This time, however, I felt it was odd that he should be in the library at this cold

311

evening hour. I ran upstairs and found him lying down. No, he was *not* all right. Going through the kitchen to look at the stove he had suddenly felt a constriction in the chest, like two bars. He took a pill and then another, but remained limp and drowsy, wanting no food and unable to face the company. I am in a spurious way so armoured against these set-backs that a dreadful unearthly calm settled down on me, partly to make me able to face his dread of my 'fussing'. But along with this grey *tristesse* was the awareness of a huge crater opening, black and menacing. Paralysed in mind and hardly able to talk, I went downstairs and cooked dinner and somehow sketched a part in the conversation until the meal was over, when I was able to go up and lie beside Ralph.

This morning he swears he is better, but is in no great hurry to get up. We must 'greet the unknown' with all possible common-sense, but I am full of doubts which I cannot voice to him.

November 29th. Throughout yesterday I sank slowly into the pit, as it became gradually clear to me that 'something or other' did happen in the stove-room on Sunday night. Ralph was comatose and fighting a desperate rearguard action against admitting himself ill. He becomes furious (frighteningly so, because bad for him) if I treat him as such, and I identify myself so completely with him that the difficulty of overriding the line he has decided to take is almost insuperable . . .

November 30th. But last night was much worse than my fears. I dropped into exhausted sleep, but soon awoke and listened to Ralph's struggling breathing for four hours, while the clock snailed round its course. But why describe such agony? We are both alive this morning – that's all I can say.

Morning calls to Red-beard and Geoff, visits from Red-beard – but I have antagonized him, I see. There is something so futile about him, and I couldn't bear the snobbish reluctance he showed to get into touch with the Reading specialist who unfortunately happens to be a Lord. Yet to some extent we depend on him, and I try to choke back my horror that this little mannikin should be relevant to the health and safety of my darling Ralph. I pressed on, screaming silently from every cranny of my brain, until I got him to arrange for the lordly cardiologist to come tomorrow. Geoff seemed to take things more seriously when I described Ralph's breathing. It seems that he took two sleeping-pills while I dozed last night, one seeming insufficient, and Geoff thought this might have affected his breathing. He has recommended a new sort for tonight. I dashed in to Hungerford to get them. Not available, I have ordered them to be brought out by taxi from Newbury, and we have got them now.

Ralph does seem a little better this evening and with more appetite for his supper. He has even read more. I went downstairs while he was eating, and listened to Berlioz' *Symphonie Fantastique* on the wireless without much pleasure. I left Ralph a walking-stick to bang on the floor if he wanted me – but I never expected to hear, nor shall I ever forget that dreadful 'thump, thump, thump' . . .

December 1st. Now I am *absolutely alone and for ever.*

Frances Partridge, *Everything to Lose: Diaries 1945–1960*

THIS IS THE LAST NIGHT

This is the last night that my love is here;
I will not sleep, I'll sit beside my dear,

Watching the worn face that I know so well,
Staring the thoughts out that no words can tell.

313

He does not speak, he gives no sign; the room
Familiar chills me, is no more a home.

Tomorrow we shall ride away, not side
By side now, but apart, like groom and bride

To church, to start another life; yes, there
I'll lose my being, alter into air,

Watch, far away, a woman stand or kneel,
Hear, absently, her voice of muffled steel,

Then, after, see her slowly turn, go back,
Unlock the door, take off her new-bought black,

And set about to do what must be done
In the still house where she now lives alone ...

This is the last night that my love is here;
He sees me not; I sit and dumbly stare.

Elizabeth Daryush (1971)

LAST LETTER

Nadezhda Mandelstam met her husband, the poet Osip Mandelstam, in May 1919. In May 1938 she watched as Stalin's secret police took him away in a truck, never to be seen again.

THIS LETTER WAS NEVER read by the person it is addressed to. It is written on two sheets of very poor paper. Millions of women wrote such letters – to their husbands, sons, brothers, fathers, or simply to sweethearts. But next to none of them have been preserved. If such things ever survived here, it could only be owing to chance, or a miracle. My letter still exists by chance. I wrote it in October 1938, and in January I learned that M. was dead. It was thrown into a trunk with other papers and lay there for nearly thirty years. I came across it the last time I went through all my papers, gladdened by every scrap of something that had survived, and lamenting all the huge, irreparable losses. I read it not at once, but only several years later. When I did, I thought, of all the other women who shared my fate. The vast majority of them thought as I, but many dared not admit it even to themselves. Nobody has yet told the story of what was done to us by other people – by those selfsame compatriots whom I do not wish to see destroyed, lest I thereby come to resemble them. Their present-day successors, the spiritual brothers of those who murdered M. and millions of others, will curse on reading this letter – why didn't they destroy the bitch (that is, me), they will ask, while they were about it? And they will also curse those who have so "relaxed vigilance" that forbidden thoughts and feelings have been allowed to break to the surface. Now again we are not supposed to remember the past and think – let alone speak – about it. Since the sole survivors of all the myriad shattered families are now only the grandchildren, there is in fact nobody left to remember and speak of it. Life goes on, and few indeed are those who wish to stir up the past. Not many years ago it was admitted that some "mistakes" had been made, but now it is denied again – nothing wrong is seen with the past. But neither can I speak of the past as a "mistake." How can one thus describe actions that were part of a system and flowed inexorably from its basic principles?

Instead of an epilogue, then, I end my book with this letter. I shall do what I can to see that both book and letter survive. There is not much hope, even though our present times are like honey and sugar compared with the past. Come what may, here is the letter:

22/10(38)

Osia, my beloved, faraway sweetheart!
I have no words, my darling, to write this letter that you may never read, perhaps. I am writing it into empty space.

Perhaps you will come back and not find me here. Then this will be all you have left to remember me by.

Osia, what a joy it was living together like children – all our squabbles and arguments, the games we played, and our love. Now I do not even look at the sky. If I see a cloud, who can I show it to?

Remember the way we brought back provisions to make our poor feasts in all the places where we pitched our tent like nomads? Remember the good taste of bread when we got it by a miracle and ate it together? And our last winter in Voronezh. Our happy poverty, and the poetry you wrote. I remember the time we were coming back once from the baths, when we bought some eggs or sausage, and a cart went by loaded with hay. It was still cold and I was freezing in my short jacket (but nothing like what we must suffer now: I know how cold you are). That day comes back to me now. I understand so clearly, and ache from the pain of it, that those winter days with all their troubles were the greatest and last happiness to be granted us in life.

My every thought is about you. My every tear and every smile is for you. I bless every day and every hour of our bitter life together, my sweetheart, my companion, my blind guide in life.

Like two blind puppies, we were, nuzzling each other and feeling so good together. And how fevered your poor head was, and how madly we frittered away the days of our life. What joy it was, and how we always knew what joy it was.

Life can last so long. How hard and long for each of us to die alone. Can this fate be for us who are inseparable? Puppies and children, did we deserve this? Did you deserve this, my angel? Everything goes on as before. I know nothing. Yet I know everything – each day and hour of your life are plain and clear to me as in a delirium.

You came to me every night in my sleep, and I kept asking what had happened, but you did not reply.

In my last dream I was buying food for you in a filthy hotel restaurant. The people with me were total strangers. When I had bought it, I realized I did not know where to take it, because I do not know where you are.

When I woke up, I said to Shura: "Osia is dead." I do not know whether you are still alive, but from the time of that dream, I have lost track of you. I do not know where you are. Will you hear me? Do you know how much I love you? I could never tell you how much I love you. I cannot tell you even now. I speak only to you, only to you. You are with me always, and I who was such a wild and angry one and never learned to weep simple tears – now I weep and weep and weep.

It's me: Nadia. Where are you?

Farewell.

Nadia.

Nadezhda Mandelstam, *Hope Abandoned* (translated by Max Hayward) (1974)

PARTED BY THE WORKHOUSE

BUT IF YOU SURVIVED melancholia and rotting lungs it was possible to live long in this valley. Joseph and Hannah Brown, for instance, appeared to be indestructible. For as long as I could remember they had lived together in the same house by the common ... They had raised a large family and sent them into the world, and had continued to live on alone, with nothing left of their noisy brood save some dog-eared letters and photographs.

It seemed that the old Browns belonged for ever, and that the miracle of their survival was made commonplace by the durability of their love – if one should call it love, such a balance. Then suddenly, within the space of two days, feebleness took them both. It was as though two machines, wound up and synchronized, had run down

317

at exactly the same time. Their interdependence was so legendary we didn't notice their plight at first. But after a week, not having been seen about, some neighbours thought it best to call. They found old Hannah on the kitchen floor feeding her man with a spoon. He was lying in a corner half-covered with matting, and they were both too weak to stand. She had chopped up a plate of peelings, she said, as she hadn't been able to manage the fire. But they were all right really, just a touch of the damp; they'd do, and it didn't matter.

Well, the Authorities were told; the Visiting Spinsters got busy; and it was decided they would have to be moved. They were too frail to help each other now, and their children were too scattered, too busy. There was but one thing to be done; it was for the best; they would have to be moved to the Workhouse.

The old couple were shocked and terrified, and lay clutching each other's hands. 'The Workhouse' – always a word of shame, grey shadow falling on the close of life, most feared by the old (even when called The Infirmary); abhorred more than debt, or prison, or beggary, or even the stain of madness.

Hannah and Joseph thanked the Visiting Spinsters but pleaded to be left at home, to be left as they wanted, to cause no trouble, just simply to stay together. The Workhouse could not give them the mercy they needed, but could only divide them in charity. Much better to hide, or die in a ditch, or to starve in one's familiar kitchen, watched by the objects one's life had gathered – the scrubbed empty table, the plates and saucepans, the cold grate, the white stopped clock ...

'You'll be well looked after,' the Spinsters said, 'and you'll see each other twice a week.' The bright busy voices cajoled with authority and the old couple were not trained to defy them. So that same afternoon, white and speechless, they were taken away to the Workhouse. Hannah Brown was put to bed in the Women's Wing, and Joseph lay in the Men's. It was the first time, in all their fifty years, that they had ever been separated. They did not see each other again, for in a week they both were dead.

Laurie Lee, *Cider with Rosie* (1959)

SIR WALTER RALEGH TO HIS WIFE, ELIZABETH

Ralegh fell from favour with James I on his accession in 1603, and was sentenced to be executed on 11th December, 1603. He wrote this letter of farewell to his wife, but on 10th December was reprieved. The sentence was not carried out until 1618.

YOU SHALL RECEAVE, deare wief, my last words in these my last lynes. My love I send you, that you may keepe it when I am dead; and my councell, that you may remember it when I am noe more. I would not, with my last Will, present you with sorrowes, deare Besse. Lett them goe to the grave with me, and be buried in the dust. And, seeing it is not the will of God that ever I shall see you in this lief, beare my destruccion gentlie and with a hart like yourself.

First, I send you all the thanks my hart cann conceive, or my penn expresse, for your many troubles and cares taken for me, which – though they have not taken effect as you wished – yet my debt is to you never the lesse; but pay it I never shall in this world.

Secondlie, I beseich you, for the love you bare me living, that you doe not hide yourself many dayes, but by your travell seeke to helpe your miserable fortunes, and the right of your poore childe. Your mourning cannot avayle me that am but dust.

You shall understand that my lands were conveyed to my child, *bonâ fide*. The wrightings were drawn at

319

Midsummer was twelvemonethes, as divers can wittnesse. My honest cosen Brett can testifie so much, and Dalberie, too, cann remember somewhat therein. And I trust my bloud will quench their mallice that desire my slaughter; and that they will not alsoe seeke to kill you and yours with extreame poverty. To what frind to direct thee I knowe not, for all mine have left mee in the true tyme of triall: and I plainly perceive that my death was determyned from the first day. Most sorry I am (as God knoweth) that, being thus surprised with death, I can leave you noe better estate. I meant you all myne office of wynes, or that I could purchase by selling it; half my stuffe, the jewells, but some few, for my boy. But God hath prevented all my determinations; the great God that worketh all in all. If you can live free from want, care for no more; for the rest is but vanity. Love God, and beginne betymes to repose yourself on Him; therein shall you find true and lastinge ritches, and endles comfort. For the rest, when you have travelled and wearied your thoughts on all sorts of worldly cogitations, you shall sit downe by Sorrow in the end. Teach your sonne alsoe to serve and feare God, while he is young; that the feare of God may grow upp in him. Then will God be a husband unto you, and a father unto him; a husband and a father which can never be taken from you.

Bayly oweth me two hundred pounds, and Adrion six hundred pounds. In Gersey, alsoe, I have much owinge me. The arrearages of the wynes will pay my debts. And, howsoever, for my soul's healthe, I beseech you pay all poore men. When I am gonne, no doubt you shalbe sought unto by many, for the world thinks that I was very ritch; but take heed of the pretences of men and of their affections; for they laste but in honest and worthy men. And no greater misery cann befall you in this life then to become a pray, and after to be despised. I speak it (God knowes) not to disswad you from marriage – for that willbe best for you – both in respect of God and the world. As for me, I am no more your's, nor you myne. Death hath cutt us asunder; and God hath devided me from the world, and you from me.

Remember your poore childe for his father's sake, that comforted you and loved you in his happiest tymes.

Gett those letters (if it bee possible) which I writt to the Lords, wherein I sued for my lief, but God knoweth that itt was for you and yours that I desired it, but itt is true that I disdaine myself for begging itt. And know itt (deare wief) that your sonne is the childe of a true man, and who, in his own respect, despiseth Death, and all his misshapen and ouglie formes.

I cannot wright much. God knowes howe hardlie I stole this tyme, when all sleep; and it is tyme to separate my thoughts from the world. Begg my dead body, which living was denyed you; and either lay itt att Sherborne if the land continue, or in Exiter church, by my father and mother. I can wright noe more. Tyme and Death call me awaye.

The everlasting, infinite powerfull, and inscrutable God, that Almightie God that is goodnes itself, mercy itself, the true lief and light, keep and yours, and have mercy on me, and teach me to forgeve my persecutors and false accusers; and send us to meete in His glorious kingdome. My true wief, farewell. Blesse my poore boye; pray for me. My true God hold you both in His armes.

Written with the dyeing hand of sometyme thy husband, but now (alasse!) overthrowne.

Your's that was; but nowe not my owne,

W. Ralegh.

FAREWELL: THE WIFE

MY OWN DEAR Husband, If I should depart this life before you, leave orders that we may be buried in the same grave at whatever distance you may die from England. And now, God bless you, my kindest, dearest! You have been a perfect husband to me. Be put by my side in the same grave. And now, farewell, my dear Dizzy. Do not live alone, dearest. Someone I earnestly hope you may find as attached to you as your own devoted Mary Anne.

Lady Beaconsfield to her husband, Benjamin Disraeli,
Earl of Beaconsfield (1856)

DAVID LIVINGSTONE TO HIS ELEVEN-YEAR-OLD SON

Shupanga
28 April 1862

My dear Oswell,
    With my tears running down my cheeks I have to tell that poor dearly beloved Mama died last night about seven o'clock. She has gone home to the House of many mansions before us. She was ill seven days but moved about for the first few days, and no alarm was taken, but at last continued vomiting came on every ten minutes or so, which nothing could stop. I was with her night and day and trust that she was tended by an all powerful arm besides. I did not apprehend the danger till she lost the power to swallow. She was so deaf from quinine that I could not converse about the rest for the soul, but on asking loud if she rested on Jesus, she looked up towards Heaven thoughtfully. I think it meant yes. I very much regret that I did not use writing as when I asked her if she were in pain, she several times replied 'No'. She saw

322

me shedding many tears in prospect of parting with my dear companion of eighteen years, and must have known that her bodily case was hopeless. She answered my kisses up to within half an hour of her departure. It was only after we had commended her soul to Him who himself passed through the gate of death, that she took no notice of me. She was then breathing with her mouth a little open, shut it quietly and breathed no more.

She has got home sooner than we – this earth is not our home. She loved you dearly and often spoke of you and all the family, especially little Baby. You must think of her now as beckoning you from Heaven, never to let the pleasures of sin cheat you out of a happy meeting with her, and above all, with Jesus who died bearing our sins on his own body on the tree.

She gave me the comb and toothbrush you kindly sent us. We find in her notes evidence that she meant to try and make us all comfortable. She is not lost but gone before ... she was collecting some curiosities for you. There are two ostrich egg shells and other shells she brought from Mozambique ... you must let Agnes divide them. She was pleased at the idea of your being a missionary of the Cross and will be pleased still if you hold steadfast to your resolution. You must all love each other more than ever now. May God our Father be your guide.... Into his care I commend you.

AN EPITAPH UPON A MARRIED COUPLE
Dead and buried together

To these, whom Death again did wed,
This grave's their second marriage-bed;
For though the hand of Fate could force
'Twixt soul and body a divorce,

It could not sunder man and wife,
Because they both lived but one life.
Peace, good Reader, do not weep.
Peace, the lovers are asleep.
They, sweet turtles, folded lie
In the last knot Love could tie.
And though they lie as they were dead,
Their pillow stone, their sheets of lead,
(Pillow hard, and sheets not warm)
Love made the bed; they'll take no harm.
Let them sleep: let them sleep on,
Till this stormy night be gone,
Till the eternal morrow dawn;
Then the curtains will be drawn
And they wake into a light,
Whose day shall never die in night.

Richard Crashaw (1652)

VIRGINIA WOOLF'S FAREWELL LETTER TO LEONARD

Friday, March 28th, 1941

Dearest,

I feel certain that I am going mad again. I feel we can't go through another of those terrible times. And I shan't recover this time. I begin to hear voices, and I can't concentrate. So I am doing what seems the best thing to do. You have given me the greatest possible happiness. You have been in every way all that anyone could be. I don't think two people could have been happier till this terrible disease came. I can't fight any longer. I know that I am spoiling your life, that without me you could work. And you will I know. You see I can't even write this properly. I can't read. What I want to say is I owe all the happiness of my life to you. You have been entirely

324

patient with me and incredibly good. I want to say that – everybody knows it. If anybody could have saved me it would have been you. Everything has gone from me but the certainty of your goodness. I can't go on spoiling your life any longer.

I don't think two people could have been happier than we have been.

V.

LEONARD WOOLF ON VIRGINIA'S DEATH

WHEN I COULD not find her anywhere in the house or garden, I felt sure that she had gone down to the river. I ran across the fields down to the river and almost immediately found her walking-stick lying upon the bank. I searched for some time and then went back to the house and informed the police. It was three weeks before her body was found when some children saw it floating in the river. The horrible business of the identification and inquest took place in the Newhaven mortuary on April 18 and 19. Virginia was cremated in Brighton on Monday, April 21. I went there by myself. I had once said to her that, if there was to be music at one's cremation, it ought to be the cavatina from the B flat quartet, op. 130, of Beethoven. There is a moment at cremations when the doors of the crematorium open and the coffin slides slowly in, and there is a moment in the middle of the cavatina when for a few bars the music, of incredible beauty, seems to hesitate with a gentle forward pulsing motion – if played at that moment it might seem to be gently pro-' pelling the dead into eternity of oblivion. Virginia agreed with me. I had always vaguely thought that the cavatina might be played at her cremation or mine so that these bars would synchronize with the opening of the doors and the music would propel us into eternal oblivion. When I made the arrangements for Virginia's funeral, I should have liked to arrange this, but I could not bring myself to do anything about it. It was partly that, when I went to old Dean at the top of the village, whom we had known for nearly a quarter of a century, to get him to make the arrangements, it seemed impossible to discuss Beethoven's cavatina with him, and impossible that he could supply the music. But it was also that the long-drawn-out horror of the previous weeks had produced in me a kind of inert anaesthesia. It was as if I had been so battered and beaten that I was like some hunted animal which exhausted can only instinctively drag itself into its hole or lair. In fact (to my surprise) at the cremation the music of the "Blessed Spirits" from Gluck's *Orfeo* was played when the doors opened and the coffin disappeared. In the evening I played the cavatina.

I buried Virginia's ashes at the foot of the great elm tree on the bank of the great lawn in the garden, called the Croft, which looks out over the field and the water-meadows. There were two great elms there with boughs interlaced which we always called Leonard and Virginia. In the first week of January 1943, in a great gale one of the elms was blown down.

Leonard Woolf, *The Journey Not the Arrival Matters* (1969)

On the day of Virginia Woolf's death, after all efforts to find her had failed, Leonard wrote a note which, creased and worn, was found among his effects when he died twenty-eight years later. It read:

THEY SAID: 'Come to tea and let us comfort you.'
But it's no good. One must be crucified on one's own private cross.

It is a strange fact that a terrible pain in the heart can be interrupted by a little pain in the fourth toe of the right foot.

I know that V. will not come across the garden from the lodge, and yet I look in that direction for her. I know that she is drowned and yet I listen for her to come in at the door. I know that it is the last page and yet I turn it over. There is no limit to one's own stupidity and selfishness.

George Spater and Ian Parsons, *A Marriage of True Minds* (1977)

ONE HUSBAND MOURNS – AND ANOTHER WIFE

Were there but a few hearts and intellects like hers, this earth would already become the hoped-for heaven.

John Stuart Mill – epitaph for his wife Harriet in the cemetery near Avignon (1860)

Epitaph on the Monument of Sir William Dyer at Culmworth (1641):

> *My dearest dust, could not they hasty day*
> *Afford thy drowsy patience leave to stay*
> *One hour longer: so that we might either*
> *Sit up, or go to bed together?*
> *But since thy finished labor hath possest*
> *Thy weary limbs with early rest,*
> *Enjoy it sweetly: and thy widow bride*
> *Shall soon repose her by thy slumbering side.*
> *Whose business, now, is only to prepare*
> *My nightly dress, and call to prayer:*

Mine eyes wax heavy and the day grows cold.
Draw, draw ye closed curtains, and make room;
My dear, my dearest dust, I come, I come.

Lady Catherine Dyer

A SAD BUT CONSTANT WIFE

This is Arundel Penruddock's last letter to her husband, John
Penruddock, a Royalist, who joined the insurrection of 1655. He
was captured at South Molton and beheaded at Exeter.

MY DEAR HEART, – My sad parting was so far
from making me forget you, that I scarce thought
upon myself since, but wholly upon you. Those dear
embraces which I yet feel, and shall never lose, being
the faithful testimonies of an indulgent husband, have
charmed my soul to such a reverence of your remembrance, that were it possible, I would, with my own blood,
cement your dead limbs to live again, and (with reverence)
think it no sin to rob Heaven a little longer of a martyr.
Oh! my dear, you must now pardon my passion, this being
my last (oh, fatal word!) that ever you will receive from
me; and know, that until the last minute that I can imagine
you shall live, I shall sacrifice the prayers of a Christian,
and the groans of an afflicted wife. And when you are not
(which sure by sympathy I shall know), I shall wish my
own dissolution with you, so that we may go hand in
hand to Heaven. 'Tis too late to tell you what I have, or
rather have not done for you; how being turned out of
doors because I came to beg mercy; the Lord lay not your
blood to their charge.

I would fain discourse longer with you, but dare not;
passion begins to drown my reason, and will rob me of
my devoirs, which is all I have left to serve you. Adieu,

therefore, ten thousand times, my dearest dear; and since I must never see you more, take this prayer – May your faith be so strengthened that your constancy may continue; and then I know Heaven will receive you; whither grief and love will in a short time (I hope) translate,

My dear,

Your sad, but constant wife, even to love your ashes when dead,

Arundel Penruddock

May the 3rd, 1655, eleven o'clock at night. Your children beg your blessing, and present their duties to you.

KARL AND JENNY MARX

In November 1881 Jenny Marx was dying, and Karl Marx (whose nickname was 'Moor') was ill with pleurisy, both nursed by their daughter Tussy. She wrote to her sister Jennychen:

OUR MOTHER LAY in the large front room – Moor in the little room behind and next to it. And they who were so used to each other, whose lives had come to form part of each other, could not be in the same room any longer. Never shall I forget the morning when he felt strong enough to go into mother's room. When they were together they were young again, she a loving girl and he a loving youth, on the threshold of life, not an old man devastated by illness and an old woman parting from each other for life ... She remained fully conscious almost to the last moment and when she could no longer speak she pressed our hands and tried to smile ... but the last word she spoke to Papa was 'good'.

329

[On the day of Jenny's death, Engels summed up what this meant for Marx by saying 'Moor is dead'. Marx lived for fifteen months after his wife, and later Tussy Marx wrote:]

It is no exaggeration to say that Karl Marx could never have been what he was without Jenny von Westphalen. Never were the lives of two people, both remarkable, so at one, so complementary of each other. Of extraordinary beauty – a beauty in which he took pleasure and pride to the end, and that wrung admiration from men like Heine ... of intellect and wit as brilliant as her beauty, Jenny von Westphalen was a woman in a million ... Truly he could say of her in Browning's words –

> *Therefore she is immortally my bride*
> *Chance cannot change my love*
> *Nor time impair.*

THE SEA-WIDOW

How fares it with you, Mrs Cooper my bride?
Long are the years since you lay by my side.
Do you wish I was back? Do you speak of me dearest?
I wish you were back for me to hold nearest.
Who then lies nearer, Mrs Cooper my bride?
A black man comes in with the evening tide.
What is his name? Tell me! How does he dare?
He comes uninvited. His name is Despair.

Stevie Smith (1971)

330

THE WIDOW'S LAMENT IN SPRINGTIME

Sorrow is my own yard
where the new grass
flames as it has flamed
often before but not
with the cold fire
that closes round me this year.
Thirty-five years
I lived with my husband.
The plumtree is white today
with masses of flowers.
Masses of flowers
loaded the cherry branches
and colour some bushes
yellow and some red
but the grief in my heart
is stronger than they
for though they were my joy
formerly, today I notice them
and turned away forgetting.
Today my son told me
that in the meadows,
at the edge of the heavy woods
in the distance, he saw
trees of white flowers.
I feel that I would like
to go there
and fall into those flowers
and sink into the marsh near them.

William Carlos Williams
(1883–1963)

THE DEATH OF LLEWELYN POWYS

OCTOBER 31, 1939: Llewelyn and I have been so happy together – as we might have been in our earliest days. He has been able to take little walks and we have had so many hours of united companionship, with no spectres to separate us.

November 19: Llewelyn had a very strange attack, like the one he had with his stomach ulcer at home. I fall like a bird shot from a branch, and *know* how short our time is together. Only last night he called me to him to say how dear I was to him, but he does this constantly. It is snowing. I have to remember the joy we have had. But Oh, if I *could* die before him.

November 21: Llewelyn said to me, while he was so ill 'No one in the world knows my follies and my weaknesses as you do. There is no one in the world I have been so happy with as with you, except perhaps with Bertie in our boyhood days'. We talk together, Llewelyn and I, and he says he is happy. Then I go away from him and feel such woe deep in my marrow that I would that the earth would swallow me up.

November 29: Llewelyn is terribly ill. I look at his beautiful head, so deathly pale his features, and all my life stops within me, and the mutinous thoughts I have sometimes had seem momentary breaths on the deep ocean of my love.

Llewelyn just said to me 'Remember the good and the bad and love me for all'.

This morning while he was being given an infusion in his vein, with three women ministering to him – Lisaly and the nurse and the doctor who is a woman – I at the foot of his bed; they laughed and chatted – and *his very life was at stake*, and yet they could laugh. He suddenly looked at them, his eyes burning and said 'Yes, that is it, laugh', but they took it that he really meant for them to laugh, and Lisaly said later 'You see how Llewelyn told us to laugh', but did not every tiniest vessel in my body tell me what he was feeling?

I looked beyond Llewelyn's pale head out of the window and saw a greenfinch poised on a fir branch, turning this way and that, so full of dainty ease, so remote from human consciousness, so integral in the soulless universe, blithe under its fanciful coat of warm feathers, able to fly free through the air, and I was comforted and knew Llewelyn's philosophy to be a true one.

Later Llewelyn said 'I wish I were the sweet web of dust'.

Llewelyn died at 2.30 A.M. Saturday, December 2. He had some moments of consciousness in the afternoon and said 'Darling', with so radiant a smile, 'I have been happiest with you. You have been so sweet to me'.

December 4: I have just looked for the last time at Llewelyn's dead body. I kissed his clay cold brow and knelt beside the body that was my whole universe, that *is* my whole universe.

> *The cold! How shall I bear my heart without its heat?*
> *My clay without its soul? . . . I am alone –*
> *More cold than you are in your grave's long night,*
> *That has my heart for covering, warmth and light.*

Alyse Gregory, *The Cry of a Gull: Journals 1923–1948*

OVER THE COFFIN

They stand confronting, the coffin between,
His wife of old and his wife of late,
And the dead man whose they both had been
Seems listening aloof, as to things past date.
– 'I have called,' says the first. 'Do you marvel or not?'
'In truth,' says the second, 'I do – somewhat.'
'Well, there was a word to be said by me! . . .'
I divorced that man because of you –
It seemed I must do it, boundenly;
But now I am older, and tell you true,
For life is little, and dead lies he;
I would I had let alone you two!
And both of us scorning parochial ways,
Had lived like the wives in the patriarchs' days.'

Thomas Hardy (1914)

WIDOW'S LAMENT

The cloth-plant grew till it covered the thorn bush;
The bindweed spread over the wilds.
My lovely one is here no more.
With whom? No, I sit alone.

The cloth-plant grew till it covered the brambles;
The bindweed spread across the borders of the field.
My lovely one is here no more.
With whom? No, I lie down alone.

The horn pillow so beautiful,
The worked coverlet so bright!
My lovely one is here no more.
With whom? No, alone I watch till dawn.

Summer days, winter nights—
Year after year of them must pass

334

Till I go to him where he dwells.
Winter nights, summer days—
Year after year of them must pass
Till I go to his home.

Chinese (7th century BC?), translated by
Arthur Waley

IN PRAISE OF SYDNEY

THERE NEVER BEFORE *was*, and never again *will be* another Sydney!!

And now dear children, I have done!! After passing nearly $\frac{1}{2}$ a century with *such* a man, I am alone without one protecting hand that I can feel *belongs* to me! and whose feelings go along with mine!!

I do not believe that anyone filling only a subordinate rank in life ever past thro' it more universally beloved, more sought after for his brilliancy and wit, his honourable bearing, his masterly talents, his truth, his honesty!

Catherine Smith, *Narrative for My Grandchildren*, written after the death of her husband in 1845

A WIDOW'S HYMN

How near me came the hand of Death,
When at my side he struck my dear,
And took away the precious breath
Which quickened my beloved peer!
How helpless am I thereby made!
By day how grieved, by night how sad!
And now my life's delight is gone,
Alas! how am I left alone!

The voice which I did more esteem
  Than music in her sweetest key,
Those eyes which unto me did seem
  More comfortable than the day;
    Those now by me, as they have been,
    Shall never more be heard or seen;
But what I once enjoyed in them
Shall seem hereafter as a dream.

Lord! keep me faithful to the trust
  Which my dear spouse reposed in me:
To him now dead preserve me just
  In all that should performèd be!
    For though our being man and wife
    Extendeth only to this life,
Yet neither life nor death should end
The being of a faithful friend.

peer – companion, bosom friend.

George Wither (17th century)

THE VOICE

Woman much missed, how you call to me, call to
  me,
Saying that now you are not as you were
When you had changed from the one who was all
  to me,
But as at first, when our day was fair.

Can it be you that I hear? Let me view you, then,
Standing as when I drew near to the town
Where you would wait for me: yes, as I knew you
  then,
Even to the original air-blue gown!

Or is it only the breeze, in its listlessness
Travelling across the wet mead to me here,
You being ever dissolved to wan wistlessness,
Heard no more again far or near?

Thus I; faltering forward,
Leaves around me falling,
Wind oozing thin through the thorn from
norward,
And the woman calling.

Thomas Hardy (1912)

'WAIT NOT TILL DEATH ...'

I DOUBT CANDIDLY, if I ever saw a nobler human soul than this which (alas, alas, never rightly valued till now!) accompanied all my steps for forty years. Blind and deaf that we are: oh, think, if thou yet love anybody living, wait not till death sweep down the paltry little dust-clouds and idle dissonances of the moment, and all be at last so mournfully clear and beautiful when it is too late!

*

She had from an early period formed her own little opinion about me (what an Eldorado to me, ungrateful being, blind, ungrateful, condemnable, and heavy laden, and crushed down into blindness by great misery as I oftenest was!), and she never flinched from it an instant, I think, or cared, or counted, what the world said to the contrary.

*

Ah me! she never knew fully, nor could I show her in my heavy-laden miserable life, how much I had at all times regarded, loved, and admired her. No telling of her now. "Five minutes more of your dear company in this world.

337

Oh that I had you yet for but five minutes, to tell you
all!" This is often my thought since April 21.

Thomas Carlyle, *Reminiscences* (1881)

MR SPARKE
In memoriam Annie Sparke

1

It was the worst winter in memory
his neighbour tells us, smoothing out
a cutting from the Hexham Courant *–*
a picture of already yellowing whiteness –
as if she thinks we don't believe her.

But we can see for ourselves: the grass
has hardly grown; spring flowers are late
coming through and in a dip behind the far wood
there's a swathe of hard grey snow
with pine needles frozen in like splinters.

Up at Allenheads, she says, a man
who'd lived there all his life
and must have known the dangers
left his car and was buried in a drift.
They thought he'd have to have his hand off.

She'd been worried Mrs Sparke
would wander out again and be lost.
That's why she called the doctor.
Her husband dug a tunnel to the phone box –
It was like standing in an igloo.

The snow was piled so high
they had to stand on chairs to watch
for the ambulance from the window.
And after that they were cut off for weeks.
He never saw her again.

2

Mr Sparke's garden is as trim as ever.
The narrow borders by the path
are lined with scarlet tulips;
the soil is freshly dug and raked
ready for potatoes and the first seeds.

Dressed in his dark blue Sunday suit
he calls to us – not as we'd expected
to sit with him in gloomy sympathy
but to admire (what must have cost him most
of the insurance) a new cassette recorder.

At the centre of the old oak sideboard,
flanked by two china shepherdesses,
it seems oddly out of place.
Like a child showing off a new toy
he won't let us go until we've heard it.

While he twists the silver buttons
we wait, uncomfortably, exchanging looks,
remembering those bulging watery eyes,
her matted unwashed hair,
the conversations leading nowhere.

He'd never seemed to notice she was ill.
He just kept on at that wall –
covering the stones with cement;
drawing the shapes of stones
on the smooth surface.

We try to think of an excuse to go.
But suddenly like ice melting in a thaw
the sound begins to flow –
an accordion band squeezing out
'What a friend we have in Jesus'.

And Mr Sparke is crying; rubbing
at his eyes with a work-swollen hand.
'What I always say is,' he shouts

above the noise: 'It's my belief
that time's a great healer.'

Vikki Feaver (1981)

ON HIS DEAD WIFE

Methought I saw my late espousèd saint
  Brought to me like Alcestis from the grave,
  Whom Jove's great son to her glad husband gave,
  Rescued from death by force, though pale and faint.
Mine, as whom washed from spot of childbed taint
  Purification in the old Law did save,
  And such as yet once more I trust to have
  Full sight of her in heaven without restraint,
Came vested all in white, pure as her mind.
  Her face was veiled, yet to my fancied sight
  Love, sweetness, goodness, in her person shined
So clear as in no face with more delight.
  But O as to embrace me she inclined,
  I waked, she fled, and day brought back my night.

John Milton, *Sonnet XXIII* (1673)

THE KALEIDOSCOPE

To climb these stairs again, bearing a tray,
Might be to find you pillowed with your books,
Your inventories listing gowns and frocks
As if preparing for a holiday.
Or, turning from the landing, I might find
My presence watched through your kaleidoscope,
A symmetry of husbands, each redesigned
In lovely forms of foresight, prayer and hope.
I climb these stairs a dozen times a day
And, by that open door, wait, looking in

340

At where you died. My hands become a tray
Offering me, my flesh, my soul, my skin.
Grief wrongs us so. I stand, and wait, and cry
For the absurd forgiveness, not knowing why.

Douglas Dunn (1985)

THE LESSON OF DEATH

'IT WAS TOO PERFECT to last,' so I am tempted to say of our marriage. But it can be meant in two ways. It may be grimly pessimistic – as if God no sooner saw two of His creatures happy than He stopped it ('None of that here!'). As if He were like the Hostess at the sherry-party who separates two guests the moment they show signs of having got into a real conversation. But it could also mean 'This had reached its proper perfection. This had become what it had in it to be. Therefore of course it would not be prolonged.' As if God said, 'Good, you have mastered that exercise. I am very pleased with it. And now you are ready to go on to the next.' When you have learned to do quadratics and enjoy doing them you will not be set them much longer. The teacher moves you on.

For we did learn and achieve something. There is, hidden or flaunted, a sword between the sexes till an entire marriage reconciles them. It is arrogance in us to call frankness, fairness, and chivalry 'masculine' when we see them in a woman; it is arrogance in them to describe a man's sensitiveness or tact or tenderness as 'feminine'. But also what poor, warped fragments of humanity most mere men and mere women must be to make the implications of that arrogance plausible. Marriage heals this. Jointly the two become fully human. 'In the image of God created he *them*.' Thus, by a paradox, this carnival of sexuality leads us out beyond our sexes.

341

And then one or other dies. And we think of this as love cut short; like a dance stopped in mid career or a flower with its head unluckily snapped off – something truncated and therefore, lacking its due shape. I wonder. If, as I can't help suspecting, the dead also feel the pains of separation (and this may be one of their purgatorial sufferings), then for both lovers, and for all pairs of lovers without exception, bereavement is a universal and integral part of our experience of love. It follows marriage as normally as marriage follows courtship or as autumn follows summer. It is not a truncation of the process but one of its phases; not the interruption of the dance, but the next figure. We are 'taken out of ourselves' by the loved one while she is here. Then comes the tragic figure of the dance in which we must learn to be still taken out of ourselves though the bodily presence is withdrawn, to love the very Her, and not fall back to loving our past, or our memory, or our sorrow, or our relief from sorrow, or our own love.

C. S. Lewis, *A Grief Observed* (1961)

ON MY DREAMING OF MY WIFE

As waked from sleep, methought I heard the voice
Of one that mourned; I listened to the noise.
I looked, and quickly found it was my dear,
Dead as she was, I little thought her there.
I questioned her with tenderness, while she
Sighed only, but would else still silent be.
I waked indeed; the lovely mourner's gone,
She sighs no more, 'tis I that sigh alone.

Musing on her, I slept again, but where
I went I know not, but I found her there.
Her lovely eyes she kindly fixed on me,
'Let Miser not be nangry then,' said she,

A language love had taught, and love alone
Could teach; we prattled as we oft had done,
But she, I know not how, was quickly gone.

With her imaginary presence blessed,
My slumbers are emphatically rest;
I of my waking thoughts can little boast,
They always sadly tell me she is lost.
Much of our happiness we always owe
To error, better to believe than know!
Return, delusion sweet, and oft return!
I joy, mistaken; undeceived, I mourn;
But all my sighs and griefs are fully paid,
When I but see the shadow of her shade.

Jonathan Richardson (c. 18th century?)

UPON THE DEATH OF SIR ALBERT MORTON'S WIFE

He first deceas'd; she for a little tried
To live without him: lik'd it not, and died.

Sir Henry Wotton (1568–1639)

ON THE DEATH OF HIS WIFE

I parted from my wife last night,
A woman's body sunk in clay:
The tender bosom that I loved
Wrapped in a sheet they took away.

The heavy blossom that had lit
The ancient boughs is tossed and blown:
Hers was the burden of delight
That long had weighed the old tree down.

And I am left alone tonight

343

And desolate is the world I see
For lovely was that woman's weight
That on last night had lain on me.

Weeping I look upon the place
Where she used to rest her head –
For yesterday her body's length
Reposed upon you too, my bed.

Yesterday that smiling face
Upon one side of you was laid
That could match the hazel bloom
In its dark delicate deep shade.

Maelva of the shadowy brows
Was the mead-cast at my side;
Fairest of all flowers that grow
Was the beauty that has died.

My body's self deserts me now,
The half of me that was her own,
Since all I knew of brightness died
Half of me lingers, half is gone.

The face that was like hawthorn bloom,
Was my right food and my right side;
And my right hand and my right eye
Were no more mine than hers who died.

Poor is the share of me that's left
Since half of me died with my wife;
I shudder at the words I speak;
Dear God, that girl was half my life.

And our first look was her first love;
No man had fondled ere I came
The little breasts so small and firm
And the long body like a flame.

For twenty years we shared a home,
Our converse milder with each year:

Eleven children in its time
Did that tall stately body bear.

It was the King of hosts and roads
Who snatched her from me in her prime:
Little she wished to leave alone
The man she loved before her time.

Now King of churches and of bells,
Though never raised to pledge a lie
That woman's hand — can it be true? —
No more beneath my head will lie.

Muireadach O'Dalaigh (c. 1180–
1250), translated by Frank
O'Connor

PÈRE ROUAULT REMEMBERS

Père Rouault seeks to console his doctor, Charles Bovary, whose
wife has recently died.

O NE MORNING OLD ROUAULT called to make
the payment to Charles for the setting of his leg:
seventy-five francs in two-franc pieces, and a turkey.   He
had heard of his berèavement and offered the best consolation he could.

"I know what it is!" said he, slapping him on the
shoulder.   "I, too, have been in your case!   After I lost
my poor dead wife I used to go into the fields to be alone;
I used to fall at the foot of a tree, weep, call on the Good
God, abuse him; I would have wished to be like the moles
I saw hanging on the branches with maggots crawling in
their bellies – dead, in a word.   And when I thought how
other men at that very moment were with their nice little
wives, holding them in their arms, I used to beat the

ground with great blows of my stick; I was pretty well mad; I hardly ate; the mere idea of going to the café disgusted me, you would not believe. Ah, well, very gradually, one day following another, spring on winter and autumn on summer, all that passed away bit by bit, little by little. It is gone, it has left me, sunk, I should rather say, for there is still something deep down as who should say ... a weight, there, about the chest. But, since it is the lot of us all, neither ought we to allow ourselves to repine, and because others are dead, wish to die ourselves ... You must shake yourself up, M. Bovary; all that will pass! Come to see us; my daughter thinks of you now and then, remember, and she says that you are forgetting her. We shall have spring here directly; we will have you shoot a rabbit at the warren by way of a little distraction."

[Not long afterwards, Charles Bovary marries Rouault's daughter, Emma. After the wedding feast, the old man sees the couple off.]

WHEN HE HAD taken about a hundred strides he stopped, and, as he watched the conveyance pass into the distance, with its wheels throwing up the dust, he heaved a deep sigh. Then he called to mind his own wedding, the old days, his wife's first pregnancy. He, also, had been very happy the day that he had led her from her father's house to his own, when he carried her on the crupper of his saddle as they trotted over the snow; for it was about Christmas time, and the country was all white. She had held him by one arm, having her basket slung on the other; the wind blew hither and thither the long pieces of lace employed in the dressing of her hair after the fashion of Caux. Sometimes they would fly across and touch his mouth, and when he turned his head he saw close to him, on his shoulder, her little rosy face,

346

smiling silently beneath the golden badge on her bonnet. To warm her fingers she would thrust them from time to time into his bosom. How old and far away it was, all that! Their son would have been thirty now! Then he looked behind him; he could see nothing on the road. He felt sad as a house stripped of its furniture; and, tender remembrances mingling with dark thoughts in his brain muddled by the fumes of the junketing, for a moment he was conscious of a lively desire to go take a stroll by the church. As he feared, however, that the sight of it might make him still sadder, he went straight back home.

Gustave Flaubert, *Madame Bovary* (1856)

from EXEQUY ON HIS WIFE

Sleep on, my Love, in thy cold bed
Never to be disquieted.
My last good night! Thou wilt not wake
Till I thy fate shall overtake:
Till age, or grief, or sickness must
Marry my body to that dust
It so much loves; and fill the room
My heart keeps empty in thy tomb.
Stay for me there: I will not fail
To meet thee in that hollow vale.
And think not much of my delay;
I am already on the way,
And follow thee with all the speed
Desire can make, or sorrows breed.
Each minute is a short degree
And every hour a step towards thee.
At night when I betake to rest,
Next morn I rise nearer my west
Of life, almost by eight hours sail
Than when sleep breathed his drowsy gale.

347

Thus from the sun my bottom steers,
And my day's compass downward bears.
Nor labour I to stem the tide
Through which to thee I swiftly glide.
      'Tis true, with shame and grief I yield;
Thou, like the van, first took'st the field
And gotten hast the victory
In thus adventuring to die
Before me, whose more years might crave
A just precedence in the grave.
But hark! my pulse, like a soft drum,
Beats my approach, tells thee I come;
And slow howe'er my marches be
I shall at last sit down by thee.
      The thought of this bids me go on
And wait my dissolution
With hope and comfort. Dear, (forgive
The crime) I am content to live
Divided, with but half a heart,
Till we shall meet and never part.

Henry King (1624)

AN EXEQUY

In wet May, in the months of change,
In a country you wouldn't visit, strange
Dreams pursue me in my sleep,
Black creatures of the upper deep —
Though you are five months dead, I see
You in guilt's iconography,
Dear Wife, lost beast, beleaguered child,
The stranded monster with the mild
Appearance, whom small waves tease,
(Andromeda upon her knees
In orthodox deliverance)

And you alone of pure substance,
The unformed form of life, the earth
Which Piero's brushes brought to birth
For all to greet as myth, a thing
Out of the box of imagining.

This introduction serves to sing
Your mortal death as Bishop King
Once hymned in tetrametric rhyme
His young wife, lost before her time;
Though he lived on for many years
His poem each day fed new tears
To that unreaching spot, her grave,
His lines a baroque architrave
The Sunday poor with bottled flowers
Would by-pass in their mourning hours,
Esteeming ragged natural life
('Most dearly loved, most gentle wife'),
Yet, looking back when at the gate
And seeing grief in formal state
Upon a sculpted angel group,
Were glad that men of god could stoop
To give the dead a public stance
And freeze them in their mortal dance.

The words and faces proper to
My misery are private – you
Would never share your heart with those
Whose only talent's to suppose,
Nor from your final childish bed
Raise a remote confessing head –
The channels of our lives are blocked,
The hand is stopped upon the clock,
No one can say why hearts will break
And marriages are all opaque:
A map of loss, some posted cards,
The living house reduced to shards,
The abstract hell of memory,

The pointlessness of poetry –
These are the instances which tell
Of something which I know full well,
I owe a death to you – one day
The time will come for me to pay
When your slim shape from photographs
Stands at my door and gently asks
If I have any work to do
Or will I come to bed with you.

O scala enigmatica,
I'll climb up to that attic where
The curtain of your life was drawn
Some time between despair and dawn—
I'll never know with what halt steps
You mounted to this plain eclipse
But each stair now will station me
A black responsibility
And point me to that shut-down room,
'This be your due appointed tomb.'

I think of us in Italy:
Gin-and-chianti-fuelled, we
Move in a trance through Paradise,
Feeding at last our starving eyes,
Two people of the English blindness
Doing each masterpiece the kindness
Of discovering it – from Baldovinetti
To Venice's most obscure jetty.
A true unfortunate traveller, I
Depend upon your nurse's eye
To pick the altars where no Grinner
Puts us off our tourists' dinner
And in hotels to bandy words
With Genevan girls and talking birds,
To wear your feet out following me
To night's end and true amity,
And call my rational fear of flying

350

A paradigm of Holy Dying—
And, oh my love, I wish you were
Once more with me, at night somewhere
In narrow streets applauding wines,
The moon above the Apennines
As large as logic and the stars,
Most middle-aged of avatars,
As bright as when they shone for truth
Upon untried and avid youth.

The rooms and days we wandered through
Shrink in my mind to one — there you
Lie quite absorbed by peace — the calm
Which life could not provide is balm
In death. Unseen by me, you look
Past bed and stairs and half-read book
Eternally upon your home,
The end of pain, the left alone.
I have no friend, or intercessor,
No psychopomp or true confessor
But only you who know my heart
In every cramped and devious part —
Then take my hand and lead me out,
The sky is overcast by doubt,
The time has come, I listen for
Your words of comfort at the door,
O guide me through the shoals of fear —
'Fürchte dich nicht, ich bin bei dir.'

Peter Porter (1978)

THE WIFE A-LOST

Since I noo mwore do zee your feäce,
*   Up steäirs or down below,*
I'll zit me in the lwonesome pleäce,
*   Where flat-bough'd beech do grow;*
Below the beeches' bough, my love,
*   Where you did never come,*
An' I don't look to meet ye now,
*   As I do look at hwome.*

Since you noo mwore be at my zide,
*   In walks in zummer het,*
I'll goo alwone where mist do ride,
*   Drough trees a-drippen wet;*
Below the raïn-wet bough, my love,
*   Where you did never come,*
An' I don't grieve to miss ye now,
*   As I do grieve at hwome.*

Since now bezide my dinner-bwoard
*   Your vaïce do never sound,*
I'll eat the bit I can avvword;
*   A-yield upon the ground;*
Below the darksome bough, my love,
*   Where you did never dine,*
An' I don't grieve to miss ye now,
*   As I at hwome do pine.*

Since I do miss your vaïce an' feäce
*   In praÿer at eventide,*
I'll pray wi' woone sad vaïce vor greäce
*   To goo where you do bide;*
Above the tree an' bough, my love,
*   Where you be gone avore,*
An' be a-waïten vor me now,
*   To come vor evermwore.*

                    William Barnes (1879)

GONE A LITTLE BEFORE ...

THIS GENTLEMAN [Mr. Allworthy] had in his youth married a very worthy and beautiful woman, of whom he had been extremely fond: by her he had three children, all of whom died in their infancy. He had likewise had the misfortune of burying this beloved wife herself, about five years before the time in which this history chuses to set out. This loss, however great, he bore like a man of sense and constancy, though it must be confest he would often talk a little whimsically on this head; for he sometimes said he looked on himself as still married, and considered his wife as only gone a little before him, a journey which he should most certainly, sooner or later, take after her; and that he had not the least doubt of meeting her again in a place where he should never part with her more – sentiments for which his sense was arraigned by one part of his neighbours, his religion by a second, and his sincerity by a third.

Henry Fielding, *Tom Jones* (1749)

REINCARNATIONS

The kitten that befriends me at its gate
Purrs, rubs against me, until I say goodbye,
Stroking its coat, and asking "Why? Why? Why?"
For now I know the shame of being late
Too late. She waits for me at home
Tonight, in the house-shadows. And I must mourn
Until Equator crawls to Capricorn
Or murder in the sun melts down
The Arctic and Antarctica. When bees collide
Against my study's windowpane, I let them in.

She nurtures dignity and pride;
She waters in my eye. She rustles in my study's palm;
She is the flower on the geranium.
Our little wooden train runs by itself
Along the windowsill, each puff-puff-puff
A breath of secret, sacred stuff.
I feel her goodness breathe, my Lady Christ.
Her treasured stories mourn her on their shelf,
In spirit-air, that watchful poltergeist.

Douglas Dunn (1985)

FROM BEYOND THE GRAVE

DURING THOSE THIRTY MINUTES, he held the pencil over the sheet of paper and it moved and filled the pages in large letters ... At one stage, the pencil said, 'The lady is here, but will not communicate with her husband directly yet. By and by, perhaps, when she is calmer. She is somewhat agitated today, since this is her first effort to communicate with her husband. She is disturbed by the grief of her husband ...'

In course of time, my wife was able to communicate directly at Mr Rao's sittings. Week after week, she gave me lessons on how to prepare myself so as to be able to communicate my thoughts or receive hers without an intermediary. At the thirty-minute sitting, she criticized my performance in the preceding week. 'It is no use, your sitting up with such rigid concentration: that's just what I do not want. I want you to relax your mind; try to make your mind passive; you can think of me without desperation and also make your mind passive ... no, no, it's not the rigour of a yogi's meditation that I suggest; this is a more difficult thing, create a channel of communication and wait. Keep your mind inactive ... I can see that you still worry too much about the child ... Take good care of her, but don't cramp her with so much anxious thought, which has grown into a habit with you ... Two nights ago, when you were about to fall asleep, your mind once again wandered off to the sick-bed scenes and the day you mourned my passing over ... No harm in your remembering those times, but at the root there is still a rawness and that interferes with your perception. Until you can think of me without pain, you will not succeed in your attempts. Train your mind properly and you will know that I am at your side. Not more than ten minutes at a time should you continue the attempt; longer than that, it is likely to harm your health ... Take care of yourself ... I am watching the child, and often times she knows I'm there, but she won't talk to you about it ... She may sometimes take it to be a dream ... For instance, the other night, you remember a wedding procession that passed down your road, you were all at the gate to watch it, leaving her asleep in your room ... I approached her at that moment; if you had ever questioned her next morning, what she dreamt, she would have told you point blank, "I dreamt of Raji ..." Sometimes she may not remember, often she will not care to talk ... Children are much more cautious than you think ... Children are precociously cautious. After coming over, I have learnt so much more about the human mind, whose working I can directly perceive ... In your plane, your handicap is the density of the matter in which you are encased. Here we exist in a more refined state, in a different medium ... I wish I could explain all that I see, think, and feel ... When you are prepared for it, I'll be able to tell you much ...'

R. K. Narayan, *My Days* (1975)

ALYSE GREGORY MOURNS LLEWELYN POWYS

APRIL 16, 1940: I wear sorrow always close to my skin. I exist within it as a snail within its shell. But this does not mean that I cannot be gay, that I cannot *look out* upon the world, that I cannot enter into the hearts of others. Every mind is a foreign country to every other mind. We can find our way only by stealth and imagination. There is not an hour of my life that I do not miss Llewelyn. I stepped out on this beautiful evening and suddenly I heard the call of the partridge and all my memories that lie ambushed in my heart opened the floodgates of sorrow, and Llewelyn was in my heart's deep core, my *only* life, my only reality, a love that has despoiled my life and even in death pursues and destroys me. We were knit together in some essential way that can never be told, and let treachery reign the whole world over, since it is at the heart of nature herself, yet there is a secret in love, fleet though it is, that has left an imprint that only death can wipe out.

April 20: I went out on this beautiful Sunday afternoon to gather gorse sticks. The sky was sapphire blue behind the curving cliffs. The little lambs, white as seagulls' breasts, frolicked on the green grass. Starlings and jackdaws rose in the air and descended again near the dozing sheep. And death, death, only death was in my heart. I heard the song of the lark, and yet this beautiful scene, this beautiful song, so miraculous on this still Sunday afternoon, did not strike joy into my being. But memories clouded my reason, and I looked at the ring on my finger and thought of Llewelyn's dead hand from which I had taken it. We punish only ourselves when we are unhappy. Oh, what is at the centre of this savage and beautiful universe, where some are tortured and others live in the light?

Last night, as I opened the door carrying out a pail for
Katie, the spring night entered my heart and I lived once
more. Each blossom on the cherry tree smote me with its
frail and magical beauty, and I was alive – alive to sorrow,
alive to joy, my memories no longer destroying me.

Alyse Gregory, *The Cry of a Gull: Journals 1923–1948*

[Alyse lived on alone until 1967. Then, terrified of failing powers
and of ending up in a hospital ward, she lay down on Llewelyn's
cloak and took her own life with the barbiturates she had been
saving for that purpose for years.]

SOME SOMERSET MEMORIALS

HERE LIETH the body of Elinor the wife of Arthur
Bartha of the City of Bristoll Marchant who departed
this life the 21st day of January Anno Dom 1683 aged 27.

> *Here lys interd by Death deprived of Life*
> *A vertious Loving and a Carfull Wife*
> *Of Honest Life and pious Conversation*
> *Noe whit neglecting of her Soul's salvation*
> *Short was her time, much more her paine*
> *Great was my Loss, much more her gain.*

(Queen Camel)

John Shutt and his wife Margaret lived together for fifty-two years
and died on the same day.

> *Their bodies buried are but not their names*
> *their vitues have inbalmed the same.*

When strength of nature did decay
their soules then hasten to away,
Unto ye author of all blis
the fountain of their happines;
A pair of doves suted of silver feathers,
Who loved and lived and died here lie together.
  Being ye 25th of September, Ano Domini Dei 1668

(Hinton Charterhouse)

A painted monument to Sarah Latch, erected in 1644, shows the dead woman in her shroud, tied at head and foot. Her poor husband John, in boots and scarlet coat, recoils in wide-eyed horror as he parts the linen over her face. It is as if they are lying in bed together and he wakes to contemplate the reality of death. Their twelve children kneel on red cushions: seven boys and four girls, and one baby wrapped in black swaddling clothes to show it died in infancy. Some of the children carry skulls to show they died before their mother. The sad, magnificent monument is finished off by a fine inscription which I like to think was written by the grieving husband.

Lyveing and dead thou seest how her we lie.
I doate on Deathe preparing now to die.
Ah fleeting life she's gone. Age somons me
Unto the grave so will posteritie
Though singling death ye sacred knot undoe,
By parteing two made one, once more in two;
I see it's Lord by thy divine decree
Thus one by one to bring us home to thee;
Whose risen Christ doth us assurance give
We'el rouse this grave, and we with him shall live.

(Churchill)

On Sara Rossiter's tomb, who died in 1747, aged 102:

> *Here lyeth two whom death again hath wed*
> *And made the grave again their marriage bed*
> *To each at first did raise some consternation,*
> *It could not make an utter sepairation.*

> (Doulting)

Remember before God Nina de Hoyer of Kacherrichy, Russia. Lived happily in Lamyatt from 1968 to 1984. She had great beauty, immense courage, outstanding humour, keen wit. Was loved by all and adored by her husband Arthur Porter.

> (Lamyatt)

> *Here lies Merrily Joules*
> *A beauty bright,*
> *Who left Isaac Joules,*
> *Her heart's delight.*

> (Yatton)

> *As God together did us joyn,*
> *So he did part us in our prime,*
> *We liv'd in love unto her end*
> *And I have lost my only Frind.*

> (Wellow, 1768)

SUSANNAH PROUT

> *Here lies my wife,*
> *Susannah Prout;*
> *She was a shrew*
> *I don't misdoubt:*
> *Yet all I have*
> *I'd give, could she*
> *But for one hour*
> *Come back to me.*

Walter de la Mare (1873–1956)

AT CASTLE BOTEREL

As I drive to the junction of lane and highway,
  And the drizzle bedrenches the waggonette,
I look behind at the fading byway,
  And see on its slope, now glistening wet,
    Distinctly yet

Myself and a girlish form benighted
  In dry March weather. We climb the road
Beside a chaise. We had just alighted
  To ease the sturdy pony's load
    When he sighed and slowed.

What we did as we climbed, and what we talked of
  Matters not much, nor to what it led, —
Something that life will not be balked of
  Without rude reason till hope is dead,
    And feeling fled.

It filled but a minute. But was there ever
  A time of such quality, since or before,
In that hill's story? To one mind never,
  Though it has been climbed, foot-swift, foot-sore,
    By thousands more.

Primaeval rocks form the road's steep border,
  And much have they faced there, first and last,
Of the transitory in Earth's long order;
  But what they record in colour and cast
    Is — that we two passed.

And to me, though Time's unflinching rigour,
  In mindless rote, has ruled from sight
The substance now, one phantom figure
  Remains on the slope, as when that night
    Saw us alight.

I look and see it there, shrinking, shrinking,
  I look back at it amid the rain
For the very last time; for my sand is sinking,
  And I shall traverse old love's domain
    Never again.

Thomas Hardy (1913)

OLD LETTERS

MISS MATTY UNDID the packet with a sigh; but she stifled it directly, as if it were hardly right to regret the flight of time, or of life either. We agreed to look them over separately, each taking a different letter out of the same bundle, and describing its contents to the other, before destroying it. I never knew what sad work the reading of old letters was before that evening, though I could hardly tell why. The letters were as happy as letters could be – at least those early letters were. There was in them a vivid and intense sense of the present time, which seemed so strong and full, as if it could never pass away, and as if the warm, living hearts that so expressed themselves could never die, and be as nothing to the sunny earth. I should have felt less melancholy, I believe, if the letters had been more so. I saw the tears stealing down the well-worn furrows of Miss Matty's cheeks, and her spectacles often wanted wiping. I trusted at last that she would light the other candle, for my own eyes were rather dim, and I wanted more light to see the pale, faded ink; but no – even through her tears, she saw and remembered her little economical ways.

The earliest set of letters were two bundles tied together, and ticketed (in Miss Jenkyns's handwriting), 'Letters interchanged between my ever-honoured father and my dearly-beloved mother, prior to their marriage, in July, 1774.' I should guess that the rector of Cranford was about twenty-seven years of age when he wrote those

361

letters; and Miss Matty told me that her mother was just eighteen at the time of her wedding. With my idea of the rector, derived from a picture in the dining-parlour, stiff and stately, in a huge full-bottomed wig, with gown, cassock, and bands, and his hand upon a copy of the only sermon he ever published, it was strange to read these letters. They were full of eager, passionate ardour; short homely sentences, right fresh from the heart – (very different from the grand Latinised, Johnsonian style of the printed sermon, preached before some judge at assize time). His letters were a curious contrast to those of his girl-bride. She was evidently rather annoyed at his demands upon her for expressions of love, and could not quite understand what he meant by repeating the same thing over in so many different ways; but what she was quite clear about was her longing for a white 'Paduasoy,' – whatever that might be; and six or seven letters were principally occupied in asking her lover to use his influence with her parents (who evidently kept her in good order) to obtain this or that article of dress, more especially the white 'Paduasoy.' He cared nothing how she was dressed; she was always lovely enough for him, as he took pains to assure her, when she begged him to express in his answers a predilection for particular pieces of finery, in order that she might show what he said to her parents. But at length he seemed to find out that she would not be married till she had a 'trousseau' to her mind; and then he sent her a letter, which had evidently accompanied a whole box full of finery, and in which he requested that she might be dressed in everything her heart desired. This was the first letter, ticketed in a frail, delicate hand, 'From my dearest John.' Shortly afterwards they were married, – I suppose, from the intermission in their correspondence.

'We must burn them, I think,' said Miss Matty, looking doubtfully at me. 'No one will care for them when I am gone.' And one by one she dropped them into the middle of the fire; watching each blaze up, die out, and rise away, in faint, white, ghostly semblance, up the chimney, before she gave another to the same fate. The room was light enough now; but I, like her, was fascinated into watching the destruction of those letters, into which the honest warmth of a manly heart had been poured forth.

Elizabeth Gaskell, *Cranford* (1851)

'WHEN I GO ...'

On 8th September, 1911, Margaret MacDonald died, after fifteen years married to Ramsay MacDonald. He was left desolate. This is what she said to him just before she died:

'When I go, I may plead to be allowed to be with you ... and if in the silences of the night or of the hills you get consolation, say to yourself that it is I being with you.'

AN ARUNDEL TOMB

Side by side, their faces blurred,
The earl and countess lie in stone,
Their proper habits vaguely shown
As jointed armour, stiffened pleat,
And that faint hint of the absurd –
The little dogs under their feet.

Such plainness of the pre-baroque
Hardly involves the eye, until
It meets his left-hand gauntlet, still
Clasped empty in the other; and
One sees, with a sharp tender shock,
His hand withdrawn, holding her hand.

They would not think to lie so long.
Such faithfulness in effigy
Was just a detail friends would see:
A sculptor's sweet commissioned grace
Thrown off in helping to prolong
The Latin names around the base.

They would not guess how early in
Their supine stationary voyage
The air would change to soundless damage,
Turn the old tenantry away;
How soon succeeding eyes begin
To look, not read. Rigidly they

Persisted, linked, through lengths and breadths
Of time. Snow fell, undated. Light
Each summer thronged the glass. A bright
Litter of birdcalls strewed the same
Bone-riddled ground. And up the paths
The endless altered people came,

Washing at their identity.
Now, helpless in the hollow of
An unarmorial age, a trough
Of smoke in slow suspended skeins
Above their scrap of history,
Only an attitude remains:

Time has transfigured them into
Untruth. The stone fidelity
They hardly meant has come to be
Their final blazon, and to prove
Our almost-instinct almost true:
What will survive of us is love.

Philip Larkin (1964)

ACKNOWLEDGEMENTS

THOUGH THIS IS a personal, deliberately idiosyncratic anthology, culled for the most part from my own library shelves, I am grateful to Margaret Elton for some helpful suggestions, and especially to Dr Graham Handley for his enthusiasm and invaluable knowledge of nineteenth-century literature.

I found the following books useful for background to the subject: Lawrence Stone, *The Family, Sex and Marriage in England 1500–1800* (London, 1977); Alan Macfarlane, *Marriage and Love in England 1300–1840* (London, 1986); Laurence Lerner, *Love and Marriage* (London, 1979); and John R. Gillis, *For Better, For Worse* (Oxford, 1985).

*

The author and publishers would like to thank the following for permission to reproduce material:

Dannie Abse, 'Epithalamion'. © Dannie Abse 1952, first published by Hutchinson in *Walking Under Water*. Reprinted by permission of Dannie Abse and Anthony Sheil Associates.

Anonymous, 'The Wife's Complaint' from *The Earliest English Poems*, translated by Michael Alexander (Penguin Classics, second edition, 1977), copyright © Michael Alexander, 1966, 1977.

'Anonymous Frontier Guard' from *The Penguin Book of Japanese Verse*, translated by Geoffrey Bownas and Anthony Thwaite (Penguin Books, 1964), copyright © Geoffrey Bownas and Anthony Thwaite, 1964.

Enid Bagnold, *Autobiography* (Heinemann, 1969). Reprinted by permission of William Heinemann Ltd.

The Book of Margery Kempe, translated by B. A. Windeatt (Penguin Classics, 1985), copyright © B. A. Windeatt, 1985.

Bertold Brecht, 'Sonnet No. 19', translated by John Willett in *Bertold Brecht: Poems 1913–1956,* edited by Willett and Manheim (Methuen London, 1976). Reprinted by permission of Methuen London.

ACKNOWLEDGEMENTS

Winston Churchill, letter quoted in *Winston S. Churchill,* Vol. 2, Companion, Part II, edited by R. S. Churchill (Heinemann, 1969). Reprinted by permission of William Heinemann Ltd.

Robert Creeley, 'The Crisis', *Collected Poems 1945–75* (Marion Boyars Publishers Ltd., 1984). Reprinted by permission of Marion Boyars Publishers Ltd.

Elizabeth Daryush, 'This is the Last Night', *Collected Poems* (Carcanet, 1971). Reprinted by permission of Carcanet Press Ltd.

Alan Dugan, 'Love Song: I and Thou', *Collected Poems* (Faber, 1970). Reprinted by permission of Faber & Faber Ltd.

Douglas Dunn, 'The Kaleidoscope' and 'Reincarnations', *Elegies* (Faber, 1985). Reprinted by permission of Faber & Faber Ltd.

T. S. Eliot, 'A Dedication to My Wife', *Collected Poems 1909–1962* (Faber, 1963). Reprinted by permission of Faber & Faber Ltd.

Vikki Feaver, 'Mr Sparke', *Close Relatives* (Secker & Warburg, 1981). Reprinted by permission of Martin Secker & Warburg Ltd.

Bert Fielder, letter. Reprinted by permission of B. F. Fielder.

E. M. Forster, *Howards End* (London, 1910). Reprinted by permission of Edward Arnold.

Julius Fucik, letter in *Dying We Live*, edited by Reinhard Kuhn (Harvill Press, 1956). Reprinted by permission of Collins Publishers.

Robert Graves, 'A Slice of Wedding Cake', *Collected Poems* (London, 1975). Reprinted by permission of A. P. Watt Ltd. on behalf of the Executors of the Estate of Robert Graves.

Alyse Gregory, *The Cry of a Gull: Journals 1923–1948* (Out of the Ark Press, 1973). Reprinted by permission of Laurence Pollinger Ltd. on behalf of the Estate of Alyse Gregory.

Edna Healey, *Wives of Fame* (Sidgwick & Jackson, 1986). Reprinted by permission of Sidgwick & Jackson Ltd.

Seamus Heaney, 'Wedding Day' and 'Summer Home', *Wintering Out* (Faber, 1972); 'An Afterwards', *Field Work* (Faber, 1979); and 'Clearances', *The Haw Lantern* (Faber, 1987). Reprinted by permission of Faber & Faber Ltd.

Ralph Hodgson, 'Silver Wedding', *Collected Poems* (London, 1961). Reprinted by permission of Mrs Hodgson and Macmillan, London and Basingstoke.

Ion Horea, 'For You', translated by Roy McGregor-Hastie, in Roy MacGregor-Hastie (ed. and trans.), *An Anthology of Contemporary Romanian Poetry* (Peter Owen Ltd., 1969). Reprinted by permission of Peter Owen Ltd., Publishers.

Lady Elspeth Howe, quoted in *Male and Female* magazine, 1988. Reprinted by permission of Lady Howe.

Anne Hughes, *The Diary of a Farmer's Wife 1796–97* (Allen Lane, 1980), copyright © Mollie Preston, 1937, 1964, 1980.

Randall Jarrell, 'In Nature There is Neither Right nor Left, Left nor Wrong', *The Complete Poem* (Faber, 1971). Reprinted by permission of Faber & Faber Ltd.

Elizabeth Jennings, 'Friendship' and 'One Flesh', *Selected Poems* (Carcanet, 1979). Reprinted by permission of Carcanet Press Ltd.

Brian Jones, 'Husband to Wife: Party Going', *Poems* (London Magazine edition, 1966). Reprinted by permission of the author.

T. Harri Jones, 'A Birthday Poem for Madeleine', *The Collected Poems of T. Harri Jones* (Gomer Press, 1977). Reprinted by permission of the author and the Gomer Press.

James Joyce, *Ulysses* (Paris, 1922). Reprinted by permission of the Society of Authors as the literary representative of the Estate of James Joyce and the Executors of the James Joyce Estate.

Philip Larkin, 'The Whitsun Weddings' and 'An Arundel Tomb', *The Whitsun Weddings* (Faber, 1964). Reprinted by permission of Faber & Faber Ltd. 'Wedding-Wind', *The Less Deceived* (Marvell Press, 1955). Reprinted by permission of the Marvell Press.

Jennie Lee, *My Life With Nye* (Jonathan Cape Ltd., 1980). Reprinted by permission of the author and Jonathan Cape Ltd.

Laurie Lee, *Cider With Rosie* (Hogarth Press, 1959). Reprinted by permission of the author and the Hogarth Press.

C. S. Lewis, *A Grief Observed* (Faber, 1961). Reprinted by permission of Faber & Faber Ltd.

David Livingstone, letters quoted in Edna Healey, *Wives of Fame* (Sidgwick & Jackson, 1986). Reprinted by permission of the author and Sidgwick & Jackson Ltd.

Robert Lowell, 'Man and Wife', *Life Studies* (Faber, 1959). Reprinted by permission of Faber & Faber Ltd.

Malcolm MacDonald, *People and Places* (Collins, 1969). Reprinted by permission of Collins Publishers.

Ramsay and Margaret MacDonald, letters quoted in Malcolm MacDonald, *A Singular Marriage* (Harrap, 1988). Reprinted by permission of Harrap Ltd.

Louis MacNeice, 'Les Sylphides', *Collected Poems* (Faber, 1966). Reprinted by permission of Faber & Faber Ltd.

Nadezha Mandelstam, *Hope Abandoned,* translated by Max Hayward (Harvill Press, 1974). Reprinted by permission of Collins Publishers.

Walter de la Mare, 'Susannah Prout'. Reprinted by permission of the Literary Trustees of Walter de la Mare and the Society of Authors as their representative.

Gabriel García Márquez, *Love in the Time of Cholera* (Jonathan Cape, 1988). © Gabriel García Márquez, 1985. Reprinted by permission of the author.

Karl and Jenny Marx, letters quoted in Edna Healey, *Wives of Fame* (Sidgwick & Jackson, 1986). Reprinted by permission of the author and Sidgwick & Jackson Ltd.

W. Somerset Maugham, *Of Human Bondage* (Heinemann, 1915). Reprinted by permission of William Heinemann Ltd.

Gerda Mayer, 'Poem About Something', *Monkey on the Analyst's Couch* (Ceolfrith Press, 1980). Reprinted by permission of Gerda Mayer.

ACKNOWLEDGEMENTS

Mrs Milburn's Diaries, edited by Peter Donnelly (London, 1980). Reprinted by permission of A. C. Morgan.

Nancy Mitford, *The Pursuit of Love* (London, 1945). Reprinted by permission of the Peters Fraser & Dunlop Group.

Blake Morrison, 'Our Domestic Graces', *Dark Glasses* (Chatto & Windus, 1984). Reprinted by permission of the author and Chatto & Windus.

R. K. Narayan, *My Days* (Chatto & Windus, 1975). Reprinted by permission of the author and Chatto & Windus.

Ogden Nash, 'I do, I will, I have' and 'Marriage Lines', *Verse from 1929 on* (Little, Brown & Co. and Curtis Brown Ltd., 1948). Reprinted by permission of André Deutsch Ltd.

Harold Nicolson, letters quoted in Nigel Nicolson, *Portrait of a Marriage* (Weidenfeld & Nicolson, 1973). Reprinted by permission of the author and George Weidenfeld & Nicolson Ltd.

Nigel Nicolson, *Portrait of a Marriage* (Weidenfeld & Nicolson, 1973). Reprinted by permission of the author and George Weidenfeld & Nicolson Ltd.

Flann O'Brien, *The Poor Mouth* (London, 1973). Reprinted by permission of Grafton Books, a division of William Collins & Sons.

Muireadach O'Dalaigh, 'The Death of his Wife', translated by Frank O'Connor. Reprinted by permission of the Peters Fraser & Dunlop Group.

Eugene O'Neill, 'Quiet Song in Time of Chaos', *Poems 1912–1944,* edited by Donald Gallup (London). Reprinted by permission of the Estate of Eugene O'Neill and Jonathan Cape Ltd.

Frances Partridge, *Everything to Lose: Diaries 1945–1960* (Gollancz, 1985). Reprinted by permission of the author and Victor Gollancz Ltd.

Boris Pasternak, *Dr Zhivago* (Collins, 1958). Reprinted by permission of Collins Publishers.

Basil Payne, 'Man and Wife', *Love in the Afternoon* (Gill and Macmillan, 1971). Reprinted by permission of Gill and Macmillan, Dublin.

Hesketh Pearson, *The Smith of Smiths* (London, 1934). Reprinted by permission of A. P. Watt Ltd. on behalf of Michael Holroyd, CBE.

Sylvia Plath, *Letters Home,* ed. Aurelia S. Plath (Faber, 1975). Reprinted by permission of Faber & Faber Ltd.

Peter Porter, 'An Exequy', © Peter Porter 1983. Reprinted from Peter Porter's *Collected Poems* (1983) by permission of Oxford University Press.

Barbara Pym, *An Academic Question* (Macmillan, 1986). Reprinted by permission of Macmillan, London and Basingstoke.

Jean Rhys, *Wide Sargasso Sea* (London, 1966). Reprinted by permission of André Deutsch Ltd.

Anne Ridler, 'A Letter' (1939). Reprinted by permission of Mrs Anne Ridler and Faber & Faber Ltd. from uncollected poems by Anne Ridler.

Rihaku, 'The River-Merchant's Wife: A Letter', translated by Ezra Pound (1915), in Ezra Pound, *Collected Shorter Poems* (Faber, 1952). Reprinted by permission of Faber & Faber Ltd.

ACKNOWLEDGEMENTS

Carol Rumens, 'Pavane for the Lost Children', *Direct Dialling* (Chatto & Windus, 1985). Reprinted by permission of the author and Chatto & Windus.

Bertrand Russell, *Marriage and Morals* (London, 1929). © Bertrand Russell, 1929. Reprinted by permission of Unwin Hyman Ltd.

Lady Sackville, diary. Excerpt from *Lady Sackville – A Biography* by Susan Mary Alsop, copyright © 1978 by Susan Mary Alsop. Used by permission of Doubleday, a division of Bantam, Doubleday, Dell Publishing Group, Inc.

Vita Sackville-West, letters, poem and diary quoted in Nigel Nicolson, *Portrait of a Marriage* (Weidenfeld & Nicolson, 1973). Reprinted by permission of the author and George Weidenfeld & Nicolson Ltd.; and letter quoted in Sir Harold Nicolson, *Diaries and Letters,* edited by Nigel Nicolson (Collins, 1966). Reprinted by permission of Collins Publishers.

Vernon Scannell, 'Five Domestic Interiors', *The Winter Man* (Allison & Busby, 1973). Reprinted by permission of the author.

George Bernard Shaw, 'Maxims for Revolutionists', *Man and Superman* (London, 1903); Preface to *Getting Married* (London, 1908); and *How He Lied To Her Husband* (London, 1905). Reprinted by permission of the Society of Authors on behalf of the Bernard Shaw Estate.

Shen Fu, *Wedded Bliss,* from *The Wisdom of China and India,* edited by Lin Yutang. Copyright 1942 and renewed 1970 by Random House, Inc. Reprinted by permission of the publisher.

Stevie Smith, 'Autumn', 'Alfred the Great', and 'The Sea-widow', *The Collected Poems of Stevie Smith* (Penguin Modern Classics, 1978). Reprinted by permission of the Executor of the Estate of Stevie Smith, James MacGibbon.

'Song of a Woman Whose Husband Had Gone to the Coast to Earn Money', in *Voices from Twentieth-Century Africa,* edited by Chinweizu (Faber, 1988).

George Spater and Ian Parsons, *A Marriage of True Minds* (Jonathan Cape and the Hogarth Press, 1977). Reprinted by permission of the authors and Jonathan Cape Ltd. and the Hogarth Press.

Bernard Spencer, 'Part of Plenty'. © Mrs Anne Humphreys 1981. Reprinted from Bernard Spencer's *Collected Poems* edited by Roger Bowen (1981) by permission of Oxford University Press.

Gertrude Stein, *Portraits and Prayers* (New York, 1934). Reprinted by permission of the Estate of Gertrude Stein.

Anne Stevenson, 'An April Epithalamium'. © Anne Stevenson 1985. Reprinted from *The Fiction-Makers* by Anne Stevenson (1985) by permission of Oxford University Press.

Heather and Robin Tanner, *A Country Book of Days* (Old Stile Press, 1986). Reprinted by permission of the authors and the Old Stile Press.

Dylan Thomas, *Under Milk Wood* (Dent, 1954). Reprinted by permission of the Trustees for the copyright of Dylan Thomas.

Helen Thomas, *World Without End* (London, 1931) (subsequently reissued as *Under Storm's Wing*). Reprinted by permission of Carcanet Press Ltd.

ACKNOWLEDGEMENTS

R. S. Thomas, 'Farm Wife', *Selected Poems 1946–1968* (London, 1958). Reprinted by permission of Grafton Books, a division of William Collins & Sons.

'Widow's Lament', translated by Arthur Waley, *Chinese Poems* (Allen & Unwin, 1946). Reprinted by permission of Unwin Hyman Ltd.

Oscar Wilde, letter, © Vyvyan Holland 1962. Reprinted from *Selected Letters of Oscar Wilde* edited by Rupert Hart-Davis (1979) by permission of Oxford University Press and the Estate of Oscar Wilde.

Nigel Williams, *My Life Closed Twice* (Faber, 1986). Reprinted by permission of Faber & Faber Ltd.

William Carlos Williams, 'The Widow's Lament in Springtime', in *Amazon Poetry, An Introductory Anthology,* edited by Donald Hall (Faber, 1969). Reprinted by permission of Carcanet Press Ltd.

Leonard Woolf, *The Journey Not the Arrival Matters* (Hogarth Press, 1969). Reprinted by permission of the Executors of the Leonard Woolf Estate and the Hogarth Press.

Virginia Woolf, *To the Lighthouse* (Hogarth Press, 1927), *The Letters of Virginia Woolf, Vol. 1, 1888–1912: The Flight of the Mind,* ed. N. Nicolson and J. Trautmann (Hogarth Press, 1975); and *The Diary of Virginia Woolf, Vol. 1, 1915–19,* ed. A. O. Bell (Hogarth Press, 1977). Reprinted by permission of the Executors of the Virginia Woolf Estate and the Hogarth Press.

E. H. Young, *Chatterton Square* (London, 1947). Reprinted by permission of the Estate of E. H. Young and Jonathan Cape Ltd.

While every effort has been made to secure permission, we may have failed in a few cases to trace the copyright holder. We apologise for any apparent negligence.

INDEX OF AUTHORS

Abse, Dannie 126
Aubrey, John 49
Austen, Jane 9, 19, 70

Bacon, Francis 35
Bagnold, Enid 297
Barnes, William 281, 352
Beaconsfield, Lady 322
Bible, The 10
Bishop, Samuel 276
Boswell, James 33, 217
Bradstreet, Ann 275
Brecht, Bertold 264
Bridges, Robert 297
Brontë, Charlotte 79
Browning, Robert 166, 303
Burns, Robert 306
Burton, Robert 37

Carew, Thomas 133
Carlyle, Thomas 269, 337
Cavendish, William, Duke of
    Devonshire 292
Cecil, Lord Robert 53
Cervantes, Miguel de 11
Chaucer, Geoffrey 144, 226
Chevalier, Albert 305
Churchill, Sir Winston 294
Cobbett, William 41, 50, 159
Congreve, William 66
Crabbe, George 136
Crashaw, Richard 323
Creeley, Robert 199
Cromwell, Oliver 268
Cunningham, John 65

Darwin, Charles 17, 113, 274
Daryush, Elizabeth 313
Dickens, Charles 85, 113, 168, 206, 238,
    282
Disraeli, Benjamin (Earl of
    Beaconsfield) 8
Donne, John 180, 267
Dugan, Alan 95
Dunn, Douglas 340, 353
Dyer, Lady Catherine 327

Eliot, George 57, 129, 244, 252, 255,
    261, 270, 309
Eliot, T. S. 279

Feaver, Vikki 338
Fielder, Bert 196
Fielding, Henry 353
Flaubert, Gustave 108, 345
Fleming, Marjory 132
Forster, E. M. 143
Fowler, Professor 47, 52, 153
Fucik, Julius 305

Gaskell, Elizabeth 22, 60, 361
Gibran, Kahlil 33
Graves, Robert 24
Gregory, Alyse 132, 214, 332, 356

Hardy, Thomas 89, 138, 187, 302, 334,
    336, 360
Harington, Sir John 216, 291
Hawthorne, Nathaniel 195
Heaney, Seamus 131, 199, 202, 311
Hebrew Prayer Book, The 106

Hegel, G. W. F. 43
Herrick, Robert 151
Hervey, Elizabeth (Countess of
  Bristol) 278
Hervey, John (1st Earl of Bristol) 277
Hodgson, Ralph 188
Hogarth, William 278
Homer 13
Horea, Ion 180
Howe, Lady Elspeth 284
Hughes, Anne 110, 184, 212

Jarrell, Randall 205
Jennings, Elizabeth vii, 222
Jones, Brian 286
Jones, T. Harri 179
Joyce, James 103

Kant, Immanuel 25
Kempe, Margery 228
King, Henry 347

Larkin, Philip 141, 156, 363
Lawrence, D. H. 25, 123, 153, 170
Lee, Jennie 102, 137
Lee, Laurie 317
Lewis, C. S. 341
Livingstone, David 198, 322
Locke, John 10
Lowell, Robert 204

MacDonald, Malcolm 275
MacDonald, Margaret 274, 363
MacDonald, Ramsay 275
MacNeice, Louis 186
Mandelstam, Nadezhda 314
Mansfield, Katherine 91
Mare, Walter de la 359
Márquez, Gabriel García 210, 298
Marx, Tussy 329
Maugham, W. Somerset 39
Mayer, Gerda 158
Meredith, George 221
Merriman, Bryan 21

Milburn, Mrs 268
Mill, John Stuart 15, 32, 327
Milton, John 9, 147, 258, 340
Mitford, Nancy 187
Monkhouse, William Cosmo 21
Montaigne 14, 15
Montesquieu, Baron de 30
More, Sir Thomas 164
Morrison, Blake 181

Narayan, R. K. 354
Nash, Ogden 34, 225
Nevar, Reverend William 148
Nicolson, Harold 218, 220, 273
Nicolson, Nigel 259

O'Brien, Flann 127
O'Dalaigh, Muireadach 343
O'Neill, Eugene 300
Overbury, Sir Thomas 16

Partridge, Frances 280, 311
Pasternak, Boris 225
Paston, Margaret 239
Payne, Basil 203
Pearson, Hesketh 126
Penruddock, Arundel 328
Plath, Sylvia 134
Porter, Peter 348
Pound, Ezra 192
Pym, Barbara 176

Ralegh, Sir Walter 319
Rhys, Jean 148
Richardson, Jonathan 342
Ridler, Anne 161
Rihaku 192
Robinson, Edwin Arlington 209
Roper, William 49
Rumens, Carol 178
Russell, Bertrand 16

Sackville-West, Victoria (Lady) 156
Sackville-West, Vita 96, 193, 217, 219,
  273, 307

Scannell, Vernon 175
Shakespeare, William 8, 9, 30, 64, 200
Shaw, George Bernard 8, 44, 262
Shen Fu 301
Skelton, John 295
Smith, Catherine 335
Smith, Stevie 63, 175, 330
Smith, Reverend Sydney 8
Spater, George, and Parsons, Ian 281, 325, 327
Spencer, Bernard 166
Spenser, Edmund 111
Steele, Richard 12, 118
Stein, Gertrude 205
Stevenson, Anne 116
Stevenson, Robert Louis 290
Suckling, Sir John 120
Swift, Jonathan 11

Tanner, Heather and Robin 106
Thomas, Dylan 85, 295
Thomas, Edward 243

Thomas, Helen 182, 284
Thomas, R. S. 167
Thurber, James 225
Tolstoy, Leo 162, 232, 289
Tournier, Paul 225
Trollope, Anthony 40, 73, 81

Victoria, Queen 63

Waley, Arthur 334
Webster, John 53
Wharton, Edith 264
Wilde, Oscar 98, 293
Williams, Nigel 77
Williams, William Carlos 331
Wither, George 335
Woolf, Leonard 325, 326
Woolf, Virginia 46, 100, 173, 248, 286, 324
Wotton, Sir Henry 343
Wordsworth, William 107, 293

Young, E. H. 250